FREEDOM OF THE AIR AND THE PUBLIC INTEREST

Freedom of the Air and the Public Interest

First Amendment Rights in
Broadcasting to 1935

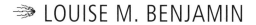 LOUISE M. BENJAMIN

Southern Illinois University Press
Carbondale and Edwardsville

Library of Congress Cataloging-in-Publication Data
Benjamin, Louise Margaret.
    Freedom of the air and the public interest : First Amendment rights in broadcasting
to 1935 / Louise M. Benjamin.
        p. cm.
    Includes bibliographical references and index.
        1. Radio—Law and legislation—United States—History—20th century.
    2. Freedom of speech—United States—History—20th century. I. Title

    KF2814 .B458 2001
    342.73'0853—dc21
                                                                            00-055711
    ISBN 0-8093-2367-2 (alk. paper)

To Maurice and Verla Benjamin

⇒ CONTENTS

⇛ PREFACE

The genesis of this book came in 1982 when I was taking courses in broadcast history, mass communication law and policy, and historical methods in mass communication during my graduate studies at the University of Iowa. All made cursory reference to radio and free speech in the 1920s, but my research on early radio at the Herbert Hoover Presidential Library in West Branch, Iowa, revealed that the 1920s were rich in perspectives on free speech and the new media of radio and motion pictures.

Throughout speeches given by Secretary of Commerce Herbert Hoover, who was in charge of radio's regulation at the time, as well as congressional hearings on free speech and radio, First Amendment concerns recurred like a Wagnerian leitmotif: government and industry censorship of programs, listeners' rights to receive information via the airwaves, and speakers' rights of access to the medium, including use by political candidates and speakers wishing to present viewpoints counter to those of mainstream society.

Tempering these free speech rights was a social and cultural preoccupation with "responsible" use of free speech in development of contemporary society. No scholar had looked in depth at the development of free speech concerns in broadcasting's first decade in the social context of the 1920s, and that topic became my dissertation on free speech issues in the development of the Radio Act of 1927.

As I completed the dissertation in December 1985, I realized that several additional chapters existed in the saga of emerging First Amendment rights in electronic media and included the evolution of free speech and the public interest to passage of the Communications Act of 1934. That investigation began soon after I received my Ph.D. and consumed more than a decade of research travel, primarily in the summer months. Over the years, my investigations included many of those dreaded dead ends and fabulous eureka moments inherent to all historical work.

Many wonderful, supportive persons graciously offered their time, talent, good humor, homes, and patient help to assist in these endeavors, and I would like to thank all of the individuals and organizations who helped make those moments and this book possible. While I want to single out those individuals meriting special thanks, to do so leaves one open to the justifiable pique of those who did not receive mention. So, to any whom I may fail to mention, my deepest thanks.

First, I thank those on my doctoral committee who, many years ago, gave me their energy and guidance in the first phases of this study: Carolyn Stewart Dyer, John Soloski, Ellis Hawley, Jeff Smith, and Bill Zima. Second, my profound thanks go to Christopher Sterling for reading very early drafts of this manuscript and offering his sage advice. Any inadequacies found herein are mine.

Since 1983, several foundations and academic institutions provided financial support to conduct this research. Their generosity made travel possible to the numerous archives and repositories containing pertinent papers related to early radio's development. I am extremely grateful to the Herbert Hoover Presidential Library Association; the National Association of Broadcasters Research Grant program; the John F. Murray Fund administered through the Iowa Center for Communications Studies at the University of Iowa; Indiana University's Research Summer Faculty Fellowship and Grant-in-Aid-of-Research programs; and the University of Georgia's Summer Faculty Research Grant program.

Numerous archives and repositories opened their doors to me for this study, and I thank them and their marvelous staffs for their support, insight, and "diligent digging" as I conducted my research: Owen D. Young Collection, St. Lawrence University, Canton, New York; AT&T Corporate Archives, Warren, New Jersey; the ACLU Collection, Seeley G. Mudd Manuscript Library, Princeton University, Princeton, New Jersey; the Herbert Hoover Presidential Library, West Branch, Iowa; the David Sarnoff Research Library, Sarnoff Corporation, Princeton, New Jersey; the Archive of Industrial Society, University of Pittsburgh, Pennsylvania; the Mass Communication History Center, State Historical Society of Wisconsin, Madison; the Payne Fund Collection, Western Reserve Historical Society, Cleveland, Ohio; the Broadcast Pioneers Collection, the Library of American Broadcasting, Hornbake Library, University of Maryland, College Park; the American Newspaper Publishers Association papers, Newspaper Association of America, Vienna, Virginia; and the National Archives, the Library of Congress, the Smithsonian Institution's Museum of American History, and the National Association of Broadcasters Library in Washington, D.C. These collections helped immeasurably in providing new and useful information about issues of free speech and the public interest that accompanied radio's early growth.

Since the mid-1980s, friends have offered their unwavering backing as I struggled with both the research and the writing of this history. I owe a debt of gratitude to Jackie Cartier, Pam Brown, Charles Cox, Ron Givens and Christina Distelhorst, Chris and Ellen Sterling, Fritz and Nola Messere, Yvonne Zecca, and Pat Carmack. They offered me their homes, sustenance, and support, and without their spectacular help, I could not have finished the research for this book. To my friends at the University of Georgia, Indiana University, and elsewhere, I also offer my thanks for support during the sometimes tedious phase of writing and rewriting and rewriting and rewriting this manuscript. Thanks for listening.

My gratitude also goes to Jim Simmons and John Gehner at Southern Illinois University Press for recognizing the value in the original manuscript sent them. To them, my editors Carol Burns and Julie Bush, and those who offered comments and suggestions for revision, I am forever indebted. This book is so much the better for their efforts.

Last, but certainly not least, I want to thank my parents, Verla and the late Maurice Benjamin, and my siblings—Louis, Leo, Joe, Ed, Frank, Regina, and Matt—and their families. Before his death, my father's encouragement of "his daughter, the doctor" and my mother's continuing confidence in my abilities aided me immeasurably. My siblings' faith in my potential also assured me that someday I would complete this book. Without their staunch and steadfast support I would never have finished this project. To my parents, I dedicate this work.

1 ⇶ SPIRIT, WHITHER GOEST THOU?

Secretary of Commerce Herbert Hoover sat in his office, listening carefully as his radio advisors David Carson and E. T. Chamberlain outlined the radio situation. Radio had grown tremendously during 1924, and now Hoover was calling another radio conference and preparing his opening remarks to conference delegates. Two previous conferences in 1922 and 1923 had been small, dealing primarily with issues of spectrum allocation, signal interference, industry selection of appropriate broadcast programs, and monopoly in ownership and sale of transmitting and receiving equipment. Now those business issues had mushroomed into concerns of what comprised broadcasting's public interest obligations. In addition, the public had misgivings about censorship of broadcast programs. Over six thousand letters had poured into Hoover's office in early October, decrying monopoly in station ownership and overt radio industry censorship of speakers and program material.

In those letters, listeners insisted upon their right to receive radio information and entertainment for free, contrary to some broadcasters and many government officials who wanted a tax placed on radio sets to pay for broadcasting. At the same time, speakers denied access to the airwaves complained bitterly about station operators' censorship. They told Hoover that a speaker's right of access to the medium should be protected so Americans could be fully informed citizens. Not so, countered broadcasters. If they could not control access to their transmitters, anyone, including Bolsheviks and anarchists, could espouse un-American views over the air or present offensive, distasteful material unsuitable for entry into American homes. Such programming would not be in the public interest.

Broadcasters and government officials realized critics of American government would also have ready access to the public via radio, and Hoover knew well that others in the Harding and Coolidge administrations had little patience with condemnation of official government policies. Newspaper editor H. V. Kaltenborn, for instance, had chided American policymakers during his talks over station WEAF for their stand against recognition of the Soviet Union and its Communist government. Secretary of State Charles Evans Hughes complained to the station's owner, the American Telephone and Telegraph Company (AT&T), and his protests resulted in nonrenewal of Kaltenborn's contract with WEAF. When the cancellation became public, cries of government and industry censorship quickly arose.

Hoover conceded that the medium's ubiquitous nature was both an asset and a liability. During the summer of 1924, thousands had been able to "attend" the presidential nominating conventions for the Republican and Democratic parties through radio's coverage. Because radio's reach was instantaneous and extensive, Hoover acknowledged it was potentially accessible to anyone, including children. He knew firsthand that with radio's development, parents had more difficulty monitoring their children's education in "sensitive" matters, as he had found his younger son listening to government health reports about syphilis on the radio. Pressure from Hoover and others halted such unseemly, government-produced material from entering American homes via radio.[1]

Consequently, as Hoover and his assistants readied themselves for the over one hundred delegates scheduled to attend the Third Radio Conference in October 1924, they realized that free speech issues and public interest concerns would comprise much of the discussion. While Hoover personally abhorred limits on freedom of expression, he surmised that limits might have to be imposed on broadcasters in the name of the public interest. But what limits were apropos? Could both free speech and the public interest be served? If not, what balance existed between the two ideals?

In preparation for the conference, Hoover and his advisors focused on three issues believed to be most salient to conferees: (1) government and industry censorship of programming, including broadcasters' rights to use the medium solely in ways they deemed appropriate; (2) listeners' rights to receive information via the airwaves clearly and without signal interference; and (3) speakers' rights of access to the medium. A fourth area of concern—monopoly ownership and control over equipment and its manufacture—touched on issues of free speech but dealt primarily with restraint of trade considerations.

By 1924, these topics had coalesced into an infrastructure underpinning discussions of broadcasting, the public interest, and freedom of expression. From the mid-1920s to passage of the Communications Act of 1934, interaction of those industry, government, and private groups having social, political, or economic interests in radio gave broadcasting its foundation for First Amendment/free speech rights. Station operators, those wanting to speak over radio, and even listeners employed the concepts of "public interest" and "free speech," or "freedom of the air" as it was called then, in the struggle to achieve their varied social, political, or economic goals. Through usage of these phrases by government, industry, and public entities, a consensus on the meaning of "public interest" and "freedom of the air" emerged during broadcasting's formative years.

The relationship of the First Amendment to radio station and government censorship of broadcasts and free speech rights of broadcasters, listeners, and speakers in broadcasting presage today's debates over electronic and telecommunications media issues. If lessons can be learned from this past new technology and its introduction into the American scene, they will help in the assessment of present and future communication technologies and their emerging free speech rights. Discussion of free speech rights during broadcasting's formation is relevant to today's considerations of First Amendment rights in the Internet evolution and in telecommunications in general.

As with today's emerging media, free speech rights in early broadcasting were influenced by events and conditions within contemporary society. Free speech concepts were intricately woven into the fabric of the times, and, with radio, "freedom of the air" focused primarily on tensions, real and perceived, between radio as a business engaged in entertainment and radio as a means of ex-

3

pression for distribution of information and entertainment. Understanding the emergence of First Amendment rights in electronic media to the mid-1930s consequently involves comprehending the fusion of cultural, social, political, and legal forces as they formed the milieu in which this new medium evolved.

The Meanings of "Free Speech" and "Public Interest" to 1934

Overall, court cases and legal scholars in the Progressive Era of the early 1900s emphasized that free press and free speech rights carried responsibilities in their exercise.[2] Subsequently, arguments advanced for free speech in radio hinged upon speakers' and broadcasters' responsibilities to use the airwaves wisely to benefit society and the public welfare. In the decades preceding broadcasting, the prevailing beliefs surrounding free speech were strongly influenced by Progressive Era beliefs that discussion of public matters had to be preserved while limitations could be devised on speech affecting private persons or influencing public welfare, if such restrictions fulfilled a public interest in preserving the overall public's well-being or maintaining an orderly society. From 1900 through the 1930s, courts held restrictions on private speech or speech inimical to the public welfare both constitutional and in the public interest.[3]

In addition, the legal definition of the "public interest" throughout broadcasting's formation was not as vague as some scholars have contended. These scholars argue that the public interest concept was so poorly defined in the early twentieth century that it was open to widely differing interpretations.[4] In two articles in *Communication Law and Policy,* Willard D. Rowland states that for nearly a century prior to broadcasting's introduction, state and federal regulators had applied the public interest concept to telegraph, telephone, transportation, and utilities and gave it a clear pro-industry meaning. In the 1920s and early 1930s, the predominant doctrine was that the public would be best served by protecting the economic viability and technological advancement of private industry. This pro-industry, "techno-economic" understanding of public interest in the 1920s had major, telling implications for broadcasting law. While this view of public interest dominated radio's evolution in the mid-1920s, another philosophical interpretation was developing at the same time. This public interest approach emphasized concepts of program, issue, and political viewpoint diversity.[5] Both views influenced concepts of freedom of the air in regulators' efforts to promote the general public welfare via radio.

Censorship and Social Trends

Societal trends also conditioned the behavior of individuals on all sides of the issue of free speech, from those who wanted to suppress "un-American" ideas and activities to those who advocated radical societal and governmental change. Shifting postwar economic, political, and social forces wrought vast changes in society and its subsequent cultural consensus. By the mid-1920s, historian Paul Murphy notes, tensions and divisions among society surfaced: the cynicism of the young toward older American values; growing disillusionment with the democratic system; the nation's wartime experience; the rise and demise of the Ku Klux Klan; American Legion and Daughters of the American Revolution sponsorship of "Americanism" contests in schools; demands by business for suppression of strikes while calling for laissez-faire or government-backed economic policy; upheavals caused by urbanization and increased mobility; and variant definitions of "liberty." These led to ambivalence in the lives of individuals and a search for societal redefinition during the Jazz Age.[6]

According to Murphy, the idea of liberty was often cast in terms of freedom of expression,[7] and broadcasting became caught up in the debate. In general, conservative groups saw "reasonable" suppression of speech as necessary to provide a safe, secure, and stable society, while liberal forces saw speech as a means of promoting social and economic justice. Murphy observed that "freedom of speech was an essential aspect of the postwar ambitions of virtually every group wishing to advance specific programs and policies."[8] Groups Murphy labeled "activist-repressionists" (such as the National Security League, the Ku Klux Klan, the American Legion, and Daughters of the American Revolution) and "activist-libertarians" (such as the Non-Partisan Leaguers, social crusaders, Industrial Workers of the World members, liberals, and reformers) used "free speech" as a shorthand shibboleth in attempts to shape society to their respective visions of a viable America. Repressionists thought true freedom of speech could exist only as an intangible symbol, while libertarians feared that, if the abstraction "free speech" were used to stifle expression, Americans would lose respect for the concept.[9]

In short, the free speech debate within society in the interwar years rose from numerous voices in the country, from those who saw abuses of free speech as intolerable to those who wished to use speech to further social goals. While never achieving full consensus, the groups and the debate they fomented kept the issue of free speech in the public consciousness, and when broadcasting entered the scene, the already smoldering and sometimes fiery discussions of permissible free speech and who could exercise speech privileges and when spilled over into debates over radio's regulation and control. Issues of access and control in radio emerged in debates and laws affecting candidates' use of the airwaves, speakers' rights to use the medium, and the formation of the radio industry's structure during the 1920s.

The 1920s also brought great economic growth, and the postwar decade saw the development of new industries, mass consumption, and mass production techniques. As corporations grew, business managers were increasingly glorified as kingpins of economic and social development. Business and government leaders saw overall adoption and promotion of cooperative values in the workplace and in society as progress toward a capitalistic utopia. A private-public sector partnership, which historian Ellis Hawley identifies as an "associative state," became a goal of government and business alike in the 1920s.[10]

Under both Presidents Warren Harding and Calvin Coolidge, government's role in society was threefold: to organize the private sector, to provide the building blocks of a modern economy, and to gather and organize information needed by private organizations to maintain the economy. In short, government's role as perceived by both government leaders and business executives was to protect and to work with private organizations, lending governmental support to the development of business and industry. These cooperative efforts—not laissez-faire, as so often has been misinterpreted—dominated the 1920s and fused public and private sector bureaucracies together to promote creation and development of governmental agencies concerned with efficiency and growth.[11]

During the interwar years, radio benefited tremendously from the interplay of government and industry as government departments worked with radio businesses to help the overall industry prosper, and this cooperation manifested itself in attempts at radio's regulation through four radio conferences held from 1922 through

1925. During these conferences, the shared cultural values and radio's contributions to an American civic consensus—or its shared cultural, social order—were discussed and debated. As detailed in the next chapter, government leaders often worked behind the scenes with dominant radio leaders AT&T and the Radio Corporation of America (RCA) to form radio policy and to set agendas for the radio conferences.[12] These confidential meetings between government and industry leaders as well as public hearings not only helped define "freedom of the air" but also delineated those meanings of "public interest" and "public welfare" used to control radio in its formative years. As radio grew in the interwar decades, questions of who was to control, use, own, and have access to the medium became crucial in discussions of broadcast radio, freedom of the air, and the public interest.

2 ➤ CORPORATIONS AND CENSORSHIP TO 1926

While at times contentious, the symbiotic relationship between government and the radio industry was firmly established during World War I. Immediately after the war, battles raged within government agencies for radio's regulatory control, and the Department of Commerce ultimately emerged victorious.[1] Private radio companies supported the Commerce Department's oversight and, during the early to mid-1920s, worked with the department's officials to bring order to the medium, especially its newest innovation, broadcasting. As the industry and government worked together, larger communication companies—RCA and AT&T—fought charges of monopoly and censorship over the medium as well as patent battles with each other and smaller companies.

Radio's overall regulation emerged during the mid-1920s through a close-knit relationship between regulator and regulated, who worked together to get radio service to the public and to set radio's agenda and policy through 1927. During the 1920s, the Commerce Department worked closely with radio industry leaders through informal meetings and four formal radio conferences to set up a practicable structure for the fledgling radio business. Regulators adopted policies espoused by the industry, especially RCA, Westinghouse, and AT&T, to get service to the public and to bring order to the airwaves, and many structures set during this time still influence broadcasting today. The collaborative policies of government and industry vividly portray historian Ellis Hawley's "associative state," as their cooperative efforts fused private and government actions into the joint undertaking of steady expansion of the broadcast industry in the 1920s.[2] These efforts also precipitated charges against the larger firms of monopoly over access to the airwaves and corporate suppression of expression. This chapter reviews the relationship of government and industry in broadcasting's formative years and charges of monopoly leveled as a restraint on freedom of the air and the public interest.

Broadcasting Begins, 1920

Most historians mark broadcasting's true beginnings from station KDKA's coverage in Pittsburgh of the 1920 presidential elections. Frank Conrad, a Westinghouse engineer, put KDKA in East Pittsburgh on the air as an experimental operation. Its first program, the returns of the Harding-Cox presidential election, were transmitted to approximately two thousand listeners. These listeners, many of them Westinghouse employees, heard news of a Republican landslide intermingled with phonograph records from the broadcast's start at 8 P.M. until after midnight.[3] After the election broadcast, KDKA instituted a daily program from 8:30 to 9:30 P.M.[4] By the end of 1922, electrical companies, newspapers, department stores, educational institutions, and state or municipal governments were operating 382 transmitting stations. Most of these stations were on the air only a few hours per week, and their broadcast messages reached between 600,000 and 1.5 million receiving sets. However, the prospect for rapid and continued growth was great—if the service could be properly regulated.[5]

As broadcasting expanded and the public's interest in it increased, the navy and various corporations—AT&T, RCA, Westinghouse, and General Electric (GE)—saw the possibilities inherent in the service. In 1920, when radio was considered wireless and a tool for commerce, radio patent holders signed cross-licensing agreements allowing all signatories to use wireless patents held by the group. As broadcasting emerged, expectation of profits made AT&T, RCA, Westinghouse, and GE hesitant to waive perceived rights under the cross-licensing agreements as each company believed it held the keys to setting up broadcast operations. None wished to relinquish its rights as the intercompany patent wars developed in the 1920s and as other independent broadcasters went on the air. Later, with these corporations' attempts at patent control came charges of monopoly and censorship adversely affecting freedom of the air.

The First Radio Conference, 1922

As broadcasting evolved, Secretary of Commerce Herbert Hoover used a rift between radio firms and the navy to cement his regulatory hold over radio under the provisions of the Radio Act of 1912. That quarrel resulted from the navy's desire for more competition in availability and manufacture of radio equipment. Large firms, especially AT&T and RCA, resisted any navy control and turned to Hoover and the Commerce Department for help. Staffers recognized that without the support of private entities, the navy would lose ground in its push for regulatory control. If the navy lost ground, civilian agencies would gain, and by mid-1922, the Commerce Department emerged from this conflict firmly in control of radio's regulation. That struggle's resolution plus the recommendations of the First Radio Conference secured Hoover's control over early radio regulation and development.[6]

The First Radio Conference met from February 27 to March 2, 1922. Called by Hoover at President Harding's request, it was attended by fewer than thirty individuals.[7] Included were persons in charge of broadcasting at various corporations: AT&T's A. H. Griswold and Lloyd Espenschied, GE's E. P. Edwards, RCA's John Elwood, and Westinghouse's L. R. Krumm. Other delegates were Representative Wallace White of Maine (later coauthor of the Radio Act of 1927), Senator Frank Kellogg of Minnesota, and noted amateur radio operators Edwin Armstrong and Hiram Percy Maxim. Naval, army, and Commerce Department representatives attended as well as spokesmen for the Department of Agriculture and the United States Post Office.[8] For this conference, government departments set the conference itinerary, unlike later years when the Commerce Department worked with industry leaders to set meeting agendas.

Before the conference, Bureau of Standards chief J. H. Dellinger told Hoover that the conference agenda should place emphasis on radio's rapid growth and needed regulatory changes. To Dellinger, radio communication was a private utility and as such was subject to control by the government. In addition, Dellinger warned Hoover that "the radio telephone used for broadcasting is such a powerful means of propaganda [which meant "publicity," not indoctrination or distortion, at this time] that there is special necessity for its control by the government."[9] A large part of this publicity was product advertising. The U.S. Army's Signal Corps agreed with Dellinger that the airwaves should be carefully guarded from improper use and that all material broadcast should be carefully regulated.[10] Consequently, Hoover's opening remarks to the conference emphasized three points for conferee consideration and implementation: (1) public interest in broadcasting was to be paramount; (2) problems to be solved included deciding who was to broadcast and to what purpose; and (3) direct advertising was to be curbed.[11]

To achieve goals related to these topics, conferees focused on three areas: preventing signal interference, selecting quality broadcast programming, and thwarting censorship and ownership monopolies. Each entity—government department, private corporation, and amateur operator—had its own ideas as to what constituted proper broadcast materials and how to prevent interference, monopoly, and censorship, and their respective ideas protected their standing and desire for control over the medium.

During the conference, delegates raised questions about who was to broadcast, who would decide broadcast program priorities, and who would have access to the medium. L. R. Krumm of Westinghouse told Hoover and the other conferees that Westinghouse's publicity department selected its broadcast materials and added, in reply to a question concerning religious programs, that all denominations had been allowed airtime.[12] Later, Representative White questioned the government's role in selecting programming for the medium, asking if the government should distinguish between program types or exercise any control over programming. Hoover suggested that priorities might eventually be established, but he hoped that enough wavelengths could be found so competition among stations would bring "high class service" to the public.[13]

White also asked Armstrong Perry, a noted amateur radio operator representing the Boy Scouts of America at the conference, about government involvement in program decision making. White questioned use of the naval radio station at Annapolis for congressional representatives' messages. "Who is going to determine what speech the navy shall broadcast?" he wondered. Perry replied that he saw little problem with the situation as he thought the navy could broadcast speeches one after another in a way similar to how the legislators' words were recorded in the *Congressional Record*. White noted that major differences existed between legislators selecting what was in the *Congressional Record* and the navy selecting what went out over its station. To White, someone had to decide priorities in broadcast programming, if the navy engaged in broadcasting.[14] According to an AT&T memorandum, Representative White fully appreciated the potential negative implications of program censorship as well as the political importance of ranking broadcasts for air and considered both in framing legislation and determining access to the medium.[15]

The first two days of the conference had been open sessions; the rest were closed executive sessions. At the end of the open sessions, the conferees recommended that indirect advertising be limited to a statement of station call letters and program sponsor. They also endorsed the concept of broadcast stations operating in the public interest.[16] Even at this early date, "public interest" was emerging with its dual technical and discursive purposes, although conferees emphasized the technical and economic aspects of providing clear signals and quality programs to as many Americans as possible and merely mentioned distribution of numerous viewpoints as serving the public interest.

The Commerce Department prepared a tentative report for distribution to conference representatives and others requesting the report. Most comments approved the preliminary report and endorsed legislation to give the secretary of commerce regulatory authority over radio. The Commerce Department then considered these suggestions at subsequent closed sessions held April 17–19.[17]

During the closed executive session, the conference's "legal committee" of Representative White, Senator Kellogg, and Commerce Department radio experts W. D. Terrell and A. J. Tyrer presented a tentative draft of proposed legislation. Both White and Kellogg agreed the Commerce Department should regulate monopolistic practices in broadcasting, so they drafted a provision granting the secretary of commerce the right to regulate any monopoly in broadcasting.[18] These anti-monopoly clauses eventually became Sections 13 and 15 of the Radio Act of 1927 and were later included in the Communications Act of 1934.

The conferees also agreed to include provisions requiring parties engaged in broadcasting to be entirely responsible for programs carried. Concerns over inappropriate material such as profane or obscene language and superfluous signals prompted this action and were precursors to Section 29 of the 1927 act, which prohibited broadcast of obscene, indecent, or profane material. (Today these provisions are Section 1464 of the U.S. Criminal Code.) The White-Kellogg legislation also included a license term of ten years and the statement that no vested property rights existed in the license or assigned wavelength. Those at the conference approved the draft, and Representative White and Senator Kellogg introduced bills into their respective houses of Congress.[19]

The bills failed, largely for fear of placing too much control in Hoover's hands and because they lacked industry backing. Hoover's hopes for a legislative outcome to radio's situation were dashed, but during the conference, Hoover had established personal contact with industry leaders and began to form alliances with these individuals. They would later work with him in setting up radio's organizational structure, a blueprint of which emerged in the Second Radio Conference. With Hoover, they also solidified the linkage of concepts of public interest and freedom of the air for radio.

The Second Radio Conference, 1923

With the bill's defeat, government and business tried to manage the spectrum as chaos in the air was "simply intolerable."[20] Exacerbating the situation was the *Hoover v. Intercity Radio Co., Inc.* decision. In this case, the court of appeals for the District of Columbia stated that while the commerce secretary could designate a channel upon which a corporation had to operate, he could not refuse the issuance of a license.[21] Hoover appealed the case to the Supreme Court, but when Intercity Radio Company went out of business, the case became moot.[22] In *Radio Digest,* Hoover called for legislation to fill an "urgent need for radio regulation" and outlined a partial solution to interference: open up those wavelengths reserved for governmental purposes to public use.[23]

Meanwhile, he stated, the radio division of the Bureau of Navigation in the Department of Commerce was setting up a new classification of broadcast stations, "Class B," with special requirements for programming and transmission.[24] He hoped this action, plus a second radio conference, would deal temporarily with the problems of legislative inactivity regarding radio and the residue of the *Intercity* decision. In a press release, Hoover stated that he wanted the conference to give him the powers to deal with radio's regulation.[25] In setting up this conference, the Commerce Department turned to government departments and larger corporations: AT&T, RCA, Westinghouse, Western Electric, and GE for agenda items.[26] At the end of November 1922, Arthur Batcheller, Commerce Department radio inspector for the East Coast, met with officials of AT&T, RCA, Western Union, and other wireless companies concerning domestic policy.[27]

By then, these companies had also begun publicity campaigns, which covertly helped the Second Radio Conference and Hoover achieve a modicum of control over the medium. In a series of speeches presented over four high-power stations in December 1922 and January 1923, Westinghouse executives told listening Americans that new national regulations were needed to replace antiquated radio laws so that the public could get excellent programs and service.[28] H. P. Davis, the Westinghouse executive in charge of broadcasting, noted that "good programs will come only when broadcasting is done by a few favorably located, high-class, high-power stations. Good reception is possible if our law makers will allow the separation of broadcasting wave bands and will hush the individual who today ruins the entertainments of thousands by the operation of an antiquated or improperly adjusted telegraph apparatus."[29] The public interest would naturally be served by companies, such as Westinghouse, which could supply high-power reception of excellent programs, and Westinghouse urged listeners to write broadcasters and congressional representatives to promote better programming and reception through adoption of this plan.[30] This vision of high-power stations offering quality programs became a prototype for American broadcast networks.

AT&T and Western Electric executives agreed with Westinghouse that high-class transmitting stations should be centered around large cities where the best talent was available, and they held a private meeting in early March 1923 to consider their strategies for the Second Radio Conference.[31] AT&T executives approved a reallocation plan in principle that favored better equipped stations as "the ideal radio broadcasting set-up" and decided to present it to the Second Radio Conference attendees.[32] To further their cause for well-financed broadcast operations, AT&T released publicity pieces to newspapers shortly before the conference began, and several of their suggestions for structural changes to improve U.S. broadcasting were close to what the conference finally adopted.[33]

During the Second Radio Conference in March 1923, representatives pushed for their special interests and for an agreeable solution to the problems of interference and setting regulations. A representative of one of the two educational institutions present, C. M. Jansky of the University of Minnesota, wanted more educational programs on the airwaves. Representatives from two stations owned by newspapers, the *Kansas City Star* and the *Detroit Evening News,* countered that their stations offered educational fare and talked about their companies' desire to go into "toll" broadcasting, or offering time for hire for programming on a first come, first serve basis. With the Department of Agriculture, they also wanted to offer market reports, lectures, and public health programs, while the large corporations pushed the allocation plans outlined in their private meetings or presented on radio to the American public.[34]

These plans raised questions of "big company" monopoly and censorship. Isaac Gregg of the *New York Evening Mail* noted that the public was suspicious of corporate broadcast interests because common people had no voice in broadcasting. David Carson of the Department of Commerce disagreed. The conference, he emphasized, was a public meeting, and the Commerce Department's aim was to protect the public interest and to provide a forum for expression. With that comment, the matter of corporate ownership monopoly was dropped without further discussion, but outright censorship of material and concerns over station signal interference and receipt of material remained as topics for discussion during the balance of the conference.[35] Conferees agreed on only two items related to free expression and the public interest: first, broadcast stations should be licensed through the Department of Commerce, and second, determining what programming the public wanted was difficult. Implicit in these discussions was the issue of listeners' rights: if signal interference caused reception problems, how could anyone obtain information or entertainment clearly?

To curb interference, conferees gave Hoover a mandate for action. In a resolution, they endorsed his authority "to regulate hours and wave lengths of operation of stations when such action is necessary to prevent interference detrimental to the public good."[36] With this public interest directive, Hoover proceeded as though the matter of his regulatory authority was settled. On his own initiative, he quickly put through a major spectrum reallocation plan and scrapped the previous system where all broadcasters were on one of three wavelengths: 618.6, 750, or 833.3 khz. Announced on April 4, the new assignments went into effect May 15, and radio began to assume the structural pattern it would have in later years.[37]

Hoover moved radio services such as maritime radio, amateur radio, and government operations from the newly created broadcast band to other frequencies, while he divided broadcast stations into three groups, each in a wide spectrum band, called Class A, Class B, and Class C stations. Class A stations were equipped to use power not exceeding 500 watts and were assigned wavelengths from 999.4 to 1365 khz; Class B stations were authorized to use from 500 to 1000 watts and operated on channels from 550 to 800 khz and 870 to 999.4 khz; and Class C stations, low-power stations whose wattage varied, were placed on 833.3 khz and were often limited to broadcasting only during daytime hours.[38]

The Commerce Department would carefully supervise technical standards for a Class B station operation, and Class B broadcasters were to maintain equipment and to offer quality programs to ensure satisfactory service to the public. Failure to sustain Class B standards resulted in forfeiture of the Class B privilege.[39] Hoover set up this plan specifically with the public interest in receiving clear signals and quality programs in mind.[40] The public welcomed the overall reallocation as it offered most listeners a scattering of stations which could be tuned in with reasonable clarity.[41] Through reallocation, the public interest and listeners' rights to receive information clearly via the airwaves had been enhanced and emphasized.

While listeners were pleased with these changes, stations left on the Class C band were not. They could not help but notice that larger corporations—AT&T, RCA, and Westinghouse—were well represented among the favored channels in the Class B spectrum. Almost all educational and religious broadcasters had been squeezed onto Class C's 833.3 khz wavelength along with other smaller stations. According to broadcast historian Erik Barnouw, the allocations seemed to reflect "a value judgment in which educational and religious interests were low on the scale."[42]

Indeed, the fortunes of larger corporations were rising. On May 15, the same day the new Hoover reallocations took effect, AT&T moved WEAF to its new headquarters in New York City, and Westinghouse turned over WJZ to RCA to be run from mid–New York. Meanwhile, RCA and AT&T were building their respective Washington, D.C., stations—WRC and WCAP. Westinghouse stations KDKA, KYW, and WBZ continued gaining audience, while GE was planning to build KGO in San Francisco and KOA in Denver.[43] In an interoffice memo, AT&T's director of broadcasting for WEAF, William Harkness, wrote Edgar Bloom, an AT&T vice president, that in his opinion, the Second Radio Conference generally conceded that AT&T and GE were the logical groups to develop high-power stations. He added that those at the conference also believed "the development or use of such stations should not be placed in the hands of irresponsible parties."[44]

AT&T believed many of these "irresponsible parties" were smaller stations, which operated with AT&T equipment purchased from sources other than AT&T. In the early 1920s, extensive sale of vacuum tubes for "amateur experimentation" made it easy for anyone to assemble a transmitter and begin broadcasting. If such a transmitter were then used for broadcasts of entertainment and news, AT&T regarded the operation as one that infringed on its patent rights. Stations, however, were largely unaware that AT&T considered them "patent infringers" and continued broadcasting with little regard for AT&T's patent rights.[45] In the spring of 1923, AT&T decided it had to protect its patents, even though the company expected charges of censorship or monopoly to arise from any action it took.

Patent Infringement Suits and Freedom of the Air

AT&T knew any action could result in a potential public relations nightmare, so the company's initial plan was to present patent infringers with what it considered a benign peace offering: AT&T would forgive any station its past infringements if the station paid AT&T a one-time license fee for using AT&T patented equipment. Fees for a lifetime license ranged from one dollar for stations operated by recognized educational institutions to two thousand dollars for 500-watt stations operated by commercial interests, an astronomical sum for commercial stations struggling to get by.[46] After payment, the forgiven station would be allowed to lease telephone wires for remote pickups and to purchase new equipment available only from AT&T or its subsidiary, Western Electric.[47] The response to AT&T's offer was underwhelming as few stations paid the fees, and AT&T officials thought more drastic measures were in order to protect patent rights and investments. The company decided to sue one station to set an example, and WHN in New York City was targeted.[48]

The suit began in February 1924, after WHN refused to obtain a patent license. After all, WHN reasoned, it already held a license from the Department of Commerce; why did it need another one from a private company? According to an AT&T internal office memo, the print media and other stations shared the same sentiment and cast AT&T in the role of an overbearing rogue, monopolizing broadcasting. Of course, AT&T thought its offer to license infringing broadcasting stations was evidence that it was not monopolizing the airwaves. To counter these allegations, the company presented itself as operating in the public interest as the protector of the public's right to receive intelligible broadcast signals.[49]

In a press release picked up by newspapers covering the suit, AT&T president H. B. Thayer stated that while protecting AT&T's patent rights, the company's actions also protected the public's ability to receive entertainment and information clearly. With so many stations on the air, Thayer said some entity needed to protect the public from destructive interference until government regulations were established. Consequently, AT&T adopted this protective role, and "whenever Congress acts we shall gladly accept its regulations as relieving us of any obligations to protect the public. We have no desire for a monopoly of the air."[50] Of course, Thayer's "gallant" actions also protected AT&T's dominant industry position and kept other broadcasters from expanding operations.

Following Thayer's lead, the company's officers portrayed themselves as protectors of the public interest as they began a campaign over AT&T's radio station WEAF that emphasized AT&T's public welfare obligations. On March 6, 1924, an announcer explained that the company's actions were made both to protect the company's patent rights and the public's ability to receive entertainment. He noted that a multitude of stations would destroy the value of broadcast entertainment and added that AT&T offered its facilities for hire with the hope that the large number of stations interfering with each other would diminish. The announcer also stated that while AT&T had no desire for a monopoly, it had to protect its patents; if the company did not defend its rights, it would lose all claims to its patents. Implied was the threat of closure of AT&T's stations with their popular programming.[51]

A few days later, WHN replied over the air. According to AT&T's accounts of the broadcast, WHN emphasized monopoly and freedom of the air and did not talk about the role patents played in the dispute. The WHN announcer suggested that government regulations were needed to keep radio from being "under the monopoly of a selfish group." He added that all Americans should be able to listen to the radio free of charge. In a then novel tactic, WHN invited WEAF's officials to use WHN's facilities to explain WEAF's position to the WHN audience. WHN's announcer also asked the audience to voice their opinions on "freedom of the air" to the House Committee on the Merchant Marine and Fisheries regarding hearings it was then conducting on new legislation.[52]

These legislators were well aware not only of the allegations of monopoly against AT&T within the WEAF-WHN suit but also of a concurrent Federal Trade Commission (FTC) investigation of the radio industry leaders for monopoly in their 1920 cross-licensing agreements. Those agreements allowed the signatories to use each other's patents while keeping other entities out of radio. The FTC had been scrutinizing the agreements for any alleged misconduct.[53] In December 1923, the FTC had issued a report on the radio industry that charged the patent holders with "the power to stifle competition."[54] While the FTC avoided conclusions as to the actual guilt of the accused companies, it continued investigating the companies' competitive practices. These inquiries lasted until 1928, when the FTC dropped its complaint against radio monopoly.[55]

The House Committee on the Merchant Marine and Fisheries not only called industry representatives to appear before it but also asked Hoover, as primary regulator of the industry, for his views on radio monopoly, censorship, and the public interest. Herbert Hoover was keenly aware of both the WHN-WEAF feud and the FTC investigation as he prepared his remarks for the congressional hearings. Immediately after the dispute began, E. E. Plummer of *Radio Digest* sent Hoover a telegram asking for his views as to whether AT&T "should be allowed to promulgate a virtual monopoly of the air" because of its patent holdings.[56] Hoover responded that, while it was impossible for him to comment on issues before the FTC or the courts, he could state emphatically it would be most unfortunate for the people of this country to whom broadcasting has become an important incident of life if its control should come into the hands of any single corporation, individual or combination. It would be in principle the same as though the entire press of the country was so controlled. The effect would be identical whether this control arose under a patent monopoly or under any form of combination and from the standpoint of the people's interest the question of whether or not the broadcasting is for profit is immaterial.[57]

Plummer published the remarks in *Radio Digest*'s March 22 issue.[58] Hoover released the same statement to afternoon papers on March 10 and reiterated the sentiments the next day in his remarks on radio regulation to the House Committee on the Merchant Marine and Fisheries.[59] Hoover told the committee he believed further legislation was needed only to preserve the public interest in the development of radio and for the service of those who used it. To him, the public should maintain control over the ether, and broadcasting should be done through grants of permits to use the ether. The ether should be kept open to free and full individual development, and there should be no monopoly over the distribution of material.[60] These sentiments were picked up by the *New York World* and highlighted in an interview Hoover granted to a *World* reporter.[61]

Hoover continued his campaign for radio regulation over radio itself. In a broadcast from Washington, D.C., on March 26, 1924, he restated sentiments expressed earlier to Plummer and others. He noted that the listening public and government officials heard a great deal about attempts to monopolize radio communication. "The only monopoly that could be developed," he reminded the audience, "would be through the restriction on the use of radio instruments; that is, a monopoly of the doors in and out of the ether." He assured his listeners that with the policies adopted by the government for control of airwaves, or "the ether," no danger existed that any vested rights would be established that would run counter to the public interest.[62]

Hoover also told his audience that another problem was beginning to confront broadcasting: the question of determining the priority of material to be broadcast. For wireless, message rankings had long been the norm with emergency and distress signals taking priority over commercial and private communications. For broadcasting, Hoover opposed both government intervention in any program decision making and any government censorship of program material. He believed it better for broadcasters to decide priority themselves, because "these stations naturally are endeavoring to please their listeners and thus there is an indirect censorship by the public. This is the place where it belongs. What we must safeguard is that there shall be no interference with free speech, that no monopoly of broadcasting stations should grow up under which any person or group could determine what material will be delivered to the public."[63]

During this time, AT&T's officials also continued their offensive against WHN. In mid-March, an AT&T spokesman appeared before the national Radio Trade Association. He said that the WHN suit prompted a lot of discussion about the air being monopolized by AT&T. He noted that within the New York metropolitan area, sixteen broadcasting stations were operating, and AT&T owned only one of these stations. He concluded that no monopoly of the air existed in New York, adding that at least fifty stations nationwide now operated under AT&T's patent licenses and stating that Western Electric would furnish radio broadcasting stations to anyone desiring to purchase them. As for AT&T's patent policy, he noted that "the freedom of the air is not in question: There is no question of depriving the public of broadcasting. There is no monopoly of equipment; it can be bought by anyone who has the price."[64]

By early April, WHN realized it could not sustain continued litigation, and it quietly paid AT&T $1,500 for a license. Both companies were relieved that the suit was settled out of court—AT&T because it did not like its villainous portrayal in the media and WHN because it could not afford continuation of a costly suit.[65] Other stations still refused to apply for an AT&T license, however. To make matters worse from AT&T's perspective, the Commerce Department continued to issue licenses for radio operations. During June alone, the Commerce Department issued licenses to twenty-three "infringing" stations.[66] Under the *Intercity* decision, of course, the Commerce Department could refuse no license application. When these station owners stated they would not get AT&T licenses, William Harkness wrote his superior at AT&T that other suits against a station in the Midwest and one on the Pacific Coast would help clear up the situation.[67] Again, no one at AT&T wanted adverse publicity, so AT&T sought other ways to bring errant stations into line.[68] Higher license fees for those who built stations without purchasing equipment from Western Electric was the most favored solution.[69]

During 1924 and 1925, AT&T's actions did nothing to alleviate the situation and fed talks about the "radio trust."[70] By October 1926, AT&T realized it was fighting a losing public relations battle. Of 571 active stations listed in government bulletins, 169 had not obtained an AT&T license. AT&T knew suits against these infringing stations would create more adverse public reaction, so by the end of 1926, the patent infringement issue was dead.[71] Stations that believed AT&T's actions constituted monopolistic practices had won. The infringers had successfully raised charges of monopoly and attempted censorship as they used "freedom of the air" to protect their businesses.

The Third Radio Conference, 1924

While the WHN-AT&T suit proceeded, the need for another radio conference became evident. Even though Hoover promoted small broadcasters and entrepreneurs under Commerce Department policies championing freedom of the air, he recognized that most innovations and expansion would come from those entities having the financial wherewithal to underwrite broadcast experimentation and technological development. To that extent, as the Third Radio Conference evolved, the Commerce Department's staff sought advice from RCA and AT&T in setting the conference's program. This agenda emerged from private meetings held between government and industry representatives as well as between the companies themselves.

In July 1924, Arthur Batcheller, Commerce Department supervisor of radio for the East Coast, forwarded AT&T officials a confidential list of twelve items proposed for discussion at the upcoming conference and later met with AT&T officers about the conference agenda. Three of the major subjects covered were establishing high-power stations, controlling broadcast advertising, and establishing a priority for broadcast material. Others covered amateur radio, frequency and power allocation, control of interference caused by power lines and electrical devices, and use of broadcast stations in emergencies. AT&T called its own interoffice conference to discuss the proposed radio conference and to develop responses to Batcheller's items. Batcheller attended the session with AT&T officials, and in the meeting they made it clear to him that AT&T wanted to encourage national, quality programming through high-power stations. Batcheller forwarded AT&T's interests to the Department of Commerce before the conference began, and Hoover incorporated some of these concepts into his conference addresses in October.[72]

Before the conference began, industry leaders held two private meetings for the purpose of conference planning. Such meetings were common during the 1920s, and "gentlemen's agreements" were often hammered out during the sessions. Attending each of these preconference sessions were representatives from RCA, GE, Westinghouse, and AT&T.[73] They agreed that three items be considered at the conference for programming improvement. First, talent had to be paid. Second, local broadcasters had to cooperate among themselves to develop and to allocate program material. Third, long distance interconnections for conveying programs, or networks, had to be developed. AT&T, Westinghouse, GE, and RCA thought they should present these subjects to the Third Radio Conference, if the companies were to continue their dominance of the industry. During the conference, these companies did focus attention on programming, although this was easy to do as other conferees were also interested in improving radio broadcast material to gain larger audiences.[74]

The Third Radio Conference began in October at the height of the 1924 presidential campaign. Just before it convened, Hoover received a flood of telegrams, over six thousand, protesting the supposed development of monopoly and radio censorship. Letters had been sent in response to smaller stations asking their listeners to write Hoover to decry the larger companies' control over the airwaves. RCA president J. G. Harbord wrote RCA board chairman Owen Young that Hoover was nervous about this development. Harbord noted that "all of Hoover's utterances and the little address which he had prepared for the President [to present before the conference] appeared to be written with one eye on the electorate and in terror of in some way or other identifying himself with monopoly."[75] Throughout the conference, Hoover publicly emphasized that the airwaves belonged to the people and that monopoly and censorship were to be avoided.

The Third Radio Conference with nearly one hundred delegates in attendance commenced the evening of October 6 so that Hoover's opening speech could reach a national radio audience. In his address, Hoover likened the ether to channels of navigation and told both his live and radio audiences that the people should retain ownership of the airwaves and that these airwaves should be regulated by the government. He added that such regulation did not mean government control. Instead, government should maintain freedom of the air so that radio would be "free of monopoly, free in program and free in speech." Hoover also recognized that programs had to be kept "free of malice and unwholesomeness,"[76] and when President Coolidge addressed the conferees with the short talk written for him by Hoover's department, he reinforced Hoover's sentiments. Coolidge emphasized that liberty of the airwaves did not mean license to broadcast irresponsibly. He recognized that "while parents may exclude corrupting literature from the home, radio reaches directly to our children." He added that there was also a great responsibility on the part of those broadcasting to do so without malice or slander. Coolidge noted that besides the legal liabilities attached to such broadcasts, great potential for injury existed because those who were wronged had no opportunity to reply.[77]

To deal with the problems before it, the Third Radio Conference divided into seven subcommittees. The third subcommittee focused on general problems facing radio broadcasting, including censorship, individual program improvement, and high-power stations. General George Squire, formerly chief signal officer of the United States Army, chaired this subcommittee, which concentrated on four areas: stations' broadcast signal power requirements and limitations to be placed upon their power; revision of station classifications; station operators' licensing; and the improvement of programs. Of these issues, the last focused on establishing a priority for broadcast materials and censoring programs.[78]

After considering possible recommendations to the full conference, the subcommittee thought it best to recommend that the Department of Commerce not regulate the material broadcast from any station. To do otherwise would mean endorsing censorship, and official government censorship was something the subcommittee could not condone.[79] Those at the conference voted unanimously to accept this recommendation and agreed that stations should be self-regulators or self-censors of program material, using "public opinion" as a guide.[80] Conferees also voted unanimously that it was "unalterably opposed to any monopoly in broadcasting."[81]

The third subcommittee also reviewed proposals by both Westinghouse and RCA for high-power "superstations" and proposals on the quality of broadcast programs. Walter Strong of the American Newspaper Publishers Association Radio Committee and Powel Crosley Jr., representing four groups—the Crosley Radio Corporation, the Radio Manufacturers' Association of Chicago, the Radio Trade Association, and the National Association of Broadcasters—expressed their apprehensions that an increase in power of a few stations, or the construction of a few superstations, would interfere with local stations and local messages.[82]

At the subcommittee's meetings, RCA's David Sarnoff noted differences between larger and smaller stations and added that the purposes of the two were not the same. Smaller stations were designed to serve local audiences, while larger entities needed higher power to serve large regions with national programming. He added that high-power had nothing to do with monopoly; the larger corporations had no desire to control the entire broadcast field. Besides, he said, the Federal Trade Commission was looking into the question of radio monopoly. With only 9 of the 583 stations operated by AT&T, RCA, Westinghouse, and GE combined, Sarnoff added that in his opinion, monopoly did not exist.[83] These public statements, however, were just the opposite of Sarnoff's many earlier, private proposals to AT&T and RCA corporate officials where he had emphasized the companies working together to control the industry's development.[84] While monopoly of ownership might not exist, John Erbstein, a broadcaster from Elgin, Illinois, complained that those companies did monopolize sales of transmitting apparatus. He said that he and others had attempted to purchase higher power equipment and had been turned down.[85]

Good programming and program balance were also discussed in the subcommittee. AT&T's William Harkness stated that AT&T stations' programming reflected a balance and conceded that the company assessed charges according to the type of programming. It gave preferential treatment to those presenting entertainment programs of a "high caliber" and charged a higher fee to those offering only talks or commercial matter. He noted AT&T took this action because of negative public reaction to too much talk on radio, not because of any desire to suppress talks. Harkness tied the fee to public entertainment value and implied the public interest was associated with this value. "The man who simply wants to talk for ten minutes is charged a higher rate, because it has not the same entertaining value to the public," Harkness said, adding that the entertainment manager at each AT&T station looked at proposed program material and asked what public reaction to it would be. If the manager thought the public would accept the program material, AT&T would air it; but if it would result in an unfavorable public reaction, AT&T would not. Harkness stated "the acceptability to the public of the matter offered" was of prime importance to AT&T stations' decisions to air programs. In reality, fees charged suppressed talks and were regarded as censorship, especially when they involved controversial speakers.[86]

The public's program acceptability concerned all conferees, and their discussion focused on mechanically reproduced music, live music, other entertainment programs, talk programs, and Class B stations. John Shepard III, representative of New England broadcasters and operator of Boston station WNAC, opposed the favored, superior Class B stations being used solely for talks on subjects only the speakers were interested in. Such "propaganda," as Shepard dubbed it, should be minimized. He proposed limiting radio talk by asking the conference to recommend the commerce secretary place a limit on the amount of talk on Class B licensees. To hold that classification, Shepard suggested that a station provide entertainment programs at least 60 percent of the time. This idea precipitated discussion as to what constituted "entertainment." Sarnoff asked if material by humorist Will Rogers was "entertainment" or "talk." Zenith's E. F. McDonald questioned why Class B stations couldn't air mechanically produced music as "entertainment." Laughter and applause greeted his comment that a player piano was often better than some of the people performing live on radio.[87]

Conferees agreed that requiring highly varied entertainment programs on Class B stations was good and in the public interest, but they concurred with subcommittee chair General Squire that they should be careful about mandating any specific program requirements. Otherwise, as Squire warned, requirements could lead to government censorship, and that was something he and the Department of Commerce wanted to avoid. Squire suggested the subcommittee drop any percentage specifications on radio program-ming, because radio should not have such standards any more than newspapers or magazines should. "The public itself will be the judge," he added.[88] Otherwise, government censorship of pro-grams could evolve. Delegates recommended a policy of noninter-ference in programs to the Commerce Department. Secretary of Commerce Hoover agreed but added that companies should make programming decisions with the "public interest" in mind. The conferees unanimously adopted a recommendation that noninter-ference in programs be government policy, as any other attitude involved censorship.[89]

While bills were introduced into Congress, once again these regulations did not pass as legislators focused on more pressing concerns of immigration control, downturns in farming and the textile industry, questions of whether Prohibition should be re-tained, and the need for continuing international relief in postwar Europe.[90] By mid-1925, the radio overcrowding situation was be-coming more acute with more stations going on the air. To deal with the situation, Hoover called for the fourth—and what would be the last—of his radio conferences to be held in November 1925.

The Fourth Radio Conference, 1925

As the Fourth Radio Conference approached, RCA and AT&T representatives met again to discuss potential conference topics. Information from the Department of Commerce was again avail-able to the companies, and among the department's agenda topics was improvement of intolerable radio interference. The two com-panies' representatives agreed that the most promising lines of im-provement were networking and a marked reduction in the num-ber of broadcasting stations. They thought that, to protect the public interest in radio, no new stations should be licensed.[91] Of course, any such action protected their own financial interest in radio as well. At another meeting solely of AT&T officials, discus-sion topics included the general Bell System policy for the confer-ence, which emphasized networking and a reduction of the num-ber of broadcast stations. Again, a Commerce Department official, this time S. B. Davis, forwarded advance questions and topics to AT&T and told AT&T officials that the subjects would be assigned to specific committees while the general session would discuss lim-iting the number of broadcasting stations.[92]

In limiting stations, one overriding question dominated: What should be the basis for granting the broadcasting privilege? AT&T officials thought that those decisions, in their words, should be made with the "public necessity and convenience" in mind. AT&T recognized that legislation would be needed to bring about a marked improvement in broadcast service, and with "public service" as the cornerstone of decision making, AT&T believed adequate legislation could provide authorization to the commerce secretary to regulate radio.[93]

The Fourth Radio Conference convened on November 9 and lasted three days. Some five hundred delegates, over five times the number for the previous conference, attended.[94] In his opening remarks, Hoover presented an outline of questions for their discussion:

1. Is it essential to limit the number of broadcasting stations to prevent further congestion?
2. If stations are to be limited in number, should the public interest, as represented by service to the listeners, be the basis for the broadcasting privilege?
3. Should regional committees, familiar with the situation and needs of their communities, be established as advisory to the Secretary of Commerce in passing upon applications for broadcasting licenses?[95]

Committees were created to handle conference business: advertising regulation, signal interference, legislation, amateur matters, copyright issues, allocation of frequencies, station operating regulations, and marine radio.

The full assembly of delegates handled those issues that seemed to be of paramount importance: licensing procedures, electromagnetic spectrum management, and support of the Commerce Department's efforts to regulate the medium. Other issues were handled in committee meetings, and reports were made to the full conference by respective committees. Each committee drafted recommendations, which the Department of Commerce published after the conference.[96]

One subcommittee dealt with radio advertising. Some delegates sought to ban all advertising, while others wished to restrict it. Debate ensued over three distinct classes of advertising—direct, or the blatant selling of a product; indirect, or the mention of a pro-

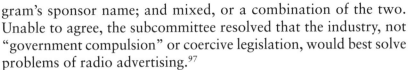

gram's sponsor name; and mixed, or a combination of the two. Unable to agree, the subcommittee resolved that the industry, not "government compulsion" or coercive legislation, would best solve problems of radio advertising.[97]

Other proposed resolutions stated more forcefully the conferees' beliefs that self-regulation was better than government oversight. Among the more vigorous statements was one submitted by WMAQ's program director, Judith Waller: "It is our recommendation that in the interest of freedom of thought and speech that no active censorship be set up to control advertising by radio." "Active censorship" meant government regulation of programming material. This sentiment was toned down to say "government compulsion" in the final resolution passed by the subcommittee.[98]

The subcommittee on station operating regulations suggested that service to the public be the basis for licensing.[99] Conferees comprising a subcommittee on legislation unanimously agreed that a limitation on the number of stations was essential and that the broadcast privilege be granted for public benefit performed. They also wanted preferential license treatment for existing stations.[100]

Conferees recommended that Congress give the secretary of commerce authorization to revoke licenses and to assign call letters, hours of operation, station location, wavelengths, and character of signal emissions. They also recommended that the secretary grant no more licenses. Hoover readily accepted this suggestion, and the day after the conference, he declared that no more broadcast applications would be accepted by the Commerce Department.[101]

As the conference concluded, Hoover addressed the public via radio and said that the major topic of the three-day conference was control of station interference. Such interference threatened what entertainment and information listeners received, and without some controls, Hoover told his listeners they would not be able to receive anything via the airwaves. According to Hoover, interference reduction was one of the conference's two outstanding results. The other was recognition of the dominance of listeners' interests in radio. His speech outlined perspectives on radio regulation that would dominate the medium for years and is worth detailing here in length:

> It may be that we shall hear a great deal about freedom of the air from some of the people who want to broadcast and who will not be able to show that their desires accord with your interests. But there are two parties to freedom of the air, and to freedom of speech for that

matter. There is the speech maker and the listener. Certainly in radio I believe in freedom for the listener. He has much less option upon what he can reject, for the other fellow is occupying his receiving set. The listener's only option is to abandon his right to use his receiver. Freedom cannot mean a license to every person or corporation who wishes to broadcast his name or his wares and thus monopolize the listener's set.

We do not get much freedom of speech if 50 people speak at the same place at the same time, nor is there any freedom in a right to come into my sitting room to make a speech whether I like it or not. So far as opportunity goes to explain one's views upon questions of controversy, political, religious or social, it would seem that 600 independent stations, many competing in each locality, might give ample opportunity for great latitude in remarks. And in any event, without trying out all this question, we can surely agree that no one can raise a cry of deprivation of free speech merely because he is compelled to prove that there is something more than naked commercial selfishness in his purpose.

The ether is a public medium, and its use must be for public benefit. The use of a radio channel is justified only if there is public benefit. The dominant element for consideration in the radio field is, and always will be, the great body of the listening public, millions in number.[102]

After the conference, Hoover made other public statements expressing his sentiments that the public interest was paramount in all deliberations on radio.[103] This definition of "public interest" coupled clear signal reception with responsible programming. The public interest standard endorsed at these conferences centered on technical issues and outcomes, with promises of program diversity brought to listeners by a reliable, corporately controlled radio industry. Such diversity was largely a promise, as will become evident in later chapters.

Until legislation passed, the Commerce Department believed the conference recommendations would assist development of appropriate laws. In the meantime, Hoover put many conference recommendations into effect. He reprimanded and threatened sanctions against stations that wandered all over the dial because of equipment defects or because they were searching for an unused portion of the spectrum. Hoover's actions infuriated some broadcasters, and challenges soon arose. One of these challenges resulted in the total breakdown of the fragile regulatory structure Hoover

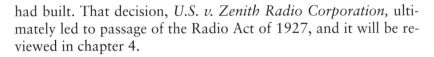

had built. That decision, *U.S. v. Zenith Radio Corporation,* ultimately led to passage of the Radio Act of 1927, and it will be reviewed in chapter 4.

Conclusion

In summary, both Secretary of Commerce Herbert Hoover and the industry wanted to create cooperative machinery to organize a socioeconomic order in broadcasting. This system involved large corporations and government agencies working together to transform the industry from amateur communication to nationwide broadcasting. A close-knit interrelationship between regulator and regulated arose as Hoover sought to control radio through four radio conferences. During these conferences, parameters for both the concepts of "public interest" and "freedom of the air" evolved. Those concepts unquestionably had a conservative, industry-oriented preference and were employed during the decade by regulators and the regulated to aid broadcast policy development favoring commercial interests. Their collaborative policies fused private and government efforts into the joint undertaking of steady expansion of the broadcast industry.

During these formative years, industry giants and government officials established their vision of American broadcasting to the later detriment of smaller commercial broadcasters and noncommercial broadcasters. Classes of stations emerged from regulatory efforts in the early to mid-1920s with larger, well-financed stations given premier status in frequency allocation. Coupled with these special apportionments was an expectation of quality programming broadcast in the public interest. "Public interest," however, was linked to clear reception of messages selected by private entities, not the government. The messages were generally conservative so as not to offend listeners and usually supported the status quo. Nothing illustrated this concept more clearly than the policies that evolved in the 1920s for broadcast coverage and treatment of politics and political candidates.

3 ⇒ TO SPEAK, OR NOT TO SPEAK, THAT IS THE QUESTION: POLITICAL SPEECH TO 1926

Over the centuries, political speech protections emerged at the apex of a hierarchy of legal protections for expression, but as speech cases from World War I show, this right was not absolute. When speech threatened the established status quo, it could be curtailed as a "clear and present danger."[1] During the Progressive Era, legal scholars emphasized social interests in freedom of expression and the importance of political discussion to democratic government. Avenues for interchange of ideas had to be kept open, but responsibility came with the exercise of speech. Whereas no valid, constitutional law could be devised in most areas of public discussion, the private domain was different, and here legal limitations could be set on freedom of speech.[2]

Public discussion focused largely on self-governance, while private speech centered upon commerce, private actions of individuals or corporations, and other expression not dealing with self-governance. Public discussion of government action could be curbed, however, if the speech threatened the public's general welfare or the public interest. This approach carried over to radio and its use in discussion of public affairs and coverage of controversial matters. Nowhere was this system of curbing speech to protect the status quo more effective than in its application to the electoral process and candidates' speech via radio.

Controlling Controversial Speech: A Question of Money

As the 1924 elections approached, concerns increased over censorship of speakers' messages, control of candidates' access to the medium, and the treatment of speakers other than politicians. Allegations of censorship, notably those involving Socialist Norman Thomas and journalist H. V. Kaltenborn of the *Brooklyn Eagle,* made politicians cautious about broadcasters' checks on messages that could affect their own ability to reach constituents. In April 1924, *The Nation,* a liberal publication, complained that broadcasters reflected the conservative views of the time and readily censored those espousing more progressive opinions. "'Mechanical trouble' in the broadcasting apparatus seems to be a disease with symptoms curiously similar to those of censorship," complained the editors. "Three times recently radio speakers have been cut short. Each time the victim has thought that the trouble was censorship, and the radio company has explained it was 'mechanical trouble.'"[3] One speaker had disapproved of Prohibition; another attacked New York drama critics; and a third had defended women's rights to keep their own names and their own jobs outside the home after marriage.

While radio companies did not want to be accused of censorship, stations feared presentation of controversial issues would create unfavorable audience reactions. AT&T was especially concerned about programming over its station WEAF, a "toll" station, one that sold its time on a first come, first serve common carrier basis. WEAF's managers thought guidelines were needed if the station were to become the leader in the radio field. They recognized they could not afford to broadcast anything unacceptable to the vast listening public, so, even though WEAF was a toll station, managers retained the right to censor all programs and to decline explanations for refusing to air programs they deemed undesirable.[4]

The most noted incident of WEAF censorship resulted in policy changes for AT&T's radio operation regarding speech criticizing government officials. WEAF gave free airtime to the *Brooklyn Eagle,* and one of its editors, H. V. Kaltenborn, began weekly, half-hour talks on October 23, 1923. Early in 1924, Kaltenborn discussed U.S.-Soviet relations. The American government had not recognized the USSR's Bolshevik government, and Kaltenborn noted that the Soviet Union's foreign commissar, Maxim Litvinov, had written the American government indicating a desire for diplomatic relations. In his memoirs, Kaltenborn stated he considered Litvinov's message "tactful and carefully phrased." The U.S. government rejected the appeal, and Kaltenborn criticized Secretary of State Charles Evans Hughes for his blunt refusal. Hughes was listening to this talk at home in the company of "a number of prominent guests." An embarrassed and angry Hughes later called a Washington representative for AT&T and "laid down the law to him." Word relayed to AT&T's New York headquarters was that broadcasts critical of the government or government officials should not be allowed.[5] Kaltenborn, however, was under contract, and nothing could be done until that agreement ran out. When it did, William Harkness, AT&T's director of broadcasting, was told to take Kaltenborn off the air.[6]

Tensions developed when the contract was not renewed. In a letter to AT&T president H. B. Thayer, the managing editor of the *Brooklyn Eagle,* H. M. Crist, criticized AT&T's discrimination and Harkness's unwillingness to present an adequate reason for discontinuing the series. In mid-September 1924, Harkness told Crist and R. M. Gunnison, the attorney who had negotiated the previous WEAF–*Brooklyn Eagle* contract, that Kaltenborn had been taken off the air in anticipation of campaign speakers' need for airtime in the upcoming election. When Crist and Gunnison asked for a post-election engagement, Harkness said various experimental matters would prevent him from giving a definite answer at that time. Puzzled and indignant, Crist felt Harkness's "flippant" manner meant he had no intention of seriously considering the *Eagle*'s application. Kaltenborn's program had drawn great listener response and was, in Crist's mind, far superior to other programs that had been renewed. Crist asked Thayer for his consideration of the matter.[7]

Thayer replied that AT&T had a prerogative to air what it pleased when it pleased over its stations and added that WEAF did not have to supply a reason for its refusal to continue Kaltenborn's talks. Crist responded that AT&T and WEAF had supplied no adequate reason for refusing to renew the *Eagle*'s agreement yet "renew[ed] the agreements for various advertising features which have very little public interest. . . . This forces on us the conclusion that you have adopted a policy of deliberate discrimination against the *Eagle.*" Later, in 1931, a wide-ranging ACLU investigation of radio censorship came to the same conclusion about this incident.[8] WEAF officials then decided the *Eagle* could buy time for ten dollars per minute, the same charge assessed any other entity desiring to broadcast. Because of these charges, the *Eagle* told its readers it was ceasing broadcasts. Letters to the *Eagle* denounced WEAF's management but did nothing to change their minds.[9] In this incident's outcome, WEAF's managers and other broadcasters learned a significant lesson: equitable charges for airtime could control speech deemed unacceptable while at the same time diminish charges of discrimination. Kaltenborn was not to be silenced, though. He resumed his talks in the fall, first over WAHG owned by Alfred Grebe, a radio set manufacturer, and later over Bamberger Department Store's Newark station, WOR.[10]

Apprehension over this type of control had been raised in congressional debates and hearings on various radio bills during 1924. In these sessions, representatives cited examples of broadcasters' power in regulating messages similar to the AT&T-*Eagle* confrontation. During debate in January, for example, Representative Marvin Jones of Texas charged that AT&T had refused its lines to a theater for transmission of a concert.[11] In hearings in March on a radio bill, Broadcasters' Society of America executive Charles Caldwell accused AT&T of refusing to sell broadcast time to religious groups for Sunday afternoon services and of withdrawing an invitation to a speaker when AT&T learned he would talk on the 1924 political campaign.[12]

Caldwell further asserted that, unless such practices were stopped immediately, monopolies and censorship would grow, and in the future "it might well be that some official of the monopoly company sitting in the quiet of his executive office, surrounded and protected and away from the public, where he can not be seen, will issue the fiat that only one kind of religion shall be talked over the radio; that only one kind of politics shall be talked over the radio; that only one candidate can give messages to the people; that only one kind of soap can be advertised."[13] While this last example caused the hearings to break into laughter, concern over message censorship continued to manifest itself in both government and industry circles, especially as the 1924 campaign drew closer.

Political Broadcasts of 1924: Setting the Stage

Politicians and broadcasters alike looked forward to the 1924 political campaign. Radio manufacturers were predicting record sales, all because of the intended broadcast coverage of the national conventions and the presidential elections.[14] In fact, in January 1924, presidential hopeful William McAdoo wanted to set up his own station to reach voters but was dissuaded by RCA president J. G. Harbord. He told McAdoo that setting up a station would cost around $100,000 and would probably reach individuals in only one locale as the effective radius of most stations was one hundred miles, at best. For national exposure, it would be cheaper for McAdoo to use already existing facilities, and Harbord encouraged McAdoo to use wire interconnections, or networks, with stations.[15]

By mid-summer, 525 stations were broadcasting, and according to Henry Marschalk of the Music Master Corporation, a Philadelphia-based music publisher, politicians were eager to try "the chief medium through which the contending parties and nominees will reach the public."[16] With this increased interest came fears that some candidates might be censored or denied access to radio. During hearings in March 1924 on radio legislation, Representative Ewin Davis, a Tennessee Democrat and later author of the Davis Amendment, which attempted to equalize geographic distribution of radio stations, crystallized sentiment in his question to AT&T representative William Harkness: "You can readily see, can you not, that one candidate might monopolize the radio field by obtaining contracts that his speeches and his propaganda, if we may use that term, might be carried and the other fellow not permitted to employ the same method of reply?"[17] Harkness denied that broadcasters would allow that to happen.

Other broadcasters, cognizant of politicians' fears, shared Harkness's views. During the first convention of the National Association of Broadcasters (NAB) on October 11, 1923, the small group of broadcasters debated the question of whether politicians should be allowed to use broadcast facilities at all. The group decided to accept the suggestion of John Shepard III of WNAC that a political party applying for airtime be required to bring a speaker from the opposing party and that both be given an equal amount of time on the same program.[18] If all viable candidates were treated equitably during the upcoming elections, broadcasters would not be perceived as playing favorites. Notes from the organization's meeting in 1925 suggest NAB members followed this policy in the 1924 campaign.[19]

As the campaign approached, concerns about "un-American" candidates vexed broadcasters. "Suppose a socialist wants to talk over the radio," one broadcaster complained to a reporter for *Colliers,* a popular mass circulation magazine. "What can I say to him, if he's a legitimate candidate? But, if I let him talk, what will happen to me and my business?"[20] As the 1924 political season unfolded, the answer to those questions became obvious: assessing charges for airtime would control access to the medium and keep speech undesirable from the broadcasters' standpoint off the air. Simply put, mainstream parties could afford time while fringe parties and undesirable candidates could not. If candidates were all charged the same price for airtime, the public would view candidates as being treated equitably, and no one could legitimately complain about overt discrimination. Lessons had been learned from the Kaltenborn-WEAF incident.

Broadcasting the 1924 Conventions

Charges aside, station operators, notably AT&T and RCA, began investigating means to broadcast the conventions, campaign, and election results, as an extensive AT&T interoffice report shows. While the primary purpose of the document was to spell out explicitly the measures used in 1924 for reference in later elections, this comprehensive summary provides conclusive documentation of radio's coverage of the campaign. According to the report, in early December 1923, the *Chicago Daily News,* owner of WMAQ, requested AT&T facilities to cover the conventions. At that time, many thought the Republican National Convention would be held in Chicago, and the *Daily News* had secured an option from the Republican National Committee to the exclusive rights to broadcast their proceedings, if they were held in Chicago. While the paper's chief desire was to serve the Chicago area, the paper's owner also thought that other stations might be connected by means of the Bell System's long distance telephone lines to carry the convention simultaneously to other points.[21]

AT&T officials told the *Daily News* editors that because of the magnitude of the engineering setup for convention coverage, the Bell System would deal directly with the Republican National Committee's convention committee rather than with the newspaper. In addition, the *Daily News*'s use of wire facilities for broadcasting during the convention was doubtful because of the engineering challenges involved in interconnection. While AT&T said it was not certain mechanical problems could be overcome, its statements masked the company's own exploration of broadcasting the conventions itself.

By April 1924, AT&T was negotiating with the Republican and Democratic parties for rights to broadcast their respective proceedings. Cleveland, not Chicago, was the site of the Republican convention, while the Democrats met in New York City. AT&T contacted both political parties' national committees to determine their needs during their respective conventions and campaigns and to organize a comprehensive plan to meet those needs. For AT&T, the primary consideration in any plan involving the use of Bell's facilities was the availability of lines that would not interfere with normal Bell System telephone traffic.[22]

Because of the lack of equipment and trained personnel, AT&T determined that no more than twelve cities in the eastern half of the country could be connected. Such a chain of stations, or network, would cost an estimated $12,000 for six days. Names of eighteen cities with a list of local stations licensed under Bell System patents were forwarded to the Republican National Committee so it could select those twelve cities to be linked. AT&T volunteered its New York and Washington, D.C., stations, while other stations would bear any expenses as a public service.[23]

AT&T also decided that the whole convention, not just the highlights, could be broadcast and that it would provide an AT&T announcer for running commentary between speeches and other events. Each station could then decide what portions of the broadcast proceedings it would carry. AT&T sent this information with charges it would assess each station to the Republican National Committee. The committee then sent letters to various stations, which had been indicated as "suitable" in the twelve cities. These stations were high-grade Class B stations using Western Electric equipment and were not in violation of AT&T patents.[24]

Details for the Democratic convention in New York were handled in similar fashion. As with the Republican convention, AT&T found it impracticable to connect more than twelve cities in the eastern half of the United States. The estimated cost of the entire service for the twelve cities for a period of twelve days was $20,000.

Again, participating stations would divide the costs. A list showing eighteen cities with their local AT&T patent-licensed stations was forwarded to the Democratic National Committee and to Stanley J. Quinn, vice chairman of the executive committee of the New York Democratic National Convention Committee. As in the case of the Republican convention, the Bell System would absorb charges for Bell's stations in New York City and Washington.[25]

As word of these contemplated hookups spread throughout the industry, AT&T officials had to deal with publicity problems regarding interconnection. In February, a complaint developed over the inability of AT&T to carry a presidential speech via its long distance lines to the Chicago area. The Rotary Club there had requested broadcast facilities for the speech too late and did not fully understand the special circuits, labor, and equipment needed for such a setup. The Zenith Corporation station WJAZ was to carry the broadcast, and its owner, Eugene McDonald, accused AT&T of stifling Chicago area listeners' ability to hear the president. This very public incident also fueled an ongoing dispute between McDonald and AT&T over sale of equipment to WJAZ. To counter McDonald's charges of censorship, AT&T mounted a publicity campaign so that no repeat performance of such misunderstandings would hamper its coverage of the upcoming convention and campaign.[26]

But, as preparations for the conventions proceeded, distrust of broadcasters, especially AT&T and RCA, threatened the proposed radio coverage of the Democratic convention. Stanley J. Quinn outlined his concerns in a confidential memorandum to Joseph Pierson of the American Publishers Committee on Cable and Radio Communications. He warned Pierson to tell "his friends in radio" that Democrats were beginning to believe that the radio industry was hostile to them, and Quinn indicated that developments over broadcasting the conventions were partially to blame.

When New York City had been seeking the Democratic convention, newspapers carried an erroneous story that the Republican National Committee had been offered $25,000 for exclusive broadcasting rights to their convention by the *Chicago Daily News* and its station, WMAQ. Democrats misinterpreted these actions and began asking AT&T and RCA to pay for broadcast rights to their convention. Both companies stated that, as a matter of principle, they would not pay for rights to programming carried in the public interest.

A conference was held among representatives of the Democratic committee, RCA, and AT&T. The companies expressed their distaste for setting the precedent of paying for the privilege of broadcasting a public event of national significance. At the meeting, Quinn suggested to William Harkness and E. S. Wilson of AT&T and David Sarnoff of RCA that they could avoid setting such a dangerous precedent by making a "contribution" to the Democratic Local New York Entertainment Fund. If the companies collectively gave $10,000 toward the entertainment of New York's visitors, the Democrats would open convention proceedings to all broadcast companies, free of charge. AT&T decided not to make a "contribution," while RCA donated $1,000.

AT&T later offered to broadcast the entire convention—for a fee assessed to the Democratic National Committee. AT&T sent Quinn a list of stations that could broadcast the convention and told him costs would be $10,000 for six days with an additional charge of about $1,100 for each successive day. When Democratic National Committee chairman Cordell Hull received word of these prices, he angrily wanted to omit broadcasting of the convention altogether.

Quinn told Pierson that danger existed for radio companies in risking the ill will of both conventioneers and the public by seeming to limit radio's coverage of the convention. He warned Pierson that the Democratic National Committee and various unnamed influential Democrats believed the radio industry was an adjunct of the Republican party. He cautioned Pierson to tell broadcasters that someday radio would need support from Democratic legislators and stated that they needed to secure legislators' goodwill before, rather than after, the election.

Even though the radio companies had stated publicly that they would treat the conventions alike in both coverage and broadcast charges, Democrats were skeptical. Quinn cited the example of George Mara, New York's local representative of the Democratic National Committee. Mara believed that whatever radio took in from the Cleveland convention, it would later pay back as a contribution to the Republican party. Quinn believed that such perceptions—indeed, the whole situation—was a serious problem for the radio industry. Pierson passed the memorandum to Owen Young, chairman of the board of RCA and a registered Democrat. Both he and Hull were involved in setting up the convention and radio's coverage. While no written record exists of meetings between Young and Hull specifically on this problem in radio's coverage, one can assume Young allayed Hull's fears of discrimination in coverage and emphasized coverage as a public service as radio stations carried the convention gavel-to-gavel and free of charge.[27]

Even with these behind-the-scenes technical and logistical problems and the doubts of Democrats of broadcasters' fairness, the conventions reached radio listeners with what seemed to be only a few hitches. The broadcasts belied the complicated technical setup and personnel dispersal necessary for the coverage. Both AT&T and RCA broadcast the proceedings of the Republican convention in Cleveland June 10–13 and the Democratic convention in New York City June 24 through July 9. For the conventions, the radio coverage setup was almost identical.

AT&T placed its announcer, Graham McNamee, and two observers in positions where they could easily watch the Republican party's proceedings and convention.[28] In addition to the WEAF network, WMAQ in Chicago and RCA's stations WJZ and WGY covered the convention. Major J. Andrew White, WJZ's star announcer, handled on-the-scene coverage for the RCA stations. Both he and McNamee provided vivid, picturesque descriptions of the proceedings.[29] As with AT&T, the RCA stations covered most convention proceedings. Most sessions were scheduled for early afternoon and evening coverage. According to WJZ's logs, when the sessions ran long, scheduled programs were canceled to carry the convention.[30]

All in all, the Republican convention ran smoothly. It opened with a fanfare from the John Philip Sousa Band, and absence of static along the East Coast allowed listeners to hear the entire session. Radio demonstration rooms in stores were packed, and the sales of radio sets soared. Coolidge was nominated almost unanimously on the first ballot. Humorist Will Rogers noted that Coolidge could have been nominated by postcard.[31]

During the convention, the radio audience heard a militant bloc led by Senator Robert LaFollette of Wisconsin fight to inject progressive planks into the Republican party platform. When his actions failed, the faction he headed bolted and set up a third party.[32] This independent party, the Progressive party, fought an uphill battle throughout the campaign to reach parity with the two major parties in monies to conduct the campaign. According to the report on Bell facility use in the 1924 election, the Progressives approached

AT&T concerning the broadcast of its convention in Cleveland July 4–5. AT&T, however, could not accommodate the request as it was still in the midst of broadcasting the Democratic convention.[33]

On July 5, the Progressives nominated LaFollette as their presidential candidate and Senator Burton Wheeler of Montana as his running mate. Soon after this, an editorial in *The Nation* questioned whether radio would cover this third party equitably. "Will LaFollette's speakers have their fair share of radio publicity?" it asked rhetorically and then answered, "We doubt it; it will be almost impossible for officials of the big radio corporations to give a new and radical movement its just allotment of time."[34]

Radio operators had learned much during the coverage of the GOP convention, and consequently, they were better prepared when the Democrats met in New York on June 24. Most observers expected this meeting to follow the pattern of the Republican convention, but the Democrats met for sixteen days instead of three when a deadlock between the two top contenders for the nomination, Alfred E. Smith and William McAdoo, lasted for over one hundred ballots. Finally, on the 103rd ballot, dark-horse candidate John W. Davis was chosen as a compromise with Charles Bryan as his running mate.[35] Twenty stations carried the convention; eighteen were in the AT&T network while RCA stations WJZ and WGY experimented with interconnection by Western Union wires.[36]

During the convention, receiving sets were installed in the hallways outside the main arena and at the headquarters of the various candidates. So complete was AT&T's coverage that some visiting reporters located in the Press Club in the basement of Madison Square Garden relied on McNamee's reports for their stories. In addition, sets in the candidates' suites enabled them to pick up the convention and kept them advised of proceedings.[37]

Unlike the Republicans, the Democratic National Committee had stationed an official censor near the speaker's microphone because it had reserved the right to cut coverage, if information it did not wish the public to hear was being aired. The committee also obtained an agreement from the broadcasters that they would not broadcast accounts of any divisiveness within the party. Neither announcers nor speakers, however, had to carry the dissension of the Democratic party to the public; the roar of the crowd clearly brought their infighting home to listeners.[38]

Historian William Leuchtenburg notes how poorly the Demo-crats came across. Democrats from the South and West emerged as racial bigots who championed the Ku Klux Klan, while New York-ers shouted down speakers and behaved like "Cockney rowdies." So closely divided was the convention that a vote not to mention the Klan by name in the platform passed by only one vote. For nine days, delegates deadlocked between McAdoo and Smith, an impasse that caused Will Rogers to quip, "This thing has got to come to an end. New York invited you people here as guests, not to live."[39]

This convention coverage, historian Gleason Archer later noted, brought a new trend in political oratory where thunderous speeches were not agreeable to radio audiences.[40] The *Saturday Evening Post* commented favorably on radio's affect on the political process: the "Democratic Convention was held in New York, but all America attended it. . . . [Radio] gives events of national importance a na-tional audience. . . . The radio is even more merciless than the printed report as a conveyer of oratory. . . . Silver-tongued orators whose fame has been won before sympathetic audiences are going to scale down to their real stature when the verdict comes from radio audiences."[41]

The conventions were not only "attended by all of America" but were the proving ground for interconnection of stations, or net-working. As the actual campaign progressed, political campaign talks helped AT&T and others refine techniques for regional and coast-to-coast network transmissions and included experiments leading to development of the National Broadcasting Company (NBC).

Broadcasting the 1924 Campaign

During the three-party presidential campaign, the Republicans pursued a strategy of concentrating their fire on LaFollette and ig-noring Davis. The Republicans insinuated that LaFollette was a Bolshevik agent and warned that a vote for him might prevent any candidate from winning a majority of electoral college votes and, thus, throw the election into the House of Representatives. "Coolidge or chaos" was the only issue, the Republicans said.[42] The Progressives based their 1924 campaign on the old cry of the evils of monopoly, and theirs was a campaign faced with almost insur-mountable odds. They had no state, county, or municipal slates; the 1924 Progressive movement was not so much a third party as it was merely a presidential and vice-presidential ticket. The Progressives were also crippled by lack of money; for every dollar Coolidge had in campaign funds, LaFollette had four cents. The Democrats made little impression on the popular mind as Davis could get neither Republicans nor the public to notice him. Consequently, his campaign coffers were less than those of the Republicans. When Coolidge swept the country with well over fifteen million votes, Davis trailed with a low total of eight million while LaFollette received under five million votes.[43]

During the campaign, varying numbers of stations were interconnected for political speeches by the more prominent members of the three leading political parties. AT&T's report on facility usage stated that the Republican National Committee requested AT&T write a guide for radio use in the campaign for various Republican state headquarters. The company complied, and the brochure stressed the vast audiences that could be reached through radio transmission, adding that radio should be used wherever practical because of the arduous nature of on-site campaigning. The booklet outlined procedures to be followed to obtain AT&T service and suggested requests be made as early as possible. The Democrats and the Progressives requested no brochures, and neither party seemed to be as aware of radio's potential as the Republicans.[44]

By 1924, AT&T was in the process of creating a continuous network of stations. Permanent installations between WEAF in New York and WCAP in Washington, D.C., were already established, and according to interoffice AT&T memoranda written shortly after the conventions, many stations in the convention network were among the twenty-one considered for a regular networking circuit. Other memos show that AT&T planned to sell airtime to national advertisers over those stations connected for simultaneous broadcasts. Such a network could also handle events of national importance, such as speeches by the president, at a relatively low cost and bring prestige and credibility to AT&T's radio operation. With a capital investment of under $100,000 and annual costs in the neighborhood of $70,000, AT&T recognized it would take only a few years to get the operation into the black. The company estimated the proposed network in the nation's top twenty-four major markets could cover 78 percent of the populace—and its purchasing power.[45]

To set up the network, negotiations with broadcast stations, some sharing the same wavelength in the same city, were proposed. Under the contract, AT&T proposed to supply "super-programs" and national advertising to stations at a set rate. AT&T believed such programs would popularize the selected broadcast stations and make it possible for the local stations to charge higher rates for local paid broadcasting. The network was to be functional by October 1924, and AT&T wanted to take steps to ensure its frequent use.[46] Broadcast of political speeches was one way to accomplish this. AT&T expected such speeches to increase listeners' interest in programming of interconnected stations. This listener interest in national programming could then be sold to national advertisers, and all broadcasters would profit.

Numerous political speeches followed the broadcast of the acceptance speeches of Democratic and Republican candidates. In all, over fifty major speeches given by individuals in the three major parties were transmitted through AT&T interconnections between the last acceptance speech on August 19 and the final speeches of Coolidge and Davis on November 3. Candidates or their respective parties paid for interconnections, so stations could carry talks for free. A review of radio stations and networks set up by AT&T shows the incumbent, Coolidge, and the Republicans interconnected groups of five or more stations more often than did the Democrats or the Progressives. Smaller networks linking four or fewer stations were also used by political speakers. Again, the Republicans used them more frequently.[47] Owen D. Young, RCA's chairman of the board, told *Wireless Age* that radio would stimulate interest in the upcoming elections and improve delivery of political speeches to Americans as the usual platform speech would not be effective with radio audiences.[48] He was right on both counts.

During the campaign, one incident became noted for alleged discrimination. In mid-October, LaFollette was denied time on WHO in Des Moines. He complained bitterly he was victim to monopoly interests that wished to keep him off the air and charged the Commerce Department with complicity in the schemes. Secretary of Commerce Herbert Hoover replied that the government, contrary to LaFollette's belief, had no say in what was broadcast. "The Department of Commerce does not and can not give orders to radio stations that they must or must not broadcast A, B, or C,"

Hoover said. "This would be a gross violation of the very foundation of free speech and would, in the end, amount to a government censorship of what goes out over the radio."[49]

As for monopoly of the airwaves, Hoover stated: "There are 530 radio stations in the United States; less than a dozen of them belong to the people that Mr. LaFollette calls the monopoly. There is no monopoly and can be none under the law. The stations are all independent and have the right to decide for themselves as to what they will or will not broadcast just as much as a newspaper has the right to decide what it will publish."[50] Under present regulations, LaFollette could erect his own station and broadcast whatever he pleased. To Hoover, broadcasters maintained control over what political messages they would transmit as well as the rules set up for requesting time. Later, the public learned that LaFollette had been denied time because he had not requested the use of WHO's facilities three weeks in advance as required by WHO's Republican owners, who had also enforced this rule against Republican senator George Pepper of Pennsylvania.[51]

With the focus on LaFollette's woes and on other radio coverage of the campaigns, the potential for control over political broadcasts was so evident to participants of the Third Radio Conference in early October 1924 that representatives of both AT&T and RCA had to defend their claims to public service and to refute charges of monopoly control over programming. David Sarnoff, RCA vice president and general manager, called charges of monopoly in sale of equipment and control over programming against AT&T and RCA "ridiculous" and said that radio was developing "in the direction of competition," not exclusivity. He noted, "Every political party, every religious sect, has had its full opportunity and its full chance to deliver its message over those stations without any charge whatsoever." Sarnoff added that no apology or defense from RCA was needed for the company's actions.[52]

During the campaign, politicians asked GE's stations to broadcast their speeches. Martin Rice, manager of broadcasting for GE, wrote a subordinate that GE had adopted a policy that its stations would not broadcast controversial subjects, unless both sides of an issue could be presented with "absolute fairness." The policy included political speeches. Rice noted that GE stations asked for advance copies of addresses to be delivered through their facilities because the GE radio managers believed if political messages were presented, the stations would be compelled to invite representatives of other points of view on the same subject to speak during the same broadcast. Otherwise, the public would infer favoritism on the part of radio operators, and Rice wanted to avoid such perceptions. To him, GE could not escape being held responsible for all addresses made on its stations because the public viewed coverage of speeches and political meetings differently. Airing a political meeting exactly as it happened showed no bias, but broadcasting speeches was perceived as endorsement of viewpoints presented.[53]

All in all, during the 1924 election, major party presidential candidates were treated equitably by the larger broadcasters. One week after the election, in a speech to an electrical engineering society, AT&T's William Harkness summed up what was then perceived as the appropriate position on political broadcasting: "During a political campaign the broadcaster either must refuse to serve any political party, or he must treat them all on the same basis. In either case he will dissatisfy some and be subject to criticism by those who do not appreciate his position."[54] For candidates, equal treatment was the rule, but stations maintained strict control over their other programming and other speakers. These policies were carried into the 1926 election year.

The Elections of 1926

Compared to the 1924 presidential campaigns, the off-year election of 1926 was lackluster and void of political sparks. Of most interest was the Socialist party's plan to erect its own station so that it did not have to rely upon any other station's magnanimity for the broadcast of its messages. During its national convention in May 1926, the Socialist Party of America voted to refer the project, including fund raising, to its national executive committee, even though some delegates doubted whether the party could actually obtain a license from the government to broadcast matters pertaining to the Socialist movement. New York's state secretary of the party, Herbert Merrill, told the convention to press on in the matter. "The Socialist Party of America *needs* a radio broadcasting station so Eugene V. Debs and other members of the party can be heard in the United States and in foreign countries," he said.[55] Debs, the Socialist candidate for president in 1920, was in poor health at the time and died in October 1926, a few weeks before the election.[56] In December, his supporters began building the radio station in his honor. The station was suggested by Debs's family as a memorial "more in keeping with Mr. Debs's record as a fearless defender of free speech" than any other memorial could be.[57] The station, WEVD, would be used after the 1926 elections to carry the messages of the Socialists, but until then, Socialists had to rely on stations owned by others to air their messages.

By autumn 1926, more than five hundred radio stations were operating, and the regulatory endeavors of the secretary of commerce had failed. Radio regulations under the laws of 1910 and 1912 had simply proved inadequate for broadcasting.[58] During discussions on what was to become the Radio Act of 1927, legislators debated provisions regarding nondiscrimination by radio stations toward all candidates. During hearings on a radio control bill in January 1926, Representative Ewin Davis returned several times to questions of equitable coverage of religious organizations as well as controversial issues and candidates. AT&T spokesman William Harkness told Davis and other representatives that AT&T gave time for religious broadcasts with the understanding that one group should not offend others. When asked how broadcasters treated political candidates, who generally did "offend" one another, Harkness replied, "We have met that situation very frequently in this way: During the last national political campaign, we presented all parties and gave them equal opportunity and they paid for the service received." All candidates, including Socialists, were treated alike: all paid for the time used.[59]

House committee members still saw likely problems, especially with potential audience deception through candidate "propaganda" and possible broadcaster censorship of information.[60] While legislators pointed out that broadcasters' "editing" was done to eliminate slanderous or seditious material, often such censorship was conducted to keep distasteful material from offending listeners.[61]

To aid them in determining if a speech might offend listeners, broadcasters often asked for advance copies of speeches. One such request in 1926 involved a political speech by Republican senator James Watson of Indiana, powerful chairman of the Senate Interstate Commerce Committee, the committee which had oversight of the Senate radio bill then under consideration. The supposed censorship of Watson's speech had far-ranging consequences for broadcasting, because the episode led directly to inclusion of the equal opportunities doctrine for political candidates in the Radio Act of 1927.

In March 1926, Cincinnati station WLW requested a copy of a speech Watson was to give on the eve of the primary election in his home state of Indiana. Watson refused. WLW said that its policy of review was consistent with the policies of the Department of Commerce, an erroneous statement but one that outraged Watson. Watson was a potential presidential candidate in 1928 and a political archrival of Herbert Hoover, another potential nominee. Watson charged Hoover with setting review policies for broadcasters and labeled Hoover the "czar" of radio. He decried WLW's action as "censorship" and introduced provisions in radio bills then before Congress for nondiscrimination, or equal opportunities, in airing speeches of political candidates and for a commission to regulate the medium.[62] Until this incident, no such equal opportunity clause had even been discussed by Congress.

Senator Burton Wheeler of Montana, the Progressive party's candidate for vice president in 1924, wrote an American Civil Liberties Union (ACLU) representative, Isabelle Kendig, that Watson was "furious" with WLW's censorship and now favored the passage of the radio bill with an amendment protecting political candidates from censorship. He stated that Watson, as chairman of the Senate Interstate Commerce Committee, would work diligently to pass the amended bill. Wheeler added that station owners' equitable treatment of speakers was brought vividly to congressional attention through WLW's request to review the Watson speech prior to broadcast.[63]

Other senators and representatives offered support for oversight of broadcasters' treatment of candidates. In debating a bill offered by Representative Wallace White, Representative Ewin Davis complained stations could discriminate against candidates by allowing some, but not all, access to the stations. Prices charged office seekers also varied as no law guaranteed equitable treatment; some candidates could be charged an exorbitant price while others could be permitted free airtime. Democratic representative Luther Johnson of Texas offered an amendment to White's bill requiring that equal facilities and rates be accorded all political parties and candidates. Johnson also wanted to extend this equal treatment to discussion of political questions or issues. While this last point was ruled out of order as not pertinent to the topic then under consideration by the House—radio licenses[64]—protection for discussion of issues would be revived in the early 1930s.

Congressional support of an equal opportunities provision for candidates upset broadcasters. The National Association of Broadcasters reviewed political candidates' rights and speakers' rights of access in general during its September 1926 meeting, and members discussed at length the Senate's proposed equal opportunities provision. Minutes of the meeting show that some labeled the clause "dynamite" and saw it as a potential menace to broadcasters' rights to use the airwaves as they chose, but Paul Klugh, executive secretary of the association, said the clause could actually be seen as a protection for broadcasters. The provision applied only to political talks and would rid broadcasters of oversight of political speeches because they would not have to review those speeches, as was then the practice.[65]

William Hedges of WMAQ countered that operators should have the right to use stations as they would any other property they owned. He added that broadcasters "should not be required to accept the addresses of any political people." Eugene McDonald of the Zenith Corporation in Chicago remarked that under the provision, all political parties, including the Soviets and the Bolsheviks, could use a station if that station opened its doors to political candidates. He saw this possibility as a threat to presentation of political issues because broadcasters would not give time to any candidate if Soviets and Bolsheviks could also claim airtime. He added that he thought congressional representatives would remove the clause when they realized that none of them would get airtime under it if un-American candidates could also have equal access.[66]

Klugh saw problems with agitating for the provision's removal. Many congressional members, he reminded the other delegates, believed the ether belonged to the people of the United States. As such, Congress could prescribe regulations that would not be permitted for newspapers or magazines. The NAB conferees could not arrive at a firm course of action concerning the provision, but they thought, at a minimum, they should reaffirm the anti-censorship resolution passed at their last annual meeting and endorsed by Hoover's Fourth Radio Conference: "BE IT RESOLVED, that it is the sense of this meeting that any agency of program censorship other than public opinion is not necessary and would be detrimental to the advancement of the art."[67] Public opinion—or, rather, broadcasters' opinion of "public opinion"—was to be the arbiter when it came to discussing political contests and broadcasting candidates' speeches.

While many stations had reviewed policies for all speeches, RCA's stations did not always request copies of speeches in advance. In the 1926 elections, the stations followed the same policy RCA had set in 1924 of treating all political candidates alike. RCA's newly formed National Broadcasting Company also continued AT&T's policy that political candidates or parties paid for any wire interconnections to distant points.[68] According to NBC's new president, Merlin Aylesworth, the company would broadcast all sides during elections without rate discrimination or censorship.[69] Charges for airtime were uniform, and facilities were made available to all political parties "without partiality, favor or affection."[70] In fact, RCA's Owen Young noted that he asked station WGY to shift its programming so that various political speeches given in particular cities and paid for by candidates might be broadcast. As a registered Democrat, Young said he leaned over backward to honor requests for airtime from other parties because he wanted to avoid the perception that RCA's stations might discriminate.[71]

During the 1926 elections, Socialists were able to purchase time on RCA's stations without discrimination. After the election, Herbert Merrill, the New York state secretary of the Socialist party, wrote station WGY that he was pleased RCA broadcast all shades of political opinion during the campaign. This action dispelled, he believed, the fear that radio would be monopolized by special interests and would be open only to the "propaganda" of those interests.[72]

Later in December, Merrill wrote WJZ to request time for Dr. Norman Thomas to broadcast a talk, "An American Labor Party."[73] Aylesworth replied that while he was not certain how many listeners would be interested in the subject between campaigns, he would be happy to authorize fifteen minutes of free airtime for Thomas's speech. This quarter-hour limit had been set by WJZ "for talks on interesting subjects."[74] The speech was delivered without a problem. Thomas told Bertha Brainard, manager of WJZ, that this speech was the first time a radio official did not wish to censor his copy. Brainard commented in a letter to Aylesworth that Thomas stuck to the fifteen-minute time allotment and left the station with goodwill for NBC.[75]

Such amiable relations had not always been the case for Thomas. In May 1926, he had been denied access to WEAF for broadcast of a speech, "Education and Peace," because his talk dealt with an allegedly controversial subject—military training in school.[76] According to Thomas, only one paragraph covered that topic; the "real" reason he was barred was because he had been arrested a few days earlier for speaking to strikers in the textile strike in Garfield, New Jersey.[77] He charged the station with censorship.[78]

Three other stations—WHAP, WMCA, and WNYC—also declined later speeches by Thomas on the WEAF episode on the grounds that those talks focused on a controversial subject.[79] Again, Thomas charged the stations with censorship. Donald Flamm, a program host for WMCA, replied to Thomas's charges of censorship in *Popular Radio,* a trade publication. He said that the people he invited to the station were his guests and that he did not believe in inviting guests who would prove to be embarrassing to the host station. Flamm added that when Thomas gave him a copy of his talk, he realized his guest might prove to be an embarrassing one. He then consulted with the program director of WMCA, who suggested that Thomas defer his talk until both sides of the subject could be presented in debate form. When Thomas insisted upon setting a definite date for the debate, WMCA stonewalled, saying it did not know when it could get someone to represent the other side.[80]

Later, another station, WRNY, held such a debate between Thomas and Hugo Gernsback, editor of *Radio News* and president of the station. Thomas asserted that radio stations should be regarded as public utilities and that their first duty was to the public. He noted that radio was dominated by a small number of closely allied stations and stated there should be no discrimination against speakers who did not espouse views held by interests controlling stations. Gernsback denied that monopoly existed. He said that less than 5 percent of the 550 stations in the United States were owned by any one interest. Gernsback advocated what he termed "censorship" of broadcasters for both material used on radio and the length of speeches made. He said the reason most radical speeches were not permitted to be broadcast was the same reason that they were not published in the major newspapers—they were not acceptable to the majority of Americans.[81]

At the same time Thomas was embroiled in this controversy, the ACLU was attacked over WEAF by a government official. The

ACLU asked permission for writer Norman Hapgood to answer the attack. WEAF refused. William Harkness wrote Norman Thomas that it was not WEAF's "custom to question statements of responsible members of government" and added, "It has been our endeavor to avoid program matter that might lead to controversy." Thomas interpreted this response to mean that a government official could say anything he pleased and it was not considered controversial but for an organization to reply to accusations was.[82] Later, in an article for *Popular Radio,* Thomas charged stations in New York City with censorship. He reiterated the same charges that statements by high public officials on radio were sacrosanct but answering their comments was not. Thomas declared that radio was so controlled and censored that "with rare exceptions" only the conservative side of public questions was presented to the public.[83]

New York newspapers had a field day with the WEAF-Thomas situation. Both columns and editorials in the papers—the *Times,* the *Morning World,* the *Evening World,* the *Herald Tribune,* the *Sun,* the *American,* and the *Brooklyn Times*—reviewed the incidents and, for the most part, sided with Thomas. Of five columns or editorials, only one columnist for the *Herald Tribune* sided with WEAF. To him, a station had a right to choose program material as it saw fit. The others thought WEAF had little to fear from broadcasting Thomas's speech because the audience would tune to someone else.[84]

After AT&T officials reviewed the incident, they believed Thomas "more or less framed this whole business and made WEAF a test case, so that he could bring about a controversy on censorship and freedom of the air."[85] They thought Thomas had planned his actions to create a market for a soon-to-be-published series of articles in *The Nation* entitled "Freedom of the Air." The series, edited by Thomas, appeared on newsstands in July.

Conclusion

In short, equitable treatment of candidates in the 1924 and 1926 elections was a goal of broadcasters. Larger broadcast companies adopted policies for equitable treatment of candidates for major political parties, but these actions effectively limited political discussion to those two parties. Radio officials did not want their medium used by advocates for what they termed "un-American" ideas. While continuation of their policies alone would have led to a quasi-equal opportunities doctrine being implemented in the industry, a turn of events in the 1926 primary election led to the inclusion of a government-mandated equal opportunities doctrine in the Radio Act of 1927. From then on, equal opportunity for political candidates was required by law.

Both government officials and industry executives feared nonconformist speech and sought to control dissidents' and government critics' access to the medium. Industry found an ideal solution to this potentially bothersome problem: impose monetary charges for access. If everyone were charged the same fees for airtime, none could complain of inequitable treatment. Subsequently, if dissenters could not buy time, their messages could not be disseminated, and broadcasters could not be held accountable. Political messages would be left to major political parties and to those who could afford the time. In essence, speech would be protected by the dollars spent on the medium.

Broadcast companies, however, recognized that public events of national significance, such as political conventions of major parties and subsequent campaigns, should be carried in public interest. Broadcasters not only earned prestige and credibility with such coverage but also garnered the goodwill of the major political parties. In carrying political programming, broadcasters also reinforced and endorsed the status quo of major political parties.

The techniques radio introduced in covering the campaigns in 1924 forever changed the face of American politics. The manner in which the candidates used the medium, their access to it, and the policies set by broadcasters to provide coverage set precedents for campaigns to come. The campaigns, especially that of 1924, also helped another facet of American broadcasting grow—networking.

4 ➤ FREE SPEECH AND THE FORMATION OF NBC

The conventions and campaigns of 1924 had shown the potential for networks, or chains of stations, to deliver programs of national importance or interest and thereby enhance political speech. Development of chain broadcasting had been discussed during radio conferences, by government officials, and by industry leaders. By mid-1924, RCA's board of directors was considering networking to bring program service to the entire nation as well as profits to the corporation. Negotiators in the developing intercompany patent wars discussed the feasibility of setting up networks. Conferees at the Third and Fourth Radio Conferences heard participants debate the pros and cons of "superpower" stations as a viable option to networking.

Concurrent with concerns over networking were concerns over the regulation of the medium. Hoover and the Department of Commerce had set up a structure for working with broadcasters to set regulatory standards, but by the time NBC was formed, new regulation was needed. Otherwise, the ability of the medium to bring programs to the listening public and the whole structure of the industry could collapse. This chapter reviews free speech concerns and how they manifested themselves in the development of NBC and the simultaneous need for new regulations to stabilize the growing multimillion-dollar radio industry after the *U.S. v. Zenith Radio*

Corporation decision in 1926 removed what little control Hoover had over radio regulation.

Patent Wars: Prelude to a National Network

Ongoing patent negotiations between signatory companies to the 1920 patent pooling agreements made clear that these arrangements were unworkable. A bitter behind-the-scenes private war brewing between AT&T and RCA over broadcasting finally boiled to the surface in the companies' patent arbitration of late 1923 and 1924. Each believed the other had moved into realms where it had no rights.

In 1920 and 1921, agreements had pooled patents among the major corporations and established various functions among the participating companies. Among the most significant points were that each major signatory—RCA, GE, Westinghouse, and AT&T—could build equipment for its own use, including broadcast transmitters. AT&T could sell broadcast transmitters, while GE and Westinghouse could manufacture radio receivers and supply them to RCA, which acted as a sales agent.[1] Under these agreements, the Telephone Group—AT&T and its subsidiary Western Electric—believed it had the right to get into broadcasting and to begin manufacturing receivers. The Radio Group—RCA, Westinghouse, and GE—believed those fields were theirs. From late 1922 through 1923, secret intercompany negotiations tried to mediate the problems between the two groups, but the factions finally had to enter arbitration.

The companies wanted to keep this rivalry as quiet as possible so as not to fuel an ongoing FTC monopoly investigation into these same agreements and charges by other companies of monopolistic practices on the part of the signatories. The FTC investigation began after it sent Congress a lengthy report in December 1923 that stated, "[T]here is no question that the pooling of all the patents pertaining to vacuum tubes had resulted in giving the Radio Corporation and its affiliated companies a monopoly in the manufacture, sale, and use thereof."[2] The FTC then followed with a formal complaint, charging patent holders had "combined and conspired for the purpose of, and with the effect of, restraining competition and creating a monopoly in the manufacture, purchase, and sale in interstate commerce of radio devices . . . and in domestic and transoceanic communication and broadcasting."[3] As the companies tried to hammer out their own agreements over who controlled what in broadcasting, the FTC held further public hearings into the corporations' practices in October 1925. As a result, the intercompany battle over patents related to broadcasting remained ultra-confidential and was resolved only with establishment of NBC in 1926.[4]

By the end of December 1923, AT&T and RCA had drawn up a patent arbitration agreement after reviewing their 1920 contracts and subsequent agreements. Each party was to present its case in the form of a concise statement before an arbitrator, Roland W. Boyden, a well-known Boston patent attorney. These statements were then to be exchanged with the other parties, and hearings on the salient points were to commence. After the hearings, Boyden's decisions were to be reported in an initial draft for reactions. Then, after he considered each company's rebuttal, Boyden would issue his final decision. While all were bound by that decision, each released the others from claims growing out of patent infringements prior to the date of Boyden's decision.[5]

During arbitration, Boyden listened to the comments of the attorneys and witnesses for the Radio Group and the Telephone Group. In these hearings, broadcasters' rights to use the airwaves and listeners' rights to receive information via the airwaves came up in discussions of "public service" operations, with broadcasters' rights receiving priority. In his opening statement to Boyden, Frederick Fish, chief counsel for RCA in the arbitration, expressed one of the earliest known sentiments of broadcasters' perceptions of public rights in broadcasting. He noted that while the telephone system was a public service corporation in the strictest sense, broadcasting was not. "It lacks every element of a public service communication system, or of a public service system," he said. "The public have no rights whatsoever to have anything to do with broadcasting. Broadcasting transmission, of course, goes out on the air. Anybody can listen to it, but they have no rights. At the present time, nobody can foresee that they ever will. . . . No one can go into a broadcasting station and say that he wants to talk or that he wants to advertise."[6] Listener rights were limited to reception of whatever broadcast operators aired, a view not limited to Fish as all participants in the arbitration accepted this perspective.

The balance of the hearings focused on business aspects of broadcasting: rights to manufacture and sell radio receiving apparatus; features and operation of telephone transmitters, telephone receivers, vacuum tubes, condensers, and carrier-current systems; the operation of station WEAF; use of telephone wires for remote hookups; radio set sales; and the functioning of wireless telephony. On June 24, the formal hearings closed. By agreement of the parties, Boyden was now to render a decision that could not be appealed.[7]

After several months of perusing piles of documents and testimony, Boyden sent a draft of his opinion to the disputants in late 1924 and told them he would consider any objections before putting the ruling in its final form. On point after point, Boyden upheld the Radio Group's contentions.[8] The Radio Group was ecstatic. RCA chief Owen Young received word of the outcome as he returned from Europe after helping to work out the Dawes Plan, a arrangement designed to save postwar Germany from economic collapse. The radiogram read: "Draft decision Boyden just received appears so far as studied to give us exclusive right sale receiving sets right to pickup wires right to install systems in hotels and apartment houses probable rights to sell loudspeakers and head phones in connection with receiving sets although stated to be in wire field and gives rights to collect tolls for broadcasting."[9] Two days later another radiogram followed: "Further study Boyden decision shows Telephone group has no rights broadcast transmission under patents Radio group."[10] Victory had been sweeping for the radio consortium. Both the Telephone and Radio Groups made comments on the referee's drafts, but no substantive changes were made in Boyden's decision. In March 1925, the ruling came out in its final form.[11]

Then AT&T played its trump card. On March 17, 1925, it presented the Radio Group with an advisory memorandum from John W. Davis, candidate for the U.S. presidency in 1924 and one of the drafters of the Clayton Anti-Trust Act a decade earlier. Davis's opinion held that if the cross-licensing agreements meant what the referee said they meant, then the 1920 contracts had been illegal in the first place: they were a conspiracy in the restraint of trade and a violation of the United States antitrust laws. Of course, AT&T noted it could not be a part of such illegal conduct. Since the contracts violated antitrust laws, AT&T would not abide by them or by Boyden's decision. AT&T had masterfully used Davis's advisory opinion to get what it wanted: entry into broadcasting on its own terms.[12]

Davis's opinion presented the Radio Group with a dilemma. How could they take AT&T to court without adding fuel to the now-pending FTC antitrust suit? In addition, Davis's memo held that only those portions of the agreement that were illegal could

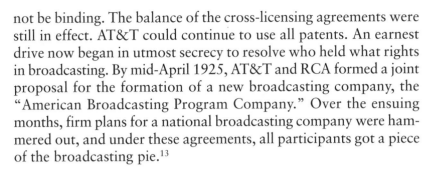

not be binding. The balance of the cross-licensing agreements were still in effect. AT&T could continue to use all patents. An earnest drive now began in utmost secrecy to resolve who held what rights in broadcasting. By mid-April 1925, AT&T and RCA formed a joint proposal for the formation of a new broadcasting company, the "American Broadcasting Program Company." Over the ensuing months, firm plans for a national broadcasting company were hammered out, and under these agreements, all participants got a piece of the broadcasting pie.[13]

Plans for a National Broadcasting Company Emerge

The idea of networking was not new. During 1921, RCA's board of directors set up a special committee to investigate the concept, and the board issued a report calling for a limited network of stations located at suitable points throughout the United States. Each station would be allocated to one of the three companies—RCA, GE, and Westinghouse—and by agreement the companies would air only material supplied by a "feature director" hired jointly by the companies. The director would also regulate privately developed programs offered for broadcast.[14] It was 1921, though, and the full board adopted a wait-and-see attitude toward networking.

Now four years later, after Boyden's decision, discussions of network structure progressed rapidly. Some, such as H. P. Davis of Westinghouse, recognized that small stations and high-power stations could coexist in any network design. Smaller stations would serve their specific locales, while superpower stations would serve both regional and national audiences. Davis also noted that programs supplied by these stations should not be subjected to formal state or federal censorship because it would stifle industry initiative. Rather, "public opinion," as discerned by broadcasters, should dictate programming.[15]

The RCA Committee on Broadcasting—David Sarnoff, H. P. Davis, and Albert Davis—took this perspective into account, and in January 1926, they issued their recommendations on chain broadcasting to the RCA board of directors. That report stated that GE, RCA, and Westinghouse stations should develop a new network to provide quality programming to national audiences but added that no station would lose its identity under the plan as each would maintain a local service. The plan would sustain and encourage both services. Contracts between the network and local stations would specify specific times for national programs.[16] On January 22, 1926, RCA's board of directors adopted the committee's recommendation, and the national network–local outlet structure of American broadcasting began to take shape.[17]

Plans advanced for formation of what would become the National Broadcasting Company. Some involved in these discussions in early 1926, notably GE's Martin Rice and Westinghouse's H. P. Davis, warned that independent broadcasters and some government officials perceived censorship might grow with the inception of this proposed network because the companies shared control over the network. Official RCA policy did not reflect these concerns, though, until a public relations firm hired by RCA to look into public reaction to a network's formation suggested RCA needed to head off potential charges of censorship.[18]

Under the board's direction, David Sarnoff contacted Isroy M. Norr of the public relations firm of Ames and Norr to study public perceptions in forming a new broadcast company. Norr submitted a fifteen-page confidential report, which began with the admonition that "to minimize the cry of 'monopoly' which is likely to greet the announcement of the broadcasting plans contemplated by the R.C.A. group," certain accommodating policies should be established and announced to the general public. Among those policies was the establishment of an advisory council that would include members of all facets of American society so that the new broadcast company would "have the cooperation of distinguished leaders in American public life." In addition to deflecting cries of censorship, the council's mission would be threefold: (1) to reflect broadcasting from a public standpoint; (2) to obtain cooperation from educational and musical enterprises for sustaining, or unsponsored, broadcast programs; and (3) to secure public support for policies a national broadcasting service might need. Norr emphasized that to further deflate charges of monopoly, RCA should also adopt a policy of local autonomy for stations that affiliated themselves with the new national service.[19] Sarnoff liked Norr's suggestions and pushed their adoption.

Critical to RCA's development of this council were announcements appearing one week later in the New York City papers that RCA and AT&T were developing a nationwide broadcast system. As Norr predicted, several newspapers alleged monopoly and censorship. On July 22, the *New York Tribune* page-one headline read:

"WEAF Sold; Air Combine Is Forecast." The paper charged that AT&T's sale of its station, WEAF, to RCA was the first step of RCA, GE, and Westinghouse "to acquire a practical monopoly of the air, through control of the important broadcasting stations." The *New York World* wrote that RCA planned to extend WEAF's chain of stations and that AT&T would supply wires for interconnections. Two *New York World* articles, headlined "Coming Monopoly of Broadcasting by WEAF Is Seen" and "WEAF Sale Only Part of Huge Deal," complained that independent stations would be hampered if they attempted to set up a rival network because interconnecting lines and competing programs would be difficult to procure. Press reports stressed the major advantage the new arrangement would have for AT&T and RCA as they could dominate broadcasting.[20]

Clearly, after these articles appeared, the new network needed to combat perceptions of possible censorship. Among the suggestions highlighted in the proposal sent to the RCA board of directors on August 10 was an advisory council to be "a court of appeal on matters of policy on programs and entertainment, as distinguished from business administration, and in cases of alleged discrimination." The council would also advise executives and suggest rules, which the company could adopt, dealing with questions of fairness in the use of facilities. In addition to the council, the recommendations outlined the business, financial, engineering, and production aspects of the new company.[21]

An Advisory Council Is Formed

The proposal suggested that the council consist of twelve to fifteen members, and the list vividly illustrates the dominant social and political components of 1920s America. Management and labor groups were represented as were farm concerns. Government officials, especially from military backgrounds, joined representatives from geographically different sections of the country and spokesmen from cultural interests such as the Metropolitan Opera and symphonic groups. Three members reflected Judeo-Christian religious beliefs—one representative each from the Catholic, Protestant, and Jewish faiths. Later, the broadcast committee added a member from the Federation of American Women's Clubs to represent women's interests, and with this amendment the general makeup of the council was established and approved.[22]

When RCA publicly announced plans for this advisory council, *Literary Digest,* a major publication of the day, heralded it as a positive step towards the elimination of discrimination. The *Digest* noted, "The general plan [for NBC] calls for the financing of a network of stations that will give a nationwide service, with improved programs supervised by an advisory council of twelve representatives of various shades of public opinion."[23]

The list of Advisory Council invitees was drawn up in a meeting held in RCA/GE chief Owen Young's office on October 28, 1926. Selected by Merlin Aylesworth, the new NBC president, and Young, individuals reflecting various facets of American life received invitations to join the council. Replies came back quickly, and the first Advisory Council was formed and formally announced by Aylesworth during NBC's inauguration ceremonies in November 1926. The council included William Green, president, American Federation of Labor; Walter Damrosch, conductor, New York Symphony Orchestra; Francis D. Farrell, president, Kansas Agricultural College; Henry M. Robinson, president, First National Bank of Los Angeles; Mary Sherman, president, General Federation of Women's Clubs of America; Dr. Henry S. Pritchett, president, Carnegie Foundation; Edwin Alderman, president, University of Virginia; Elihu Root, Nobel Peace Prize laureate, attorney, statesman, and secretary of state under Theodore Roosevelt; Charles Evans Hughes, attorney and later Supreme Court chief justice; General Guy E. Tripp, chairman of the board, Westinghouse; Major General J. G. Harbord, president, RCA; Owen Young, chairman of the board, GE and RCA; John W. Davis, attorney and 1924 Democratic nominee for president; Dwight W. Morrow, financier with the J. P. Morgan Company; Julius Rosenwald, president, Sears-Roebuck Company; Morgan J. O'Brien, attorney from New York; and Reverend Charles F. MacFarland, general secretary, Federal Council of the Churches of Christ in America. (Rosenwald, O'Brien, and MacFarland were seen as the council's representatives for the Jewish, Catholic, and Protestant faiths respectively.)[24]

Young personally championed the council and sincerely believed it would advance the nation and American principles as radio's popularity grew. He wrote letters of invitation to each individual and told them that NBC's selection of national programs carried with it a corresponding responsibility that could more wisely be exercised with the advice of "a disinterested and impartial body of American citizens representing widely different interests." Young added that "while a Democracy is learning to handle an instrument of such power [as radio], it is most important that the decisions of its executives relating to broadcasting programs and public service should be subject to review and correction by an Advisory Council."[25]

Replies came quickly. In his letter of acceptance, Edwin Alderman told Young it seemed to him to be perfectly clear that a free radio was as important to the liberties of the people as a free press, while Morgan O'Brien complimented Young on his highly regarded international reputation in dealing with German reparation payments from World War I, adding, "[N]othing could be more agreeable to me than to work with, or under you, in one of your many useful and patriotic endeavors."[26]

When prospective members accepted Young's invitation, he wrote to thank them and to reiterate his vision of the council. "It will act as a restraint on the broadcasting organization and will tend to make them consider carefully all questions affecting the use of their facilities. . . . It will likewise be a restraint upon the foolish complaints from people who, without any consideration at all, just assume they may be discriminated against." Finally, he said the council would give the public at large the feeling that they have a right to go to a competent and impartial body regarding the misuse of the facilities. According to Young, the preservation of this right of appeal was perhaps more important than the council's ability to make programming suggestions.[27]

The council's makeup was announced on NBC's inaugural program in what Young and Merlin Aylesworth called "the most prestigious broadcasting program ever presented."[28] The program brought an enthusiastic response of approximately 140,000 letters and telegrams from all over the United States.[29] In early December, NBC's board of directors formally approved the council, and its first meeting was held February 18, 1927—five days before the Radio Act was signed by President Coolidge.[30]

At this meeting, Young explained the circumstances leading to NBC's formation and noted "the purpose of that organization [NBC] is to provide the best programs available for broadcasting in the United States and to secure their distribution over the widest possible area." He added, "[T]he wise guidance of able men of diversified experience located in different parts of the country is sought in order that the facilities of the National Broadcasting Company may be put to their best possible use in the public interest, which is the only way to serve the business interests of the founders of the plan."[31] Later, he stated his vision for the council:

> [We] hope the Advisory Council may be considered as a court of appeal for complaints. There will be less complaints because of its existence. I should expect few will ever come to your attention unless they are really serious and difficult cases. In that case, they should be decided in the public interest. But the fact that you exist means that the National Broadcasting Company's organization itself will be most careful to avoid unfair discrimination or misuse knowing that an appeal lies over them. . . . The fact of your existence for the purposes indicated is undoubtedly of more importance than the work you will have to do in this particular field. To my mind, your most important service will be in the way of constructive suggestion as to how we can enlarge and improve broadcasting service from time to time.[32]

The first meeting of the council was largely organizational, and discussion focused on hopes for the council to be a viable contributor to network programming decisions.[33]

As minutes of the 1928 council meeting show, no complaints were filed with the Advisory Council during NBC's first year.[34] The council lasted until the mid-1940s, when it was disbanded as a redundancy to Federal Communications Commission (FCC) oversight. During its tenure, its members heard few complaints, but those few protests contained issues vital to free speech on network radio. Perhaps the greatest contribution the council made to NBC was in the network's initial months when, as Isroy Norr suggested, the council acted to deflect monopoly and censorship charges leveled at NBC.

RCA, NBC, and the Question of Financing

With the acquisition of WEAF, NBC formed two networks—the Red and the Blue. The Red Network originated its programming from WEAF while WJZ, the original RCA flagship station, originated programming for the Blue Network. NBC records show that during NBC's first week, WEAF and the Red Network were on the air approximately twelve hours per day during the week and nine hours on Sunday, while WJZ and the Blue Network broadcast eight hours daily. WEAF came on the air at 6:45 A.M. while WJZ began broadcasting at 1:00 P.M. Both stations broadcast until midnight, but there were "dead spots," or time off the air, in their schedules. WEAF was off the air in the morning from 8:00 to 11:00 and in the afternoon from 1:15 to 4:00. WJZ was usually off the air from 2:40 to 4:30 and from 6:00 to 7:00 in the evening.[35]

By 1920s standards, this amount of programming was substantial. In 1925, Hiram Jome, author of the *Economics of the Radio Industry*, noted many stations operated at irregular intervals, and the average operation time was five hours *per week*. Schools, churches, and hobbyists owned most of these stations.[36] Another study by AT&T supported Jome's findings and confirmed that nearly 60 percent of the stations then in existence—230 out of 537—were on the air fewer than five hours per week.[37]

As NBC went on the air, RCA executives discussed how it would pay for itself. They knew that many government officials still saw direct advertising via radio—or blatantly selling products or services with mention of their prices—as undesirable, even though advertising was growing in every other medium. In discussions, the executives recalled other methods suggested for financing the business, including taxes on sets. This plan had been suggested as early as 1924 when the House Finance Committee submitted a bill including taxes on receivers as a means of raising general revenues for the government.[38] Broadcasters roundly criticized this plan then as imposing upon "freedom of the air" and listeners' rights to receive information.

This 1924 tax-on-receiver plan began as an amendment to an overall tax bill in the 68th Congress. During debate, Senator Reed Smoot of Utah said this amendment proposing a 10 percent tax on receivers was actually a tax on the manufacturers of sets, not a tax aimed at set purchasers. In Smoot's opinion, RCA had a monopoly on the manufacture of sets, so this tax was aimed solely at it.[39] Because RCA feared negative congressional and public reaction, it decided not to use its radio facilities to combat the tax. Otherwise, Congress might perceive the action as an improper marshalling of public opinion for private gain. In April 1924, RCA president J. G. Harbord announced that RCA would not use its stations to argue the pros and cons of the proposed 10 percent tax on radio sets but would use other means to oppose this "unjust and discriminatory" tax.[40] While RCA maintained a neutral position over the air, Harbord sent a letter to the Senate Finance Committee opposing the tax. The letter stated that the tax was unwarranted and would hamper the development of an instrument "of such vital use for education and instructive purposes."[41]

Senators opposed to the tax—notably Clarence Dill of Washington, Royal Copeland and James Wadsworth of New York, and Ellison Smith of South Carolina—picked up on these themes and also argued any assessment was not in the public interest and would simply be passed to consumers. The tax not only would discourage radio's development but also would dampen set purchases. Consequently, any tariff would curb reception of educational material and information by radio, especially in poor rural districts.[42]

Dill argued that the tax would also obstruct free speech through inhibiting the listeners' ability to receive information. "[J]ust as firmly as I believe that the press ought to be kept free and that speech ought to be kept free, I believe the right to use radio ought to be kept free because I believe it will eventually be a greater blessing than the free press has ever been in this country," he said.[43] When the senators voted on the receiver tax amendment, it was overwhelmingly rejected, and RCA officials were understandably ecstatic with its failure. Ultimately, advertising became the method of financing for not only NBC but also all commercial broadcast facilities. In the 1930s, radio advertising would become an issue between newspapers and radio as the Depression deepened and competition for revenue increased.

While the act failed, it drew attention of senators and representatives to listeners' rights to receive information and entertainment free via radio. This right and broadcasters' rights to use the airwaves as they pleased later surfaced in discussion leading to passage of the Radio Act of 1927. In those discussions, rejection of the receiver set tax was seen as part of a distinctly superior American broadcast system that enhanced the listening public's right to receive education and information freely over the airwaves. Threatening this ability, though, was the dissatisfaction of a few broadcasters over the regulations Hoover developed following the Fourth Radio Conference. A challenge to his power soon resulted in threats to the very existence of broadcasting.

The Zenith Decision

Eugene McDonald of the Zenith Corporation and president of the National Association of Broadcasters objected to what he termed the "one-man control of radio with the Secretary of Commerce as supreme czar."[44] His station, WJAZ, shared a wavelength with GE station KOA in Denver. WJAZ was allotted only two hours of operating time per week, and that time—10:00 P.M. to midnight on Thursday—was to be used only if KOA did not want it. Since Hoover had said he wanted a case to test his authority to regulate the medium, McDonald accommodated him. He moved, or "jumped," WJAZ to a more attractive channel—one assigned by international agreement to Canada.[45] This move threatened international relations, and the Commerce Department was forced to bring suit. Decided on April 16, 1926, *U.S. v. Zenith Radio Corporation* held that the secretary of commerce had "no express grant of power in the [1912] act . . . to establish regulations" and added that the secretary could only issue licenses "subject to the regulations in the Act" of 1912.[46] In other words, Hoover's ability to regulate broadcasting was nonexistent.

In a public statement, Hoover noted the *Zenith* decision affected not only broadcasting but amateur services as well and added that if stations proceeded to select their own wavelengths and broadcast times, effective public service would end. Hoover called for passage of the Dill and White radio bills. He knew they would give the Commerce Department the authority to determine who could broadcast, to minimize interference, and to further radio's development in the interest of both listeners and industry.[47]

Hoover also argued that the *Zenith* ruling conflicted with the *Intercity Radio* decision of 1923, which held that the secretary could control the assignment of wavelengths, so he asked the U.S. attorney general for his opinion on the Commerce Department's powers.[48] In early July, the attorney general agreed with the *Zenith* decision, concluding that under the Radio Act of 1912, the Commerce Department lacked discretionary powers.[49] Overall regulation would have to wait until new laws were enacted.

The National Association of Broadcasters told stations that until new legislation passed, broadcasters would have to regulate themselves. It asked station cooperation in keeping the industry free from "undesirable practices and operations during the intervening months" before legislation could be enacted.[50] As constant change could jeopardize the entire industry, the NAB asked stations to sign certificates promising to stay on previously assigned wavelengths.[51] Within ten days, over 150 stations complied.[52] However, by the end of December, some nonsignatory stations changed their wavelengths, power, and time of operation. Fear that more would follow finally forced Congress to act.

Conclusion

Fear over network power and ability to control all forms of speech broadcast via radio led to development of an advisory council to the newly formed NBC networks. While its apparent purpose was to rule on complaints of discrimination in programming and to counsel NBC on its operation, the council also was a public relations tool used to allay fears of monopoly, censorship, and NBC network domination over radio. Concurrent with apprehension over network control were concerns over radio's regulation. During the mid-1920s, the Commerce Department's regulatory efforts disintegrated, and broadcasting faced challenges that could cause the industry to collapse. As the existence of stations was threatened, so too was the ability to bring listeners entertainment and information. Consequently, legislation was needed to enhance listeners' rights to receive information—and stations' ability to speak. Passage of the Radio Act of 1927 brought about necessary changes, and then the Federal Radio Commission (FRC) faced the daunting challenge of cleaning up the airwaves and enhancing freedom of the air and the public interest for both listener and broadcaster.

5 ⇒ IN THE PUBLIC INTEREST: THE RADIO ACT OF 1927 AND ACTIONS OF THE FEDERAL RADIO COMMISSION TO 1933

The Radio Act of 1927 resulted from increasing industry and public pressure to remedy the potentially disruptive influence of the *Zenith* decision. Passage of the act depended upon the talents, compromises, and efforts of key legislators who built upon nineteen bills introduced into Congress between 1921 and 1927 that would have repealed or amended the Radio Act of 1912.[1] Key supporters in Congress for a new radio law were Representative Wallace White of Maine, Senator Clarence Dill of Washington, and Senator James Watson of Indiana. The most noteworthy opponents were Representative Ewin Davis of Tennessee and Senator Key Pittman of Nevada.[2]

These individuals helped decide the meaning of public interest and central issues of freedom of the air: censorship, broadcasters' rights to use the medium, listeners' rights to receive information via radio, and speakers' rights of access to the airwaves. Much of their initial congressional debate was instructional, as few legislators had any working knowledge of the radio situation.[3] During the bill's introduction in both houses of Congress, long explanations on broadcast history and the need for legislation were made by the bills' sponsors, Wallace White in the House and Clarence Dill in the Senate.[4] This chapter reviews passage of that act in light of issues involving freedom of the air and public interest and shows how the Federal Radio Commission brought structure to the industry through its regulatory powers, related ancillary orders, and use of both public interest and free speech issues.

A New Law

In hearings, congressional representatives and senators debated possible broadcaster censorship and potential abuse by proposed regulatory powers. Representative Luther Johnson of Texas summarized one view when he pointedly asserted that because of radio's limitless potential as a medium for entertainment, education, information, and communication, it should be carefully guarded. He added, "The power of the press will not be comparable to that of broadcasting stations when the industry is fully developed. . . . [I]t will only be a few years before these broadcasting stations, if operated by chain stations, will simultaneously reach an audience of over half of our entire citizenship." He concluded that radio's ability to mold and to crystallize sentiment was unequaled and that, because of this power, discrimination by stations must be made illegal. If not, he added, then "American thought and American politics will be largely at the mercy of those who operate these stations . . . then woe to those who differ with them [the station operators]. It will be impossible to compete with them in reaching the ears of the American public."[5]

Under proposals in the House in 1926, license renewal was left in the hands of the secretary of commerce. During hearings before the House Committee on the Merchant Marine and Fisheries, representatives questioned Commerce Department officials about this discretionary power to issue and to revoke or renew licenses. Representative Frank Reid of Illinois asked Stephen Davis of the Commerce Department and advisor to Secretary Hoover his opinion on protection for broadcasters against a vindictive commerce secretary: "[S]uppose some broadcasting station during the Republican administration of the Government is broadcasting a lot of Democratic documents which we thought were not for the good of the country. Would it be possible for him [the secretary] to refuse the license if, in his discretion, he thought that [it was not good for the country]? Would it not be a limitation of the freedom of speech?" Davis replied, "If you can imagine a secretary doing that, he would have the power, but his action would be reviewable by a court on a direct appeal, under the terms of the bill." Davis believed revocation would not happen unless the broadcaster had been found guilty of monopolistic practices.[6]

Throughout the hearings, Representative Ewin Davis returned to questions of religious programming and equitable coverage of issues and candidates on radio. When questioned by Davis, AT&T spokesperson William Harkness told legislators that AT&T acted as any editor of a paper would. He said, "We feel if the matter is unfair or contains matter which the public would not care to hear we may reject it."[7] The company edited material in the public interest; it did not censor it.

The Senate, too, held several hearings in early 1926 on its version of a radio control bill. Senator James Watson raised concerns about curbs on broadcast speeches and educational materials. When he asked Harkness about treatment of speakers from political parties and religious denominations, Harkness again described AT&T's policy as treating all religious and political groups equitably. Harkness also told Watson that AT&T balanced speakers with other programming so stations could maintain their audiences.[8]

Stephen Davis of the Commerce Department also testified before the Senate committee and presented the committee with the official recommendations of the Fourth Radio Conference. Included was a recommendation prohibiting censorship by the secretary of commerce. It read in part: "No regulation or condition shall be promulgated or fixed by the Secretary of Commerce which shall interfere with the right of free speech and free entertainment by means of radio communication." Davis added that while he could not imagine a commerce secretary censoring radio, he thought perhaps it was wise to embody a noncensorship policy in the law.[9] When the Radio Act of 1927 was passed, a noncensorship provision was incorporated as Section 29.

Morris Ernst of the ACLU testified that the ACLU was concerned with the bill's provisions on censorship and freedom of speech. Ernst complained that "free speech is a misnomer when one has to pay $400 an hour on one of the good New York stations." He added that some speakers were lucky to get on radio at all, especially if they wanted to criticize the government. He then cited six instances in which speakers had either been requested not to criticize the Coolidge administration or had been denied airtime on unnamed stations in New York or New Jersey because their views were deemed too controversial.[10]

One solution to this censorship, Ernst told the Senate committee, was to give preference to nonprofit organizations in the licensing of stations. Ernst believed nonprofit stations would not be as likely as commercial stations to discriminate because they were more interested in the public good than were commercial stations, which feared offending audiences. Ernst also wanted the Department of Commerce to oversee chain broadcasting, not just stations, because he feared possible network control over programming. A network's ability to cover the entire country through linking stations made it far more powerful than newspapers because newspapers were primarily local in coverage. Because of broadcasting's power, Ernst wanted laws developed so the public would have the right to hear various viewpoints and also have the opportunity to charge stations with not filling a public necessity.[11]

Senators did not adopt Ernst's suggestions. To them, the answer to these potential problems lay in changing the regulatory body from the secretary of commerce to an independent commission. By mid-April, the Senate version of the radio bill provided for such a commission, which, according to Senator Dill, was to "prevent monopolization of the use of the ether by any person, firm, corporation, or association . . . and [to] encourage and assist in the development and improvement of the use of radio." Dill and Senator Watson also wanted to empower "the Commission [with the right] to refuse or revoke licenses in cases of monopoly or attempted monopoly."[12]

President Coolidge opposed the creation of a new commission to oversee radio, if such a commission were not responsible to the White House. Coolidge and congressional advocates of executive branch control over radio believed that independent commissions were not as responsible as executive branch departments in halting monopoly and curbing private interests in industry. They feared that commissions in general were not efficient, as they fostered bureaucracy. Opponents, though, thought an agency devoted solely to radio would be better than one also concerned with other government business.[13]

Senators debated who or what was to be the regulatory authority—an independent commission or the secretary of commerce. Dill stated that a commission was necessary because license renewal under the Commerce Department made broadcasters feel an "obligation" to that department and the administration in power. He added that some stations were reluctant to air views attacking the administration because "they were compelled to go to Washington to get their licenses renewed and could not afford to take the chance of displeasing the administration."[14]

During further debate on censorship and control of the airwaves, some senators argued for provisions extending a form of equal opportunity for use of the airwaves to discussions of issues, while others wished to eliminate a portion of the bill that stated that broadcasters could deny use of facilities to all potential candidates.[15] Both would enhance free speech, but senators recognized not everyone could build a separate broadcast system because of spectrum scarcity. Senator Robert Howell of Nebraska differentiated between electronic and print media: "Are we to consent to the building up of a great publicity vehicle and allow it to be controlled by a few men, and empower those few men to determine what the public shall hear? It may be argued that we do that with the newspapers. Yes, that is true; but anyone is at liberty to start a newspaper and reply. Not so with a broadcasting station."[16] Every applicant could not be granted a license; there were not enough wavelengths to go around.

Dill also emphasized that "freedom of the air" meant that listeners had the right to receive programs for free over the airwaves so that

> anybody anywhere may listen in to any broadcast whatsoever . . . without any restraint or hindrance whatsoever by the Government. This freedom of radio reception by the American people is the feature of radio that distinguishes and differentiates radio conditions in every other country in the world. In practically every other country the government levies a tax on receiving sets. In some countries the government has prevented listeners-in from having sets that will receive broadcasting on more than two or three wavelengths.[17]

Other conditions distinguished American broadcasting from systems in other countries. Notable to Dill were private ownership and lack of government control over stations. What, Dill asked rhetorically, was "the result of this policy of freedom for radio broadcasting and radio reception? . . . With only 6 percent of the world's population, we have more than 80 percent of all the receiving sets on earth and five times as many broadcast stations as all the rest of the world combined." He added that to preserve radio's freedom from too much government regulation or from monopolistic tendencies by private companies, Congress had to pass legislation conforming with the public interest.[18]

Dill recommended that a commission handle allocation of stations because he "did not feel that any one man, however good and however wise he might be, ought to be entrusted with the discretion of saying who shall and who shall not have a monopoly of the air in a particular community." Senator J. Thomas Heflin of Alabama agreed wholeheartedly that an independent commission could act to stifle monopoly and could also control broadcaster censorship.[19]

Senator Simeon D. Fess of Ohio argued broadcasters had to take responsibility for what was broadcast as they were not common carriers. The Senate Interstate Commerce Committee had changed common carrier provisions in an earlier version of the radio bill to state that there should be no discrimination in charges or service to advertisers. The committee also added that no licensee could discriminate against any political candidate or censor a candidate's speeches. Dill said that while broadcasters did not like limitations on their operations, they did not find this provision objectionable.[20]

The next day, however, Senator Albert Cummins of Iowa raised an objection to the part of an amendment forbidding discrimination against advertisers. He argued that a lack of discrimination on the part of broadcasters in the acceptance of advertising made radio a common carrier.[21] Cummins said he thought this provision would take away the broadcasters' oversight of programming material. Dill argued that this amendment did not prohibit stations from refusing material; rather, it stated that all advertisers had to be charged the same rate. The Senate was hesitant to accept this position, and that portion of the provision was not included in the final version of the Senate's bill, which passed July 2.[22] Because it differed from the House bill on provisions establishing a commission as the regulatory agency and providing equitable treatment of political candidates, a conference committee formed to reconcile the two versions of the legislation, including Senators James Watson, Albert Cummins (later replaced by Frank Godding of Idaho), and Clarence Dill and Representatives Wallace White, Frederick Lehback of New Jersey, Frank Scott of Michigan, and Ladislas Lazaro of Louisiana.[23]

In the conference meetings, Dill was able to achieve an important compromise on the regulatory body. The House version held that the Commerce Department was to regulate radio; the Senate version provided for an independent commission. The compromise stated that a commission would be established for a period of one year to regulate the medium. After the year ended, it would then act as an appellate body for decisions made by the secretary of commerce. White was willing to accept this solution to the impasse.[24] Dill was convinced that after the commission had been operating for a year, it would be allowed to continue. In an interview years later, he commented, "I knew if we ever got a commission, we would never get rid of it."[25] With this major compromise and the agreement that political candidates should receive equal opportunity from broadcasters, the conferees agreed to the bill and sent it back in late January 1927 to both houses of Congress for review.[26]

The conference report passed the House on January 30 and made it through the Senate on February 19. Conferees warned their colleagues that rejection of the bill would halt any chance of getting radio regulation passed as Congress was due to adjourn March 4. White told the House that while he was far from satisfied with the bill, he still supported its passage. To wait would endanger a radio industry threatened by chaos because of the court decisions that stated the commerce secretary could no longer regulate the medium.[27]

The only outspoken criticism on the conference bill in the House came from Ewin Davis, who continued to fight against the unequal geographical distribution of stations throughout the United States. Davis wanted a permanent commission to regulate broadcasting and pushed for clarification of the commission's powers. He also asked if the anti-monopoly language in Section 14, which dealt with license revocation, meant that the commission could prevent discrimination by broadcasters toward others who wished to use the radio for messages.[28]

Davis wanted the commission to prevent discrimination, but Representative Frank Scott, who served on the conference committee, reminded Davis that in his desire to prevent discrimination, Davis was treading close to controlling the exercise of free speech. Davis countered that the public needed three protections in the act to enhance free speech: (1) stiffer provisions to prevent radio monopolies, (2) creation of an independent, bipartisan commission comprised of representatives of different geographic regions, and (3) development of "radio zones" so that the equitable allocation of stations in the United States could be effected. Davis feared a monopoly in geographical coverage of one entity's signal, not a monopoly in the number of stations owned by a single entity. The fear of this type of monopoly—one of station signal coverage—had surfaced in the radio conferences under the guise of superstations, but it seemed to be a new concern to the members of the House who had seen monopoly only in terms of station ownership concentration.[29]

Senators' debate on the conference report focused on provisions stating that the government owned the airwaves and broadcasters would receive limited licenses to the spectrum. Senator Key Pittman was the bill's major adversary in the Senate, much as Davis was the main antagonist in the House. Pittman also raised the issue of monopoly. Pittman believed legislation could not control the development of monopolies, especially by RCA, and he attempted to have the bill sent back to conference. Clarence Dill, the bill's chief proponent, told Pittman and the other senators repeatedly that the bill's provisions prevented monopoly. He said these provisions were found in Section 13, which allowed the commission to refuse to grant a construction permit to entities found guilty of unlawfully controlling or attempting to control the manufacture or sale of radio apparatus, and in Section 15, which granted the commission the power to refuse or to revoke the license of any entity found guilty of monopoly.[30]

Senator James Watson, another member of the conference committee, joined Dill in defending the bill. During the second day of Senate debate, both Watson and Davis explained that the bill included curbs to claims of ownership of the ether by private companies. Dill stated that the inclusion of the basic principle of requiring stations to operate in the public interest, convenience, or necessity (or PICON) gave the commission the right to prevent anyone from claiming a vested right to own the ether and to prevent monopolies.[31]

Pittman wanted a permanent commission, not one that would dissolve after one year. Dill countered that while he also wanted a permanent commission, the House of Representatives was adamantly opposed to its creation. The one-year commission was a compromise, Dill said. He reminded Pittman that after the year, the commission would not dissolve; it would remain to act as an appellate body for the opinions of the commerce secretary. If anyone objected to the actions of the secretary, the objections would be sent to the commission. In Dill's opinion, this right of appeal shifted the ultimate decision-making power from the secretary of commerce to the commission. Because the commission would decide all disputed matters, Dill stated that it would probably sit continuously. After more discussion on the merits of the commission, the senators voted to agree to the conference report, and the legislation was sent to President Coolidge on February 22. He signed it the next day.[32]

Thus, the passage of the Radio Act of 1927 resulted from compromise and necessity—compromise on the bill's provisions on monopoly and a commission and the necessity to combat chaos, real and perceived, in the radio spectrum. The Radio Act of 1927 codified the views of Wallace White and Clarence Dill into law. Hoover and the industry supported the bill because they knew regulation was needed to curb interference and to set regulatory standards for the medium. As radio control passed from the secretary of commerce to the Federal Radio Commission on February 23, 1927, a new regulatory era was under way.

Order Out of Chaos: Enhancing Listener Rights

The newly created Federal Radio Commission faced the daunting task of cleaning up the airwaves. Congress formed the commission to bring order out of chaos, but it neglected to allocate resources to accomplish the task. Before adjourning in 1927, Congress had confirmed commissioners Eugene Sykes, Admiral W. H. G. Bullard, and Colonel John Dillion but had not confirmed Orestes Caldwell and Henry Bellows. So, the FRC began shakily with three confirmed commissioners, two unconfirmed commissioners, and "one desk, two chairs, a table and a packing box."[33] The engineering division was not formed until August 1928, while its legal division began June 25, 1928, when Louis Caldwell joined the staff as general counsel. Until then, Bethuel Webster Jr. of the Justice Department assisted the commission in its hearings.

Meanwhile, the navy loaned the FRC the able Captain Stanford Hooper as a technical advisor, and the Department of Agriculture assigned Sam Pickard to act as the commission's secretary. The Department of Commerce provided temporary quarters, clerical help, and assistance from J. H. Dellinger, now chief of the Commerce Department's radio division.[34] Unfortunately, before the

commission could complete its task of allocating frequencies, Colonel Dillion and Admiral Bullard died on October 8 and November
24, respectively. Henry Bellows and Orestes Caldwell, both unconfirmed, had worked without pay since the commission's inception,
but Bellows resigned in frustration on November 1. Sam Pickard was
appointed to replace him, while Harold A. LaFount took Dillion's
place. Neither man was confirmed until March 1928. Bullard's successor, Ira E. Robinson, was not appointed until April 1928. So, in
late November 1927, Eugene Sykes was the commission's only
confirmed member, a tenuous situation at best and one that illustrates the overall lack of concern Congress had with communication issues at the time.[35]

Shortly after the commission's formation, Sykes addressed the
radio audience over NBC, outlining the commission's hopes for
clearing up the spectrum. He placed emphasis on the public interest standard in serving listeners' rights to receive radio signals
clearly. "In the determination of every radio question," he noted,
"the dominant influence is and must be public interest. This doctrine, that broadcasting exists only for the purpose of properly serving the listening public, is the constitutional basis for every action
the Commission may take." He urged the public to help determine
what comprised "public interest" and asked for public participa-
tion in open hearings on radio, set for March 29 through April 1.[36]

At these hearings, reducing interference dominated discussion,
and issues of free speech were raised only on the last day by Morris Ernst of the ACLU. Ernst noted censorship existed in both program selection and license allocation. He cited examples of discrimination in programs: Protestants refused time to speak on religious
issues; a professor asked to drop several paragraphs of a speech
critical of American foreign policy; the inability of the Women's
International League for Peace to get time; and outright denials of
airtime to Norman Thomas and H. V. Kaltenborn. While licensing
decisions had to be made for the limited spectrum space, Ernst
believed that censorship of any kind was anathema as radio could
control political election outcomes and the mood of the nation.

Ernst offered a seven-point plan to better the situation. First,
complete logging of all programming was a must. By keeping track
of programs and listener responses, stations would know if they had
balanced programming listeners wanted to receive. In addition, the
commission would be better able to discern what programming was

in the public interest and necessity. Second, diversity in ownership of the stations was needed to enhance free speech. If one group with one point of view operated no more than one station, more diversity of opinion would exist. Third, prohibiting trading or trafficking in licenses would keep unfit broadcasters from purchasing a controlling interest in a radio company. Fourth, the commission should hold hearings on questions of program discrimination and censorship. Fifth, equal opportunities should be extended to include spokespersons for political candidates. Political candidates could not monopolize the process through presenting their viewpoints over the airwaves through their spokespersons, who were not covered by Section 18. Other candidates' spokespersons should be allowed equal access. Sixth, preferences in licensing should be given to nonprofit, eleemosynary organizations, which would present distinct, assorted views. Last, as stations were eliminated from the crowded airwaves, the commission should give preferences to stations that air all sides of every argument. Such stations, he noted, lived up to the American standard of free speech.[37]

Merlin Aylesworth, president of NBC, echoed these sentiments when he addressed the ACLU one month later. He noted that charges of censorship rose most often when stations selected programs but warned, "[F]reedom of the air does not and can never mean unlimited license of speech, or the right to bore, insult or outrage the radio listening public." He likened freedom of the air to freedom of the press in its ability to reflect the interests of readers or listeners and claimed the "public interest" lay behind every NBC programming decision. NBC had the right to select programs, although he emphasized that no political, racial, or religious lines were drawn in allocating NBC's facilities. Balanced programming was key.[38]

NBC employees clearly decided which speakers provided that balance. Writer Oliver Garrett interviewed various NBC officials and noted that "[c]harges of censorship, with varying degrees of justice, are made against a number of the most important stations. One broadcasting official explains that 'we censor the speaker, not the speech,' meaning that the prominence and position of the speaker in his community is regarded as the matter of first importance, not his views."[39] As NBC judged a speaker's quality and public acceptance, those decisions generally underscored conservative viewpoints.

At the end of November 1927, NBC engineer Alfred Goldsmith told the National Electrical Manufacturers Association in Chicago that pessimists had predicted curtailment of program choices available to listeners. He acknowledged that, by raising the level of program fare, network programming would restrict choices for the listener who "for some mysterious reason, wants a very poor program." He called such programs "undesirable" and told the audience that it would be much better for the industry to concentrate on providing the "freedom for the listener to select from among as many high quality programs as possible."[40]

FRC commissioners also emphasized listener choice. In April 1927, Commissioner Henry Bellows spoke to the League of Women Voters in Washington, D.C., and emphasized that both interference reduction and societal betterment through radio served the public interest. "The law tells us that we shall have no right of censorship over radio programs, but the physical facts of radio transmission compel what is, in effect, a censorship of the most extraordinary kind. . . . The demand from every section of the country is to cut down the number of broadcasting stations in the interests of the listening public," he said. Consequently, the commission had to decide which stations were rendering service in the "interest, convenience, or necessity" of the public, and the dilemma facing it was one of measuring "the conflicting claims of grand opera and religious services, of market reports and direct advertising, or jazz orchestras and lectures on the disease of hogs." Because Congress denied the commission the right to interfere with programs, "safeguarding of that right of free speech [for minority opinions] which is essential to intellectual growth lies in the hands of the broadcasters themselves" as well as listeners. Listeners must demand "that kind of radio service which will make our country a better and happier and finer place in which to live."[41]

Later, the FRC included these sentiments in its 1927 annual report. Of the 732 licensed stations existing as the commission began operation, only 696 remained by midsummer.[42] Some decrease was due to General Order No. 12, issued May 26, 1927, which granted sixty-day licenses to all stations and stated licensees not serving the public interest, convenience, or necessity would be eliminated. Any station dissatisfied with the allocation of frequency, power, or time assigned them could appeal in writing by June 15. Then the commission would call a hearing on the case.[43]

With the breakdown in regulation in 1926, 250 new stations had come on the air, and older stations had jumped wavelengths or increased power five to ten times their former output. Radio stations in some markets were separated by as little as two kilocycles instead of the more common fifty kilocycles for stations in the same towns. Canadian stations were threatened with interference, in spite of frequent warnings from the federal government and personal appeals from Coolidge's cabinet to errant broadcasters that international goodwill was at stake. Thus, the FRC's first steps were to transfer all stations to authorized channels on "even tens" of kilocycles, to clear six Canadian channels of American broadcasters and reassign them to other wavelengths, and to place remaining interfering stations in the spectrum "wherever possible."[44] While these actions enhanced listeners' rights to receive information, it also emphasized and reinforced the commercial status quo.

Listeners' rights were superior to those of broadcasting stations, and the legal test of stations operating in the public interest, convenience, or necessity ensured those rights, according to J. H. Dellinger. In a speech to radio listeners on NBC, Dellinger noted that public interest meant that both city and rural listeners deserved service; "too much" duplication of programs could not be permitted; and the total number of stations had to be reduced to eliminate interference.[45]

At the fifth annual convention of the National Association of Broadcasters in September 1927, Commissioners Bullard, Caldwell, and Bellows also emphasized listener rights, even though only one-quarter of American homes were equipped with receivers. While sorting out interference problems captured the bulk of industry presentations, commissioners raised concerns about freedom of speech and public service. According to Bellows, public service meant two things: entertainment and presentation of a variety of programs that the public would not otherwise receive. The key, difficult to define, was that program material should have value to the general public. Commissioner Caldwell recognized that questions of freedom of speech would arise in deciding who would have access to the airwaves. He noted that "all types of political, social, and religious propaganda" have their places on the airwaves, and with more stations wanting to come on the air, the situation would change.[46] Those wanting licenses, though, found them difficult to obtain, and new stations as well as smaller, independent stations faced a nebulous future.

A confidential memorandum outlined a guide for the commission's future transfers and deletions. Channels 1350 to 1500 kHz were designated for future high-power stations, while the band 1310 to 1350 kHz was selected as "the languishing band or region for packing into close proximity poor stations whose records show that they have been rendering service of little public value." Moving poorer stations to this band could be accomplished with less resistance than if these stations were reassigned to lower channels, because these middle band frequencies were within reach of all receiving sets. According to the memo, through a Darwinian survival of the fittest, this closely packed, "languishing" band would eventually be reclaimed without legal hassles attendant to outright elimination of stations. Thus, the radio band would be reconfigured to look like this: 550–590, regional channels; 600–1000, clear channels; 1000–1190, regional channels; 1210–1300, 100-watt local stations; 1310–1350, languishing band; and 1360–1500, reassigned with what the memo dubbed stations of "deserving quality." Of course, deserving stations were largely commercial and were becoming affiliates of the newly formed networks. While the FRC privately considered implementing this unpublicized plan, it never did.[47] By the end of March 1928, with the passage of the Davis Amendment, the FRC had abandoned this particular allocation scheme. But the fact that the FRC considered the plan as an option shows the commission's low regard for stations it deemed unworthy.

The Davis Amendment

The Davis Amendment came through the efforts of Representative Ewin Davis, who was concerned that stations in the South were neglected in favor of stations in the Northeast and upper Midwest, which dominated radio. As first outlined in debates leading up to the Radio Act of 1927, Davis wanted to equalize station numbers, power, and airtime among five geographic zones in the United States, roughly Northeast, South, Great Lakes, Midwest, and Mountain/Pacific States or West. After it passed, the Davis Amendment modified Section 9 of the Radio Act and required equal allocation of licenses to states within each of these five zones and according to population within the states.[48] FRC implementation of the amendment was inconsistent and erratic. Sometimes the FRC used it to close unwanted stations or force them off the air, while on other occasions commissioners ignored the amendment in implementing policy.

Under the amendment, the FRC established limits on the number of stations that could operate simultaneously at any given time. After exhaustive study, the commission and its engineers determined that no more than 40 clear channel stations of 5,000 watts or more, 125 regional stations of 500 to 1,000 watts, and 150 local stations of 10 to 100 watts could operate at one time. A larger number of transmitters could operate by sharing daytime periods, but the total could not exceed those limits at night, if good radio reception was to be safeguarded.[49]

General Orders No. 32 and No. 40 were passed to implement the Davis Amendment, and they effectively shut down or forced many stations off the air. General Order No. 32 of May 1928 stated that the commission was not satisfied that the "public interest, convenience or necessity" standard would be served by granting renewal applications to 164 stations. Of these stations, 37 were in the first zone, 31 in the second, 91 in the fourth, and 5 in the fifth. Only the third zone, largely made up of southern states, escaped cuts. Most of the stations slated for deletion protested, and 110 appeared at hearings on July 9. The hearings reduced the number of stations by 62. Twenty-six were closed outright by the commission; another 32 because they did not appear at the hearings; and 4 by surrendering their licenses voluntarily. In addition, another 47 stations voluntarily surrendered their licenses before June 30. Thus, a total reduction of 109 stations was made.[50]

General Order No. 40 had even wider, long-range implications for the industry. It outlined the FRC's station classification plan, which allocated ninety-six frequencies, each 10 kHz wide. Of these, forty were clear channels, eight for each zone; thirty-five were regional, seven for each zone; and the remaining twenty-one channels were local. This allocation effectively cut the total number of stations thought possible at the time because only one station would operate on clear channels at night, while only two or three stations would operate on regional assignments. Stations with these valuable assignments rapidly affiliated themselves with the evolving national networks. The remaining twenty-one local channels could accommodate numerous low-power stations. The FRC's 1928 annual report stated the allocation "provides, or at least makes possible, excellent radio reception on 80 per cent of the channels. The few other channels will suffer from heterodyne interference except in a small area close to each station."[51]

These assignments were not without powerful critics. Senator Dill, for instance, attacked the commission for failing to assign clear channels to independent, non-network affiliated stations.[52] Affected stations also reacted with lawsuits, attacking the FRC's authority to make regulations.[53] One station whose hours of operation were curtailed appealed the FRC decision, contending it was deprived of its property rights. The appeals court held that Congress had the right to pass laws regulating radio, as without national regulation, chaos would reign. Station construction and operation under a license did not create property rights, the court noted. In another case, the commission's right to deny a license at renewal was upheld. In general, the court said the FRC had the right to use the "public interest" in determining if a station license should be continued.[54]

Deciding "public interest" claims among applicants continued to be a part of the FRC's responsibilities. But what did "public interest" mean to the FRC? In August 1927, in its only explicit statement on the concept, the FRC acknowledged that "a precise definition of such a phrase which will foresee all eventualities is manifestly impossible" but added that a few general principles were applicable. First and foremost was "freedom from interference of various types as well as good quality in operation of the broadcasting station." Clear signal reception was the chief goal in serving the public interest. The FRC also saw channel allocation for various types of geographically defined service as enhancing the public interest. Needed were stations covering as large a geographic area as possible in addition to regional and local stations. In programming, the FRC wanted stations to avoid too much duplication of both programming and program types. The commissioners also believed broadcasting's limited facilities should not be used for service readily available in other forms, such as phonograph records. Presenting original material was a must. While recognizing advertising's economic base for radio, the FRC stated that benefits "derived by advertisers must be incidental and entirely secondary to the interest of the public" and added, "Advertising should be only incidental to some real service rendered to the public, and not the main object of a program." A licensee or applicant's character, financial responsibility, and past record could also be used to determine fitness for broadcast. Definitely not in the public interest were using radio for distinctly private matters and not operating "on a regular schedule made known in the public through announcements in the press." The statement concluded that the "public interest, convenience, or necessity" test was comparative; the number of channels was limited while the number of persons wanting to broadcast was far greater than could be accommodated. The commission's duty was to "determine from among the applicants it has before it which of them will, if licensed, best serve the public."[55]

On February 16, 1929, the FRC issued additional guidelines, known as the Great Lakes Statement, to delineate further what "public interest" meant when deciding conflicting claims between broadcast stations. Stations having the longest period of service should be given priority, the commission said. This viewpoint endorsed broadcasters' beliefs that longevity in public service was most important in protecting their rights to use the airwaves. In this statement, instead of using the analogy of telephone and telegraph service where the rights of senders of messages were distinguished from the rights of recipients, the commission stated that broadcasting stations would be considered public utilities. Broadcast stations furnished a commodity, in this case instruction and entertainment, just as an electric light company furnished a commodity—electricity. Consequently, stations should provide well-rounded programming designed for the tastes, needs, and desires of all substantial groups of listeners and not operate exclusively in the private interest of individuals or groups. Since the broadcast band could not accommodate stations for every school of thought, "propaganda" stations—or stations emphasizing one issue or one particular religious, political, social, or economic viewpoint—had less claim to the airwaves than did more general public service stations.[56]

This statement drew upon FRC general counsel Bethuel Webster's January 1929 statement on FRC censorship powers. Extrapolating from state statutes providing censorship over theaters and moving pictures, Webster noted the FRC could not approve or disapprove programs before broadcast. Since Section 9 of the Radio Act provided grant of licenses only if the public interest, convenience, or necessity were served, the commission could later review programs and station records to see if stations had rendered good service. Such review did not interfere with free speech rights, nor was it censorship. Webster concluded, "[T]he programs of any station may be compared with those of any other station in order to ascertain which would better serve public convenience, interest, or necessity, and the licensing of one in preference to the other on the basis of such a comparison is not contrary to the non-censorship provisions of Section 29 of the Radio Act."[57]

Other implementation of the Davis Amendment also brought about tortuous reasoning by FRC commissioners. During 1932, for example, WKBB in Joliet, Illinois, applied for a permit to move to East Dubuque, Illinois, to serve Dubuque, Iowa, across the river. The FRC granted the application without a hearing because the station wanted to move to another Illinois location, even though its stated purpose was to serve the Iowa city. The *Dubuque Telegraph-Herald* protested vigorously as it had sought a license for Dubuque for some time and had been told it could not get a license because Iowa was over quota in radio stations. After the protest, the commission suspended the initial WKBB grant and held a hearing, which reaffirmed its original action.[58]

The U.S. Court of Appeals then denied the *Telegraph-Herald*'s appeal because the newspaper lacked standing in the original WKBB request. The court noted that the newspaper was "not a corporation aggrieved or whose interests were adversely affected by the decision of the Commission modifying the license of WKBB."[59] The American Newspaper Publishers Association (ANPA) claimed WKBB's chief purpose was to compete with the newspaper for advertising accounts in the Dubuque area and dubbed such a tactic "unfair competition" because the quota system kept the *Telegraph-Herald* from obtaining a station license.[60]

Other stations brought further challenges to this quota system, and by February 1933, 116 separate cases were pending before the FRC that involved substantially the same issue—reassignment of a station to another channel in an attempt to equalize broadcast facilities among states and geographic zones. In another case dealing with purely quota grounds, the FRC ordered deletion of WIBO and WPCC, two Chicago stations that shared time on 560 kc, in favor of WJKS of Gary, Indiana. The Court of Appeals reversed the FRC decision, holding it was "arbitrary and capricious" and that the Davis Amendment did not dictate mathematical equality in the states and zone distribution of facilities. On behalf of the FRC, the Department of Justice filed a petition for Supreme Court review on February 3, 1933. If the decision were reversed, the FRC could have a free hand in eliminating facilities in the twenty-seven over-quota states and reassigning them to under-quota areas, regardless of property rights, station investments, public service, or free speech issues.[61]

In May 1933, the Supreme Court upheld the FRC's original decision, finding that the agency implemented congressional power to regulate radio as interstate commerce. The decision added that stations had no property rights in channel assignments and that the quota system was valid and in compliance with the Radio Act. The Court noted that a fair distribution of power did not mean a mathematical distribution but rather an apportionment of facilities that would equally serve all persons. The Court added that the Court of Appeals was not a "super–Radio Commission" and could deal only in questions of law. In writing for the Court, Chief Justice Charles Evans Hughes held that the channel shared by WIBO and WPPC in Chicago could be reassigned to WJKS in Gary, Indiana, as Indiana was 22 percent under quota while Illinois was 55 percent over quota.[62] Critics of the decision noted it made little sense as Gary was just outside Illinois's boundaries and the station's object was to serve audiences in the Chicago area.

Conclusion

In their public pronouncements and speeches to industry groups, FRC commissioners placed emphasis on the public interest standard in serving listeners' rights to receive clear radio signals. Cutting the number of stations serving the nation reduced interference and enhanced the public interest in receiving intelligible signals. In initial FRC hearings and pronouncements, reducing interference dominated discussion, and issues of free speech became important as they were tied to clear reception of programming offered by stations to the general public. Balanced programs were also key to the public interest, but broadcasters decided what programs provided that balance. Freedom of the air and station operation in the public interest began to take on a meaning defined, in part, through airing programs that the public would not otherwise receive and that had value for a general audience. The statements made concerning public interest also endorsed the economic and commercial constructs that pervaded the four radio conferences.

The spectrum allocation shake-ups during 1927–28 won both

praise and protest and served to extend the FRC's existence. The commission created forty clear channels, most of which went to network affiliates, with a host of regional and local assignments. Virtually all stations operated by educational institutions received part-time assignments, in most cases confined to daytime hours, which many considered useless for adult education. Although noncommercial stations were relegated to undesirable channels, hours of operation, and coverage areas, they protested and fomented a set-aside of spectrum for educational and noncommercial use, discussed in chapter 11.

All in all, the FRC's policies were largely shaped by personal, sectional, or political considerations and did little more than crystallize the commercial status quo. By the early 1930s, radio's structure set in the mid-1920s was essentially reaffirmed and adopted. License limitations and implementation of the Davis Amendment resulted in a system of program service on a few channels with the most valuable facilities operated by electrical manufacturers, newspapers, and commercial establishments. By 1932, NBC and the Columbia Broadcasting System (CBS) controlled the best program facilities through affiliation with the best stations. The FRC made no fundamental changes in the system, and while station numbers declined, substantial improvement in remaining operations did not necessarily occur. Handicapped with insufficient appropriations, especially for technical and legal personnel, the commission concerned itself with piecemeal realignment devised only to lessen signal interference.

In short, broadcasting had to operate in the public interest, a definition based on economic, technical, and financial concerns that primarily meant preventing interference and presenting programming for a general audience. During hearings, though, seeds of another perspective on "public interest" that emphasized viewpoint diversity were planted. As they grew, the FRC was destined to deal with what programming in the public interest meant. Differing interpretations arose and often resulted in court cases that further clarified the meaning of freedom of the air.

6 ⇒ "BY THEIR FRUITS YE SHALL KNOW THEM": BRINKLEY, BAKER, AND SHULER

By their fruits ye shall know them" soon became a major FRC slogan, and "if those fruits are distasteful to the commissioners, a trifle sour, off-color or odoriferous perhaps, they may swing the big stick and ordain that the license of the offender not be renewed," FRC critics asserted.[1] In many cases decided from 1927 to 1934, the FRC held it was not in the public interest to use radio for personal controversy, slanderous attacks on individuals, or the exploitation of the personal views and business of the licensee. On this ground, Jacob Conn of Providence, Rhode Island, lost his license in 1928, and several Pennsylvania stations were placed on probation for carrying what the *American Mercury* dubbed "a back-fence squabble" over the air. In his *Hello World* programs, W. K. Henderson of Shreveport, Louisiana, gave "picturesque hell" to chain stores. So, in 1932, when he applied for license renewal, he was initially turned down because he used the airwaves "primarily as a personal mouthpiece and that his derisive and abusive language was inimical to the moral and aesthetic development of the youth of America."[2]

The most severe charges of programming impropriety by station owners were leveled against "Dr." John Brinkley of KFKB, Milford, Kansas; Norman Baker of KTNT, Muscatine, Iowa; and

Reverend Robert Shuler of KGEF, Los Angeles, California. These men fought for their licenses in the name of "freedom of the air," and in Shuler's case, also in the name of religious rights for viewpoints and public revelations he thought beneficial to the public interest. The Baker and Brinkley cases focused on presenting and promoting medical information over the air in a fashion inimical to the public welfare, while the Shuler case revolved around his personal attacks and comments on government, politics, the courts, and religious groups. In each case, the FRC decided the broadcasters' actions were in their personal interests and not in the broader public interest.

Protecting the Public Welfare

Concerns over Brinkley and Baker and their brand of broadcasting began in late December 1929, when Dr. Shirley Wynne, commissioner of health for the state of New York, wrote to the FRC to ask its help in getting medical quacks off the air. He wanted to know if something in the federal law could be invoked to halt the broadcasts, as he believed radio's "fake doctors" constituted a greater hazard to the public than did ads in print media because radio reached a wider audience. While constitutionally opposed to censorship, he thought that stations could submit their sponsors' health claims to a local health department for approval.[3] Wynne's proposal was opposed by the Citizens' Medical Reference Bureau, which saw such actions as enabling regular, or "allopathic," physicians to disparage other forms of healing.[4] Wynne's crusade clearly demonstrated the battles within the medical establishment between acceptable practices and those discredited by the majority of doctors. Disdained procedures ran the spectrum from valid homeopathic and chiropractic methods to potentially deadly homemade cancer cures.[5]

Initially, the FRC ruled that under the Radio Act, it could do nothing to stop alleged false medical advertisements on radio. In a decision issued in December 1929, FRC vice chair Eugene Sykes noted that the commission could not exercise any kind of censorship, as Congress had repeatedly refused to give the commission such powers. The lone dissenter, Harold LaFount, stated that the commission had the authority to act if the programs were not in the public interest, convenience, or necessity,[6] and this view ultimately gained the majority in just a few months for fear of major negative social consequences perpetuated by radio quacks. Foremost among questionable practitioners were Dr. John R. Brinkley and Norman Baker.

John Brinkley and KFKB

In addition to operating KFKB ("Kansas First, Kansas Best"), Brinkley owned the Brinkley Hospital and Brinkley Pharmaceutical Association in Milford, Kansas. Three times each day for half an hour, Brinkley ran a *Medical Question Box* program over KFKB. During the program, he would answer letters from listeners and prescribe cures for their ailments, generally advising the use of Brinkley Pharmaceutical medicines. In 1930, the FRC refused to renew his license on the ground that the station was being operated for Brinkley's personal and financial interest. In February 1931, the court of appeals upheld this decision, and Brinkley moved his business to Mexico.[7]

Brinkley came to Milford, a town of several hundred persons, after World War I in response to an ad for a town doctor.[8] Born in 1885 in Beta, North Carolina, Brinkley had a medical education that can be described as spotty at best. Just before World War I, he was granted a diploma from the Eclectic Medical University of Kansas City and the Kansas City College of Medicine and Surgery. According to Dr. Morris Fishbein, head of the American Medical Association, both schools were "diploma mills." Brinkley later claimed he graduated from the National University of Arts and Sciences in St. Louis, but his name did not appear in any school records.[9]

Brinkley began broadcasting in 1923 and quickly made KFKB one of the most popular stations in Kansas and the Midwest. KFKB carried Brinkley's talks, including his notorious claims to restore potency in men by grafting live tissue from goats. In hearings before the FRC in 1930, the commissioners noted KFKB carried Brinkley's talks on this alleged rejuvenation procedure and other medical subjects about one and a half hours per fifteen-hour broadcast day, while the Brinkley Hospital used the station another one and a half hours daily. Other station programs included music, lectures, weather broadcasts, political discussions, baseball reports, and national events. The over-the-air prescriptions brought the station between $15,000 and $20,000 each month. Brinkley and his staff performed thousands of operations at fees ranging from $250 to $1,500. The average was $750, a considerable sum in the Depression years. Through distributing large amounts of money to the town and financing building projects that employed residents, Brinkley made himself popular in the community. Among his projects were a large sanatorium and the Brinkley Methodist Memorial Church.[10]

The commissioners questioned not only advertisement of "goat gland" operations and Brinkley's *Medical Question Box* but also Brinkley's claims that he did not control the station's full operations; they also raised concerns over sexual material in Brinkley's broadcasts that they believed bordered on indecency. One of Brinkley's detractors, a Dr. Stewart, testified that Brinkley aired a letter from a woman who said her husband was so virile that he constantly annoyed her at night. She wanted to know what to do, and Brinkley allegedly said, "All I can say is, tell your husband to sleep in the barn." To counter charges of indecency, Brinkley's attorney presented thousands of affidavits from people, including other medical personnel and station monitors, who said they heard nothing obscene or indecent over KFKB, including this alleged broadcast. Commissioner Ira E. Robinson then reminded George Strong, Brinkley's attorney, that the Radio Act provided for license revocation if broadcasts were obscene, indecent, or profane and added that the Brinkley comment could be deemed indecent.[11]

The commission denied KFKB's license renewal, and the court of appeals upheld that decision on February 2, 1931. The court found Brinkley in control of the station and his *Medical Question Box* devoted to "diagnosing and prescribing treatments of cases from symptoms given in letters" written by patients he had never seen. The court ruled that KFKB was operated solely for Brinkley's personal interest and that the *Medical Question Box* was "inimical" to public health and safety. The court held that in considering an application for license renewal, an important consideration was past performance, adding the biblical declaration "by their fruits ye shall know them." The court noted censorship was not involved, as the FRC did not subject Brinkley's broadcasts to scrutiny prior to release. Prohibitions against censorship in the Radio Act, however, did not preclude the commission from its right to note a station's past conduct at license renewal.[12]

The FRC denied his license, and the Kansas Medical Board revoked his medical license for "unprofessional conduct." Afterwards, he ran for governor of Kansas and nearly won. While interested in the governorship, Brinkley was undoubtedly just as interested in getting the right to dictate members of the State Board of Medical Examiners, which had revoked his license. Brinkley had filed his candidacy too late to be included on the ballot, so he was dependent on write-in votes. Consequently, he conducted one of the most colorful and effective campaigns in Kansas history. Flying around Kansas in his private plane, Brinkley made hundreds of speeches, promising to cut taxes while providing free textbooks and driver's licenses and constructing highways and lakes in every county of landlocked Kansas.

His speeches consisted of quotations from poetry and the Bible and a spelling lesson. As many as two dozen times during a speech, Brinkley got the audience to spell his name aloud so they would not misspell it on the ballot and consequently invalidate their votes. "He would say: 'Now once again. Let's spell the name of the candidate you're going to vote for.' Then beating time he would lead his audience in J-O-H-N—B-R-I-N-K-L-E-Y." Election clerks were told to throw out any Brinkley vote for misspelling or any other technicality, and in the end Brinkley came in second with 183,278 votes to Harry Woodring's 217,171. Brinkley also carried three counties in Oklahoma, where he was neither running nor qualified for office. He ran again in both 1932 and 1934, when Alf Landon roundly defeated him. Meanwhile, he headed to Texas and Mexico, where he continued his broadcasts.[13]

In 1931, Mexican authorities banned his physical entry, but by using Mexican citizens as a front, Brinkley erected a station in Villa Acuna, Coahila, Mexico, opposite his new hometown of Del Rio, Texas. Using telephone hookups from his home in Del Rio, he began broadcasting from station XER in October. Again, he gave medical advice over the station and answered letters sent to his *Medical Question Box*. He directed people to contact his hospital in Milford, Kansas, for further treatment. Broadcasting at 50,000 watts, XER drowned out U.S. stations close to it on the dial at 735 kilocycles, including WSB in Atlanta, and interfered with CKAC in Montreal, Canada, a disruption the Canadian government wanted stopped.[14]

Protests from Mexican citizens also arose and focused on station employees, who were all American, and broadcasts, which were rarely in Spanish. Criticism of this "Yankee imperialism" grew as did complaints by United States officials until the Mexican government forced him to close XER by mid-1934. He then continued his broadcasts by purchasing broadcast time over XEPN in Piedras Negras, Mexico, and using telephone line hookups to both Mexico and Abilene, Kansas, from Del Rio for his broadcasts. Other broadcasts were carried through a studio at Eagle Pass, Texas, just across the Rio Grande from Piedras Negras.[15]

Mexico, meanwhile, promulgated a set of regulations for broadcasters that eliminated a number of conflicts with broadcasters in the United States. Among the regulations were laws providing for two sets of stations—educational and commercial. Commercial stations could be licensed only to Mexicans, had to be operated by Mexicans, and had to employ a staff composed of no less than 80 percent Mexican citizens. All advertising rates had to be approved by Mexico's Department of Commerce, and all medical advertising had to receive approval of the Minister of Health before broadcast. All programs had to be carried in Spanish except by special approval of the government.[16] In part, the Mexican government acted in response to an influx of radio mystics, astrologers, and fortune tellers who transferred their activities to stations south of the border when FRC pressure halted such broadcasts in the United States.[17]

In January 1935, Brinkley was charged with violating Section 325(b) of the Communications Act. This provision made it illegal to maintain, use, or locate a studio or apparatus in the United States for the purpose of transmitting sound waves electrically to a radio station in a foreign country and for the purpose of being broadcast from a station having a power output sufficient to be heard consistently in the United States without first securing a permit from the commission.[18] For five more years, though, Brinkley continued to sidestep the law until the Mexican government finally forced him off the air in 1940 with the signing of the North American Regional Broadcasting Agreement (NARBA).[19]

Norman Baker and KTNT

Another broadcaster feeling the FRC's wrath at the same time as Brinkley was Norman Baker. Baker began operating station KTNT in Muscatine, Iowa, on October 14, 1925. Baker said he fancied the "explosive" nature of the call letters he selected and adopted a station motto, *"Know The Naked Truth."* Throughout his operation, he claimed newspapers in his reception area, especially those owned by Lee Newspapers, were hostile to him. He maintained that the papers' publication of false, colored, and misleading news articles forced listeners to rely on KTNT as the sole agent for truth on matters of public interest.[20]

Clashes with the local *Muscatine Journal* were common, and when Baker became totally dissatisfied with the paper, he solicited cancellations of *Journal* subscriptions over the air. He then organized the Progressive Publishing Company (of which he was president) to establish another Muscatine newspaper. He sold stock in the company over KTNT. In making sales, which amounted to more than $100,000, Baker promised a return of four times the investment.[21]

Baker also used the station to sell his KTNT magazine, plus tires, gasoline, books, and radio equipment handled by his sales organizations. In addition, he operated the People's Protective Association and used the station to solicit funds. The purpose of the association, according to Baker, was to fight for the public, "not only to fight medical things, but other things for the benefit of the public."[22]

The American Medical Association became the subject of the station's venomous attacks because the AMA disagreed with Baker's medical theories and the practices of the Baker Institute in the treatment of cancer. Over the air, Baker referred to the AMA as the "Amateur Meat-Cutters Association" and labeled members as unscrupulous, immoral, inefficient, money-mad malpractitioners. He also assailed individual doctors with scathing personal and professional attacks. State officials faced comparable disparagement, as did the officials of the *Muscatine Journal*. In personal attacks over the station, Baker referred to them as "immoral, drunkards, damned liars, contemptible curs, scoundrels and cowards." In his attacks on individuals, he also used the words "prostitute" and "abortionist," words considered inappropriate for broadcast at the time.[23]

In his report about KTNT in March 1931, FRC radio examiner Ellis Yost noted that a radio station license imposed an inescapable obligation on the licensee to serve the public interest and to promote the public welfare. Promoting personal or community strife and turmoil by means of radio communications was not in the public interest, nor were a station's unjust attacks or attempts to destroy legitimate organizations or individuals to further personal interests and business. Yost noted that "a proper respect for the rights, privileges and opinions of all peoples should be observed and maintained by all licensees" and that "since the home is the principal listening post in the broad field of radio reception, nothing which tends to vulgarity, immorality or indecency has any place in radio communications." Yost concluded that Baker operated the station for his personal rather than the public interest. Hence, in his opinion, KTNT's license should not be renewed. In addition, because the state of Iowa was in the oversubscribed Fourth Radio Zone, deleting KTNT would further the goals of the Davis Amendment to equalize radio facility assignments among zones and states.[24]

Baker protested Yost's report as "censorship" and demanded a hearing before the FRC. One was scheduled for mid-May. Meanwhile, the ACLU offered Baker help in the name of free speech, an offer he welcomed.[25] Baker and his attorney, W. D. Randall, contended that Yost's report was not sustained by evidence. Randall also noted that Baker was "denied a proper opportunity to show by the record that KTNT had served the public interest, convenience and necessity." While supplying no evidence of such programming, Randall stated KTNT never deviated from its assigned frequency; did not play phonograph records but provided high-grade, live programs; and supplied its listeners with special features such as market reports, religious programs, news bulletins, and publicity on local events.[26]

Randall also raised questions about implementation of the Davis Amendment. While admitting Iowa had more stations within its borders than the Davis Amendment quotas allowed, he argued that "the denial of the renewal of this license would work a grave injustice on many thousands of people. What Congress unquestionably meant was that the people who listen to radio, the public, should be considered in the allocation of licenses to broadcast. Congress did not mean that the privilege of broadcasting should be mathematically distributed among the States according to population."[27] If the interpretation of the law were such, he added that New Jersey would be a forest of radio towers. Randall also charged that Baker was the victim of the American Medical Association and the powerful Lee Newspapers, concluding his remarks by asking, "Are you going to deprive thousands of people living in Muscatine and its broadcast area of their favorite station because a jealous newspaper and a group of money-mad doctors ask you to do so?"[28]

Arguing that Baker used his frequency for his personal rather than the public interest, the FRC answered "Yes" to Randall's question on June 5, 1931, and denied KTNT's license renewal. Baker's attacks were unfounded, the FRC noted, adding that "surely his infliction of all this on the listeners is not the proper use of a broadcasting license. Many of his utterances are vulgar, if not indeed indecent. Assuredly, they are not uplifting or entertaining." In denying the renewal, the commission acknowledged that "though we may not censor, it is our duty to see that broadcasting licenses do not afford mere personal organs, and also to see that a standard of refinement fitting our day and generation is maintained." The FRC concluded that KTNT programming contained bitter, personal attacks on individuals and organizations and obscene or indecent language in violation of Section 29 of the Radio Act. Consequently, Baker lost his broadcast license and, like Brinkley, moved his operations to Mexico.[29] In 1934, he was running a 150,000-watt station on 1115 kc from Nuevo Laredo, Mexico, across the border from Laredo, Texas. Like Brinkley, Baker was finally forced off the air by NARBA in 1940.[30]

Reverend Robert Shuler and KGEF

Of the cases of station license revocation, that of Reverend Robert Shuler and KGEF proved most directly salient to issues of both public interest and free speech, as Shuler raised such rights in his defense. Shuler was pastor of Trinity Methodist Church of Los Angeles, and his problems began almost immediately after the inception of KGEF in December 1926. Owned by the church and supported by voluntary donations from church members, this noncommercial station went on the air after receiving a $25,000 contribution from Mrs. Lillie Glide, a wealthy widow. She had stipulated that her gift be used specifically to finance KGEF's broadcast of Shuler's sermons and his comments on politics, politicians, and other public matters.[31]

Sharing time with KFAC, KGEF broadcast 23 1/4 hours each week. Of these, Shuler used three, for half-hour sermons Sunday morning and evening and hour-long broadcasts Tuesday and Thursday from 8:00 P.M. to 9:00 P.M. Other hours were used by other Protestant churches in the area and by several civic and nonprofit clubs such as the Poetry and Music Club, the Southern Conservatory of Music, and the Los Angeles Conservatory of Music.[32] According to critics, Shuler was a crusading puritan as well as something of a showman. Among those whom Shuler denounced were institutions, including the Catholic Church and government agencies, and promoters (he called them "swindlers") of Julian oil stock in which forty thousand investors lost $20 million. Critics noted his audiences "were delighted to have their imaginations stimulated with ideas of sexual and other vices at the same time that they were emphatically assured of their own superior righteousness and even allowed as it were to have a hand in bringing the wicked to judgment."[33]

Shuler's problems began when he filed for KGEF's license renewal in September 1930 and was granted a thirty-day license instead of the customary ninety-day one. His application was challenged by George D. Lyon, a prominent Los Angeles businessman and past commander of the Los Angeles American Legion Post, which numbered over twenty thousand veterans. Shuler requested a hearing, which began in Los Angeles on January 8, 1931, and concluded January 24. During proceedings, Shuler's supporters presented letters and petitions containing more than 144,000 names of persons who thought KGEF operated in the public interest and asked that the license be renewed. They also introduced a radio popularity contest conducted by a Los Angeles radio magazine in which KGEF came in fourth out of twenty stations in southern California. Forty-eight witnesses testified on Shuler's behalf and fifty for critic George Lyon. Among the witnesses for both sides were lawyers, judges, doctors, ministers, educators, businessmen, police officers, and the present and former mayors of Los Angeles.[34]

Introduced into the hearings were transcripts of Shuler's broadcasts and contempt-of-court proceedings growing out of Shuler's statements about the California courts and the cases before them. More than twenty-three hundred pages of transcripts and testimony were developed during the hearings, including transcriptions of some of Shuler's diatribes against individuals and organizations he disdained. Targets included Jews, the Catholic Church, government and civic leaders, and the California judiciary.

In testimony, Shuler stated his free speech rights came both as a citizen and as a "teacher" of Jesus Christ's doctrine, and he readily admitted naming over the air men he considered unlawful or unethical. Shuler had said Albert Marco was "well known as the King of the Underworld" and cited Farmer Page "as the King of Gamblers of the City of Los Angeles." Both men were then serving jail terms. Shuler claimed he drove another alleged gambler from the city by broadcasting both his place of business and his home address. During one six-month period, Shuler noted, "I would broadcast his street number on Tuesday night, and then his new street number on Thursday night." He also claimed his broadcasts caused the downfall of Los Angeles district attorney Asa Keyes.[35]

Shuler admitted attacking other religious denominations over the air, especially Jews and Catholics, and stated he would not allow these groups access to station facilities for any purpose. He repeatedly attacked the Catholic Church and condemned anyone he believed "flew the banner of Rome." One of his targets in 1928 had been then Democratic presidential candidate Al Smith, a Catholic. Shuler said, in a typical broadcast, "If Al Smith is elected, God help us! This nation is billed for years of turmoil and strife, of discontent and struggle, for hate and venom, the life of which your nation has not seen since slavery lifted its head. . . . For Rome and liquor, through an organized force, is going to try to take over this nation and wring the life out of this country and make law to be a puny stigma while she grows to be a giant."[36] During FRC testimony, Shuler was asked if such attacks were in the public interest and if freedom of speech gave broadcaster speakers the right to slander religious denominations. Slander—no, he replied, but speakers should be allowed to tell "the truth," and Shuler's "truth" allowed him to oppose the Catholic Church on the air.[37]

In his report, FRC examiner Yost recognized Shuler's popularity. He noted that time for commercial broadcasts over other Los Angeles stations was easier to get during the times Shuler was personally on the air and added that Shuler probably had a greater number of listeners when broadcasting than any regular broadcaster on the Pacific Coast. Yost conceded some listeners tuned to the broadcasts out of curiosity or because they expected to hear sensational tidbits. Others, he acknowledged, listened expecting or fearing that they might be attacked,[38] and these were the ones who understandably wanted Shuler off the air.

Yost noted that Shuler exercised a great deal of liberty in opposing, criticizing, denouncing, and attacking persons, organizations, political parties, courts, judges, juries, candidates for public office, and public office holders. Shuler claimed his comments and attacks promoted the public welfare but also admitted that he had made attacks via radio without knowing all facts surrounding the matters. On the other hand, Lyon asserted the broadcasts were biased, prejudiced, unjust, unfair, and based on false and frivolous reports and rumors. Lyon insisted that Shuler's talks stirred up strife, engendered racial hatred, increased religious prejudice, and fostered unjust suspicion of public officials.[39]

Shuler admitted that he attacked persons over the air, "believing that there is no way to cure the ills of society today except by attacking the men who are preying upon society, and expose their acts to the light of day." He added that he proceeded, "knowing when I did so that there are libel laws intended to protect the good name of every man in this community." He claimed a new California slander statute was "expressly passed for my station, and conceded all over the State to have been passed with my station in mind, knowing that every man had his recourse through the courts if I should say anything whatsoever that would defame their character or harm or hurt their good names."[40]

Shuler said that as both a minister and a civic and moral leader, he was privileged to make such speeches. The courts specifically stated no precedent existed for Shuler's claims to privilege as a minister, although they did recognize his right to free speech. This right, though, was tempered by the equally fundamental rights of due process and fair trial. The judiciary had to be free from improper interference with cases before them. While courts recognized that the judiciary, their officers, and decisions were open to public criticism, the courts stated that Shuler's radio broadcasts interfered with judicial proceedings and were clearly in contempt. Later, courts recognized Shuler's claims of free speech but dismissed any declaration to ministerial privilege in his broadcasts. Consequently, Shuler adroitly continued to play on free speech sentiments, although he made no further claims to any rights or privileges as a minister or to exercising any First Amendment rights under the religious clause guarantees.[41]

In mid-July 1930, one highly publicized, ill-fated event evolved from Shuler's broadcasts and publications about the Julian stock fraud. An officer of the First National Bank allegedly involved in the Julian scandal, Motley Flint, was murdered in a Los Angeles courtroom by Frank Keaton, a fifty-eight-year-old real estate investor. Keaton lost virtually his whole fortune, $35,000—a princely sum at the height of the Depression—in the fraud and confessed that Shuler's criticism of Flint and others involved in the scandal caused him to confront Flint and kill him.[42] At the end of July, a mass anti-Shuler rally was held at Olympic Auditorium. With more than

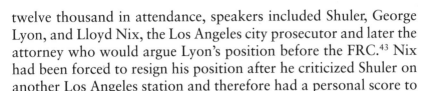

twelve thousand in attendance, speakers included Shuler, George Lyon, and Lloyd Nix, the Los Angeles city prosecutor and later the attorney who would argue Lyon's position before the FRC.[43] Nix had been forced to resign his position after he criticized Shuler on another Los Angeles station and therefore had a personal score to settle with Shuler.[44]

In his appeals before FRC examiner Yost and the FRC, Nix asserted that, simply because Shuler was a minister, the public had not repudiated him. Had he been a political agitator or an ordinary character assassin, public indignation and quick condemnation would have followed his attacks. Nix contended Shuler had taken advantage of his position as a minister to present himself as a champion of the public interest. Because he was a minister, listeners believed not only in his sincerity but also in the reliability of his charges against police and other government officials.[45]

A grand jury investigated Shuler's charge that Los Angeles police and police officials were extorting money from persons accused of violating the law. Their inquest concluded that the charges were unjustified. Shuler admitted to the grand jury that he did not know whether his accusations were true and said he had no means of obtaining the facts. They replied, "No public good has been accomplished by his methods . . . no public abuses corrected, and innocent persons by innuendo and irresponsible gossip have been unjustly suspected and accused."[46] Echoing the grand jury, Shuler's opponents did not ask his privilege of "legitimate" freedom of speech be abridged. Rather, they wanted him to be "strictly regulated so that he may be controlled in what they consider his illegitimate use of the air to the harm of the individual and the community."[47]

Yost firmly believed Shuler had been "extremely indiscreet" in his broadcasts and asked whether KGEF had violated broadcasting's obligation to render true public service. Yost stated that no one had the right, under the guise of free speech, to use radio to injure others through broadcasts based solely on rumors and unverified reports. Such programs were indefensible, as reputations could be irreparably damaged. Similarly, unjust attacks on religious denominations increased prejudice and aroused community strife and antagonism, while unwarranted criticism of courts and public officials destroyed people's confidence in government. Both were counter to the public interest.[48]

Yost knew two factors limited his powers to determine how far Shuler and KGEF could go in their broadcasts. First, the Radio Act prohibited program censorship, and second, he had to evaluate all of KGEF's programs, not just Shuler's broadcasts, in making his decision. After reviewing the entire public service record of KGEF, Yost found that the station did broadcast in the public interest, convenience, and necessity, and his report, issued August 7, recommended license renewal because the totality of the station's programs justified renewal of its license, in spite of Shuler's offenses.[49]

On September 1, Lyon filed formal exceptions to Yost's report and requested oral argument before the commission. The first issue raised was Shuler's "verbal lease" of KGEF to Trinity Methodist Church. Examiner Yost had stated in his report that Shuler did not maintain control over the station because he leased it to the church. Such arrangements defeated the purpose of the formal licensing process, as proper assignment of stations was undermined. Second, Lyon asserted Yost had misread the law when he weighed Shuler's actions against the public service of all other broadcasts over KGEF. Lyon argued that if such a principle were adopted, "then our histories must certainly be rewritten and Benedict Arnold will stand forth as a national hero because he spent years of service with a marvelous military record in behalf of his country and only betrayed it once."[50] This argument was again emphasized in the hearing before the commission.[51]

Third, Lyon contended that Shuler's three hours of weekly airtime resulted in more damage to targeted groups and individuals than the good done during other broadcasts over KGEF. If Yost's report stood, then he had "fixed a standard of permissible misuse of radio stations to three hours per week" and had overruled the commission in the Brinkley-KFKB and Baker-KTNT cases. Citing the latter case, Lyon contended KGEF's use had stirred up "personal and community strife and turmoil," one main reason given for denying KTNT's renewal. Lyon also noted that Yost had made that argument when he reviewed KTNT's case and added that "as a community trouble-maker Shuler stands in a class by himself and that Norman Baker and [John] Brinkley are mere kindergarten boys in short pants in comparison."[52] To Lyon, Yost had glossed over the slander, falsehood, and attacks on institutions and individuals in describing Shuler's broadcasts as "indiscreet."[53]

Last of all, Lyon agreed with Yost's assertion that Shuler's status as a minister did not entitle him to more privilege in broadcasting than other American citizens but added that Yost's actions actually accorded Shuler more, as any other broadcaster would have lost a license under the same circumstances. Lyon asked that KGEF's license renewal be set for hearing before the commission.[54] His petition was granted, and the hearing began September 26.[55]

In their oral arguments, Lyon's attorneys emphasized Shuler's propagation of religious intolerance and racial prejudice and the maligning of public officials, none of which was protected by free speech principles. Lyon's attorneys cited the California Supreme Court's decision, in reviewing Shuler's radio diatribes against the judiciary, as not protected by constitutional guarantees of free speech. No one had the right to interfere with the orderly administration of justice, including ministers, broadcasters, soapbox orators, or newspaper editors.[56]

Lyon's attorneys emphasized Shuler's attacks on the judiciary, Catholics, Jews, and prominent Los Angeles citizens, including publisher Harry Chandler. Free speech protected none of his invectives. Religious attacks were malevolent slurs, promoting religious strife and not open, informative discussion of religious topics, while attacks on the judiciary impeded justice. Attacks on citizens usually were groundless, filled with innuendo. Citing the *KTNT* case, Lyon's attorneys reminded the commission that the public interest was not served when a station promoted personal and community strife through its broadcasts, reasons given for denying the licenses of Brinkley's KFKB and Baker's KTNT stations. If KGEF were allowed to remain in Shuler's hands, the commission would have effectively overruled itself in the *KTNT* and *KFAB-Sorenson* cases and would also be in conflict with the court of appeals in the *KFKB* case.[57]

In addition, the attorneys charged Shuler with blackmail through his broadcasts and in using language and terms that were inappropriate for broadcast. Shuler admitted that during one plea for money, he had said, "I know a man listening in, if he doesn't give a hundred dollars, I will go on the air next Tuesday night and tell what I know about him." Shuler got more money than he expected. He also admitted using terms such as "pimps," "king pimps," "prostitutes," and "prostitution," which some listeners found offensive.[58]

In his defense, Shuler cited petitions signed in favor of his broadcasts and the names of prominent citizens, including the mayor of Los Angeles and the police chief, who appeared before Yost to testify to the good done by KGEF. In a lengthy, rambling speech, Shuler added that Lyon's attorneys took examples presented to the commission out of context. He defended his attacks on the judiciary and on individuals later convicted of crimes.[59]

In some broadcasts, Shuler had said it was rumored that three of the FRC commissioners were against him and that the "Catholic commissioner might be against him" because he was a Methodist minister. When asked to identify the "Catholic commissioner," Shuler could not do so and was told that no commissioner was Catholic and that two commissioners were Methodist. Shuler asked pardon for being misinformed. To this apology, Commissioner Ira Robinson asked if the purpose of a broadcast station was to discuss personal controversy over the air. Shuler replied he thought it necessary to acquaint people with anything of interest unless it betrayed some confidence or unless some obligation not to make a statement existed.[60]

In a telling exchange, Robinson then asked Shuler about his statements that the commission had already decided to reverse Yost's findings. Shuler said he had been so informed. Robinson reproached Shuler for broadcasting an untruth and added that the commission had an open mind on Shuler's case. He speculated about other judicial matters Shuler broadcast, asking if they had also been reckless and unnecessarily aired. Shuler said these broadcasts were in the public interest, but Robinson remained unconvinced.[61]

In closing remarks, Lyon's attorneys built their remarks on the "Catholic commissioner" broadcast to emphasize Shuler's broadcasts based on rumor or unfounded allegations. Shuler simply did not get the facts before he went on the air. Therefore, they asked, did a station serve the public interest when it constantly and consistently carried misinformation and innuendo? Should a station be used for slander and scandal?[62]

No, the commission decided. Citing Shuler's statements against Catholics, Jews, the judiciary, and civic and government leaders, the FRC stated that "in almost every instance appearing in this record, the attacks made by Shuler, and the methods employed therefore, are certainly not in the interests of the public or the rendition of a commendable broadcasting service." Shuler's misstatement of facts, insinuations based on those false or ignorant declarations, and his reckless use of assertions with little or no effort to ascertain truth made him unfit to hold a license. His attacks on religious organi-

zations promoted religious antagonism, while his repeated denigra-
tion of public officials and the courts were "bitter and personal"
in nature and often ignorant of the facts. Such attacks had resulted
in two convictions for contempt of court, and these radio talks did
not meet the statutory standard for a licensee. In addition, deletion
of KGEF would make a more equitable distribution of radio facilities under the Davis Amendment. Seventeen stations would remain
to serve the Los Angeles area. Reassigning KGEF's 1300-kc frequency would help equalize broadcast signal distribution. Consequently, on November 13, 1931, the commission reversed its examiner and denied KGEF's license.[63]

Naturally, Shuler appealed, and among the organizations supporting his appeal was the ACLU.[64] Shuler wrote of his gratitude
to that organization for its support, noting, "Undoubtedly this case
will be the one that finally settles the matter of whether or not men
shall be free to speak their convictions over the air. Otherwise the air
must be completely surrendered to commercialization and a form
of entertainment such as is largely occupying the dials at this time."[65]

Liberal publications such as the *Open Forum* rallied to Shuler's
cause, even though they disagreed with his ultraconservative views.
Writer George Shoaf noted Shuler had "ignorantly and blatantly
criticized and condemned virtually everything which intelligent radicalism represents . . . and yet, no intelligent and far-seeing radical
will rejoice at Shuler's downfall." Denial of his license "is a deliberate and premeditated assault upon the traditional American and
Constitutional right of free speech." The editorial concluded that
while Shuler was uninformed and ignorant, every liberal and radical should decry the FRC decision, "not for Bob Shuler's sake, but
for the preservation of free speech, free press, and free assembly—
for the very integrity of the Constitution of the United States."[66]

On November 29, 1932, the court of appeals upheld the commission's right to deny Shuler's license. Citing *Near v. Minnesota,*
the court noted that citizens may freely utter or publish their sentiments on condition that they are responsible for any abuse of that
right.[67] For broadcasting, airing defamatory and untrue material
was an abuse of the broadcast license. License denial was not an
infringement on free speech or censorship but an exercise of FRC
authority to determine licensees. It was within the FRC's decision-
making powers to determine whether Shuler's past programming
was presented in the "public interest." If it was not, the license could

be revoked. Shuler was still free to speak; he just could not use radio as his pulpit.[68] He appealed his case to the Supreme Court, which denied *certiorari* on January 16, 1933.[69]

Without commenting on the substance of his broadcasts, the ACLU criticized the Shuler decision, stating it established a dangerous precedent that could give the FRC unlimited powers to suppress stations it wanted to silence.[70] ACLU attorney Morris Ernst compared the situation to silencing a newspaper for publication of an offensive article.[71] Ernst told the *New York Times* that this first important case on censorship was "against all previous rules laid down by the Supreme Court to gag a man in the future for something he said in the past. On this principle a newspaper publishing an offensive article would be punished by suspension of publication, something the Supreme Court has refused to permit in the past."[72]

Shuler's attorney, Louis Caldwell, and other ACLU attorneys, in a last-ditch effort, filed a petition for a rehearing, even though they and ACLU officers and members held no counsel for Shuler as an individual.[73] On February 13, 1933, the Supreme Court denied this second petition, and the case was closed.[74] The *Christian Century* editorialized, deploring the ruling and calling for congressional action to rectify the Shuler case through amendment of radio law.[75]

Even though the ACLU had offered Shuler help in the past, Shuler expressed amazement after the Court's pronouncement that the ACLU again had offered assistance while other more conservative organizations ignored his situation or agreed with the case's outcome. Over radio and in his syndicated column, Shuler noted that the only organization to come to his defense was a group he had denounced in the past as "red" or, at best, "pink." "I battled for my government for 35 years and find my government with her fingers on my throat, while the Civil Liberties Union comes to my rescue. . . . Can you beat it!!" he wrote and added, "I shall never forget that my government's supposed foes and my foes came to my rescue when my constitutional rights were imperiled."[76] Other writers were amazed that Morris Ernst, a Jew, would defend the rights of an obvious anti-Semite.[77] Of course, the reason Ernst and the ACLU championed Shuler's cause was because they knew that if the FRC could cancel his license, the FRC could cancel the license of any station expressing minority viewpoints.[78]

Conclusion

By the early 1930s, the FRC clearly prohibited the types of speech promoted by such broadcasters as Brinkley, Baker, and Shuler, and the courts upheld the FRC's revocation authority under the public interest clauses of the Radio Act. In many ways, KTNT, KFKB, and KGEF were easy targets. While they had vast listening audiences, they were opposed by powerful constituencies such as state and local government officials, the American Medical Association, and major religious denominations. Deciding that these stations had not operated in the public interest would—and did—bring protests, but these denunciations came from organizations considered more fringe at the time, such as the ACLU, or from poorly united individuals or groups having little clout in the political system.

To the FRC, a station licensee had an indisputable obligation to serve the public interest and promote the public welfare, not his own private interests. Creating turmoil through attacks on others or promoting personal goals via radio was not in the public interest, nor were any station's unjust attacks on other religious groups or government agencies, especially the courts, to be tolerated. In addition, because the home was the main base of radio reception, broadcasts judged vulgar, immoral, or indecent by contemporary standards were forbidden. The home, and especially children, had to be protected from potentially injurious material.

No station operator, under the guise of free speech, could use radio to injure others through broadcasts based solely on rumors and unverified reports. Such programs were indefensible, as reputations could be irreparably damaged. Similarly, unjust attacks on religious denominations increased prejudice and aroused community strife and antagonism, while unwarranted criticism of courts and public officials destroyed people's confidence in government. Religious intolerance, racial prejudice, and maligning of public officials were not protected by free speech principles. No one had the right to interfere with the orderly administration of justice, including ministers, broadcasters, soapbox orators, or newspaper editors. In radio, ministers were not entitled to more privileges than other American citizens when it came to station ownership or operation. Politicians made up the only special group entitled to special protections and advantages, thanks to Section 18 of the Radio Act.

7 ⇒ TO REACH THE VOTERS: POLITICAL SPEECH, 1928–1934

By the 1928 elections, many procedures had been established to enhance political speech—at least the speech of major political parties. While passage of the Radio Act offered protection for all political candidates in Section 18's equal opportunities provision, corresponding policies for airtime initiated by radio networks and individual stations favored major political parties. Many of these policies centered on the purchase of airtime, and minor parties found it virtually impossible to obtain it. Candidates got time largely if they could afford increasing program costs, while those who were not candidates or who espoused more controversial ideas had difficulty gaining access to the medium at all.

By early 1928, Governor Al Smith of New York noted that radio's potential had been demonstrated during the 1926 elections and observed, "Radio is entitled to its place with the newspapers and motion pictures as a forceful agency for public education and the formation of public opinion on the leading questions of governmental policy."[1] RCA radio engineer Alfred Goldsmith noted that radio and motion pictures ushered in a new political campaign era. With candidates' ability to reach listeners in large theaters or at home, the two media "restore that intimate contact of the ancient Roman forum, where all the people gathered to hear all the candidates."[2]

Obviously, listeners' ability to participate more fully in the mainstream political process enhanced both democracy and freedom of speech, but overall, broadcast policies and practices enhanced the status quo. This chapter traces the coalescence of broadcaster and government policies begun in 1924 to their virtually unquestioned acceptance by 1934 by the majority of broadcasters, listeners, and government officials as enhancing the democratic process, freedom of the air, and the public interest.

The Elections of 1928

As 1928 elections grew near, both industry and political party strategists planned their campaigns carefully. Radio's value to the voter lay in bringing candidates and issues into "the calm and quiet" of listeners' homes, according to RCA president J. G. Harbord. "The magnetism of the orator cools when transmitted through the microphone," he noted in an interview in March for the *New York Times*. He predicted listeners would be free of mob psychology because broadcasting political talks in the upcoming election would hurt demagogues and help "honest politicians."[3] Tennessee congressman Ewin Davis agreed. Brevity and appeal to reason were two main factors that candidates had to keep in mind for the upcoming election. Audiences would not tolerate verbosity and appeals to emotion, nor would voters sanction unfair treatment of candidates. They wanted all sides of the issues to be presented, Davis told a *New York Times* reporter.[4]

In January, stations and networks applied to the Republican and Democratic National Committees for permission to carry their conventions. Again, a chief question was cost: Who would pay for coverage? Various alternatives were offered. For instance, the national committees could pay costs, or an advertiser might sponsor proceedings. CBS said it would carry conventions free of charge to both political parties as an "institutional service" to the public and added that no charge would be assessed national committees. NBC was not as certain. While agreeing that such coverage was a public service and was in the public interest, NBC officials said they had not decided costs because they were still seeking permission to broadcast.[5] The *New York Times* editorialized that conventions should be carried in their entirety because the American public expected it. The *Times* suggested that radio's "wealthy interests" work out a way to report both the Republican convention in Kansas City and the Democratic convention in Houston "verbatim, stridentem, and loquentum."[6]

Candidates would pay for other time used and were expected to purchase that time well in advance for scheduling purposes.[7] In Chicago, the going rate for airtime was $360 per hour. While some candidates deemed this price exorbitant, others considered pooling resources with three or four to buy one hour and divide time among themselves. One candidate bought time on election eve so that he could "scotch any eleventh hour canards or whispering campaigns which might be started in the last minute, and which would be otherwise difficult to correct." For smaller, struggling stations, such purchases of airtime were lifesavers. Monies brought in supplied a large portion of their yearly income for 1928.[8]

While Republicans and Democrats had no problem in general in securing time, other political parties faced obstacles arranging convention coverage. WEVD, located in New York City, announced in mid-March that it would carry the April meeting of the Socialist party, but Anton Gerber of WEVD stated the station could not carry proceedings gavel-to-gavel as it shared time with other stations. In an attempt to gain wider network coverage for the party, Norman Thomas accused NBC of violating federal law through favoring the Republican and Democratic parties. When Thomas complained of the impossibility of getting airtime over NBC, the pressure worked. After complaints became public, NBC arranged daily twenty-minute convention summaries at 11:00 P.M. over WEAF.[9] In addition to carrying these summaries, NBC also planned in April to hook up affiliates on its Red, Blue, and then-existing Orange networks for convention coverage. All networks rejoiced after the Republican and Democratic National Committees granted permission to broadcast their conventions. Independent station WGN of Chicago also requested and received permission for such broadcasts.[10]

When convention coverage began in the summer of 1928, NBC's networks boasted over forty affiliates, with more than 500 persons, including 375 engineers, aiding in coverage of both conventions. NBC veteran announcer Graham McNamee, who had covered the 1924 presidential conventions for AT&T, again provided commentary, peppered with quips provided by humorist Will Rogers.[11]

Other stations followed program formats similar to the ones broadcast in the 1924 elections. During 1928, for instance, WMAQ carried speeches, paid political programs, and election returns.[12] In setting up coverage for 1928, NBC studied difficulties and successes of the 1924 and 1926 campaigns. It estimated that nearly eight million receiving sets were being used, twice those existing in 1924.[13]

Speakers were coached for best radio voice presentations; candidates knew delivery counted. Strategists recognized that listeners tolerated no dull, flat speeches or flowery oratory, and "in a closely and hotly waged contest it is possible that the man with the best radio personality might win a nomination or election over a field of aspirants possessed of less power to sway through the microphone." In recognition of radio's power, convention speakers' platforms included a "corral," or fenced enclosure, to compel speakers to stay within the range of the microphone. During the 1924 Democratic convention, a chalk square had been etched onto the speaker's podium at Madison Square Garden, "like a batter's box," in a vain attempt to keep speakers such as William Jennings Bryan within microphone range. Bryan had "dashed this way and that, hanging over the speaker's rail and gesticulating at his hearers, causing the radio to lose large portions of his address." To prevent wandering in 1928, a narrow physical enclosure kept orators from leaping right or left and forced them to face the mike at all times.[14]

Another admonition came from the major parties' national committees: avoid "asides." Sensitive microphones often picked up comments made near the platform speakers. During the lengthy Democratic convention in 1924, millions of radio listeners heard so-called rough words over the air, including mutterings of "Sit down, you damn fool" during one speech at Madison Square Garden. Both Democrats and Republicans worked during their 1928 conventions to keep platform gossip and wisecracks out of mike range.[15]

No Democrat wanted a repeat of the 1924 convention, as many believed broadcasting that prolonged agony of candidate selection dealt a damaging blow to the party. One newspaper account noted that the "long deadlock, with its quarrels, would have been annoying to the country years ago, when all information would have been received through the newspapers, but the radio exaggerated and rubbed it in. . . . It is admitted by most Democratic leaders that another long-winded convention like that of 1924 would be disastrous."[16] Senator Frank Willis of Ohio observed that listeners would not appreciate long-winded speeches and would rather "listen to brief, pithy statements as to the position of parties and candidates."[17]

Indeed, both parties took radio audiences into account. The Democratic convention keynote address was moved to nighttime to reach the largest possible audience, while Republicans covered a table with a soft piece of wall board so the rap of the gavel would "sound right" over the air instead of its usual timbre of "someone breaking dishes." Radio loudspeakers were set up in department stores and outside radio studios and shops. Women gave porch parties with radio furnishing political entertainment, and hospital patients kept up with the conventions through headsets. Cleveland's baseball team even carried a portable set to monitor both gatherings. Not counting shortwave transmissions to Canada, Europe, and South America, NBC hooked up forty-two stations for the Republican convention and forty-four for the Democrats. Graham McNamee noted that the "Republican Convention cost $1.07 per second to broadcast. The Democratic Convention cost $1.15 per second." Because the Democratic convention was again longer than the Republican, NBC footed a bill of $105,000 for the Democrats and $75,000 for the Republicans.[18]

Over one hundred broadcasters carried the Republican party's notification ceremonies to nominee Herbert Hoover and his acceptance speech. Both NBC and CBS organized the largest chains of stations to date to carry the speeches and Hoover's acceptance; NBC's networks linked at least seventy-three stations while Columbia's totaled twenty-three. More than 46,000 miles of telephone wire linked stations together for speeches and music, while another 22,200 miles of telegraph lines coordinated the networks' efforts. A backup system of over 20,000 miles of wire stood in readiness for any emergency. Augmenting networks were shortwave stations.[19]

On radio, candidates were introduced by tunes the public quickly recognized. "East Side, West Side" became the official song of Democratic candidate Al Smith, while refrains of "California, Here I Come" introduced Republican Herbert Hoover. Parodies on the issues were also set to music. The fight over Prohibition prompted renditions of "How Dry I Am" in jazz time and as a funeral dirge, while Governor Smith's campaign song became "East Side, Wet's Side" and "Yeast Side–Wet Side." After the campaign and election, which Hoover won, political commentator Frank Kent noted that in 1928, both sides spent a total of $1.5 million on radio, or twenty-five times the 1924 total of $60,000.[20]

After the elections, programs assumed their old form until the March inauguration approached and networks and stations worked to bring the ceremony to the public. On March 4, 1929, over one hundred stations carried Herbert Hoover's presidential inauguration so that nearly every American could tune in. NBC alone had over thirty microphones picking up the festivities. While an estimated 20 million heard the 1925 inauguration of Coolidge, 63 million would hear Chief Justice Taft administer the oath of office to Hoover.

Broadcasts began at 10:00 A.M. from the sentry's box at the White House with descriptions of the first official callers on the Hoovers. After the Hoovers and the Coolidges left the White House, radio achieved a new first when microphones picked up the swearing-in of Vice President Charles Curtis and the new senators in the Senate chambers through a special soundproof booth built to blend into the decor. From the Senate chambers, the broadcast moved to the Capitol steps, where announcers had full view of Hoover's swearing-in. Analysts explained each phase of the ceremony, and microphones carried the proceedings. Announcers then described the inaugural parade and other pageantries through their conclusion at 4:00 P.M. Announcers in aircraft above the White House and along the parade route brought listeners a bird's-eye view of the festivities.

That night, inaugural galas reached the same millions, as the inaugural ball was broadcast beginning at 11:00 P.M. and ending around 12:30 A.M. During the day, schools devoted several hours to this practical history and civics lesson. Hospitals and passenger trains also picked up broadcasts, while restaurants and theaters in large cities advertised their radio facilities as a special inducement to patrons.[21]

While seven states did not have transmitters carrying the broadcasts—North and South Dakota, Idaho, Wyoming, Nevada, Arizona, and New Mexico—residents were able to pick up at least one of the more than one hundred distant stations carrying the swearing-in. The FRC asked stations not broadcasting the ceremonies and festivities to cease operation during the inaugural program in Washington, between 11:00 A.M. and 4:00 P.M. eastern standard time.

Announcers, including Graham McNamee, Milton Cross, Ted Husing, William Hedges, and Norman Brokenshire, provided commentary throughout the day.[22]

After the inaugural, GE and RCA chief Owen Young told the annual meeting of the NBC Advisory Council that radio would continue having a profound effect on politics as politicians would have to take into account the vast invisible audience "coolly sitting in judgment around the family fireside." He foresaw an equalizing effect upon sections of the country where one political party held a great deal of power over others. He claimed radio "evens the scales and affords a fair hearing to both sides" and added, "Who can say what radio may not accomplish in destroying sectionalism and creating a new national unity?"[23]

Political coverage was not without its critics, though. In March, the *Forum* carried an article condemning the use of radio for advertising and politics.[24] One month later, RCA president J. G. Harbord replied to the magazine that radio was the greatest boon to democracy since the early Greeks envisioned self-governance. Broadcasts of national conventions and candidates' acceptance speeches vividly demonstrated the effectiveness of radio to voters and candidates alike. The networks treated both events as "news" and carried them at their own expense. He credited radio with creating greater interest in politics and for allowing this unique service to eliminate the mob feeling of live political audiences. Each listener in the privacy of the home was free from the contagion of the crowd and could judge the politician through the logic of the issue presented. Radio was more than the advertising agency that Jack Woodford, the article's author, claimed it was. Harbord predicted that radio would probably contribute more to democracy than any other single influence.[25] This influence remained largely for more conventional ideas, though. Dissident speech found little outlet over the air, especially as the Depression deepened.

The Depression, Radio, and Social Change

The early 1930s brought changes to society as economic collapse and its repercussions encompassed America and the world. For the average American, the most notable change was a decline in the overall standard of living. By 1931, businesses cut wages dramatically, and mortgage foreclosures were eight times what they had been in 1929. Net income was halved, but not all socioeconomic classes were evenly affected. The poor and middle class suffered more, and their misery created a new radicalism, feared by the status quo, which found radio voices in agitators such as Huey Long, Father Charles Coughlin, and Reverend Francis Townsend.[26]

Americans had falsely believed a permanent plateau of prosperity had been achieved in the 1920s, because they saw business planning overcoming the ills that had brought about past recessions. Government and business leaders thought balance had been achieved through rational decision making, but these perceptions diverged from actual economic reality. The system was hardly balanced and was conducive to excess instead of protective against excess. For example, investors speculated in stocks and land as "sure things," and the bubble finally burst in the fall of 1929. Throughout the early Depression years, fraudulent dealings on the London stock markets, nations moving off the gold standard, troubles checking the flow of gold out of the U.S., increases in interest rates, and investors pulling out of stocks hit stock markets negatively worldwide and shook public confidence. The bottom fell out of the U.S. market, and stocks' aggregate worth of $87 billion in 1929 plummeted to $18 billion by 1933.[27]

President Hoover tried to correct these problems by putting supposed recovery machinery into effect. He called a series of industrial conferences in Washington, D.C., to combat panic. Out of them came action to bolster farm prices and reform business and labor practices. By late 1930, Hoover seemed to be correct when he said that recovery was just around the corner. That, of course, was not the case, as further unforeseen economic woes struck: banks collapsed, severe drought hit the South and Southwest, and agricultural product dumping on world markets grew. The economy kept contracting, and this collapse became the greatest, most severe compression in American history.[28]

During the early 1930s, industrial production declined by 50 percent; national income dropped 40 percent; unemployment rose to 25 percent of the population; and farm prices dropped another 55 percent from lows of the 1920s.[29] In contrast, radio was one area of growth during these harsh years. Few listeners gave up their sets, and by 1938, more than 91 percent of urban homes and nearly 70 percent of rural homes had at least one radio.[30] Radio joined recovery efforts by deemphasizing economic plight, often censoring speakers, including minor party candidates, who wanted to address economic recovery efforts that relied on more radical methods to correct public ills. While Hoover remained active in combating the Depression, the public blamed him and his administration for economic misery. His image in the press shifted from one of a progressive activist to an inept presidential misfit. Changes were in the wind, and those changes began with the election of 1930.

The Elections of 1930: Dissident Candidates' Speech

Radio increased in popularity as the country languished. Even though unemployment was at an all-time high and income for Americans on the whole had dropped precipitously, the broadcast audience consisted of 43 percent of the nation's 29 million families. They used radio an average of two and a half hours per day and were reluctant to give up this free entertainment as hard times got even harder.[31] But, with the economy's downturn, many individuals "who had never had a radical thought before in their lives began to question the virtues of American capitalism."[32]

As the 1930 election approached, the Communist party planned to capitalize on discontent, and radio became one tool to reach the masses. In mid-September, the Communist party tried to buy time on WEAF and the NBC Red network to reach millions of Americans, but the organization's letters requesting time were ignored until late October. Then, in a vain and somewhat halfhearted attempt to rectify the situation belatedly, NBC executive John Elwood tried to reach the party's campaign manager, Jack Perilla, by phone to arrange airtime. An assistant said Perilla would return his call. When Perilla did not, Elwood made no further attempts to contact him. Complaints of discrimination followed, and NBC president Merlin Aylesworth admonished Elwood to get written records in the future so that the Communist party could not claim bias.[33]

Unlike the Communists, Socialist party candidates were not ignored by broadcasters, largely because they were not perceived as threatening as the Communists, who advocated massive changes in American government. In addition, Socialists had previous experience in campaigns, so they knew the appropriate procedures for requesting and buying airtime. In fact, at the end of the campaign, NBC received a thank-you note complimenting the company for carrying the campaign addresses of Socialist candidates on an equitable basis.[34] By disregarding Communist candidates in favor of other, more temperate dissident viewpoints, broadcasters censored what listeners received, closing down more upsetting political speech and supporting advocates wanting change within acceptable standards as determined by broadcasters.

The Elections of 1930 and 1932: A Question of Libel

During the campaigns of 1930 and 1932, another major anxiety arose for networks and stations—they would be held legally responsible for candidates engaging in over-the-air slander. New regulations and court cases had extended state libel and slander laws to radio, and broadcasters feared possible repercussions during the political campaigns. In June 1929, California governor Clement C. Young signed a "slander bill" that was partly influenced by Reverend Robert Shuler's attacks on government officials over KGEF. The new law extended libel law to radio and expressly limited criminal liability to slander uttered "willfully and with a malicious attempt to injure another."[35] Another libel bill introduced in mid-March 1930 in Texas made it unlawful for any person to broadcast a verbal defamation of another or for the owner of the station to permit such a broadcast.[36]

In April 1930, a defeated candidate from Berwyn, Illinois, a town near Chicago, was fined ten dollars and costs for slander committed during the campaign over radio under a libel law that Illinois had adopted in 1927. In the case, John H. Ehardt, the police magistrate-elect of Berwyn, charged defeated candidate Fred Broucek with uttering defamatory remarks during the campaign. While Broucek offered no defense, his attorney, Harry Levitan, asked, "Since Broucek made his remarks in Cicero, how can he be tried in Berwyn?" The Berwyn judge ruled that he had jurisdiction as the ether waves traveled to both places, and damage had been done to Ehardt's reputation in both suburbs.[37]

By late 1930, other states enacted laws or introduced bills covering libel and slander over the airwaves.[38] Because state libel laws carried heavy damages and held broadcasters responsible for speech mandated by Section 18 of the Radio Act and FRC General Order No. 31, station owners wanted answers spelling out their rights, obligations, and responsibilities when broadcasting political speech: Did radio speech that a station had to carry by law fall under libel or slander laws, or both? Answers finally came in a case begun in 1930 and decided in the summer of 1932, just in time for the presidential election.

Sorenson v. Wood held broadcasters responsible for defamatory speech against a candidate for public office in Nebraska. The Nebraska Supreme Court found that the Radio Act conferred no privilege to stations to publish defamatory statements in campaign speeches and added that when someone wrote libelous words and then read them over the air with the consent of the owner of the station, the reader and the owner were both responsible for the action.[39]

The case began at 6:30 P.M. on August 11, 1930, the eve of the Nebraska primary election, when Richard Wood broadcast an attack on C. A. Sorenson, candidate for reelection as attorney general, over Omaha station KFAB. Wood said, "In his [Sorenson's] acceptance of the attorney general's office he took an oath before God and man that he would uphold the law justly and honestly. His promises to man are for naught, and his oath to God is a sacrilege, for he is a nonbeliever, an irreligious libertine, a mad man and a fool." Wood also accused Sorenson of protecting and condoning gambling houses in Omaha in clear violation of his oath of office.[40]

Complicating the case was the fact that Wood attacked someone who was not his immediate opponent. Wood was running for railway commissioner, not attorney general, and his speech was on behalf of a candidate for the Republican nomination for the U.S. Senate, W. M. Stebbins. Stebbins had introduced Wood and told the audience that Wood was speaking for him in response to a speech made by Senator George Norris, who was Stebbins's opponent. In the speech, Wood got carried away and moved from his original topic to criticism of Sorenson's political record. Sorenson sued both Wood and the station for $100,000. In its defense, KFAB stated an advance copy of the speech was not available prior to broadcast. The station also argued that because Wood's speech was made on behalf of Stebbins as a political candidate, it could not be censored under Section 18 and the FRC's General Order No. 31. That order reproduced Section 18 and made clear a licensee had no power of censorship over the material broadcast under Section 18. The jury agreed with KFAB and brought no verdict against the station. In addition, it awarded Sorenson only one dollar in his charges against Wood.[41]

On appeal, however, the Nebraska Supreme Court stated that in enacting Section 18 of the Radio Act, Congress had not approved libelous language used in the campaign, as such sanctions were contrary to constitutional protections under the Fifth Amendment prohibiting taking property without due process. It sided with Sorenson and noted that Wood assigned "the attributes of Judas Iscariot" through innuendo to Sorenson: treachery, unfairness, baseness, avarice, and dishonesty. It added, "We are of the opinion that the prohibition of censorship of material broadcast over the radio station of a licensee merely prevents the licensee from censoring the words as to their political and partisan trend but does not give a licensee any privilege to join and assist in the publication of a libel nor grant any immunity from the consequences of such action."[42]

The court pointed out that no distinction in this case existed between radio and the print media. Station employees could have cut off the speech at any time and should have done so.[43] The court did not address the issue of candidacy, and it was this point, addressed in 1959 in *Farmers Educational and Cooperative Union v. WDAY*,[44] that later changed the interpretation of broadcaster liability in cases of libel involving political candidates. For now, though, stations assumed they were liable for all statements made in candidates' broadcasts, even though they had no opportunity to read speeches in advance and believed they could not censor the candidates anyway.[45]

Station managers wrote the FRC asking the commission for guidance. The commission stated that it did not deal in hypothetical situations and would not give legal advice to stations about carriage of candidates' speeches unless it had a specific case before it. The commission called the broadcasters' attention to Section 18, which provided that if they permitted a candidate for political office to make a speech from their stations, they were required to allow opponents to answer under the same terms. While Harold LaFount, acting FRC chair, declared that the Radio Act permitted broadcasters to refuse requests for any and all candidate speeches, he added that such action would be shortsighted. He also noted that broadcasters had no right of censorship other than prevention of obscene, indecent, profane, or defamatory language.[46] Thus, broadcasters were caught in a bind and reacted by watching candidates closely.

While the NAB voted immediately to appeal the *Sorenson v. Wood* case to the U.S. Supreme Court, member stations reacted without delay by laying down rules for both candidates and spokespersons for candidates. Minneapolis station WCCO's guidelines were typical: No person speaking in behalf of any candidate for office would be permitted to broadcast unless a written copy of the speech was submitted to station management not less than twenty-four hours before broadcast. Management would then make any necessary changes to conform the speech to local libel law. The station emphasized that candidates who spoke in person would not be subject to the advance copy requirement. The station also reserved the right to refuse time to candidates who violated the libel and slander laws of Minnesota.[47]

In November, WCCO cut off a political broadcast by F. H. Shoemaker, a candidate for Congress. Shoemaker reserved two fifteen-minute periods just before the election. A few minutes into the first address, WCCO's program director telephoned the president of Northwestern Broadcasting, Inc., WCCO's parent company, to ask him to listen to the broadcast as the program director believed Shoemaker was violating state libel laws in referring to a former Minnesota governor. After listening a few moments, the president agreed, and the broadcast was immediately halted.[48]

The next morning, the former governor declared he had been subjected to libel and threatened to sue both the candidate and the station. WCCO management agreed with him that the speech was libelous and said they had cut off the speech as soon as they could. They also told the former governor they would welcome a suit to test the law. That same morning, WCCO refunded Shoemaker the cost of his entire broadcast and told him he would not be permitted on the air again unless he submitted a manuscript of his speech and no deviations were made from the text. Shoemaker protested, citing Section 18, and threatened to countersue. Those at WCCO said again they would welcome such a suit to test the constitutionality of Section 18. Four hours before broadcast of his second address, Shoemaker and his attorney submitted a manuscript, including a brief denunciation of WCCO, for approval. The station gave it, and Shoemaker delivered the speech as written, including the condemnation.[49]

In correspondence following this episode, the National Council on Freedom from Censorship, a group formed by the ACLU, thought a challenge to WCCO and the earlier *Sorenson* decision would be necessary "if we are to have free and open political discussions over the radio," adding, "[I]t will be a rather sad commentary upon our governmental system if candidates for office are to be prevented from calling attention of the listening public to malfeasance in public office, or to demonstrated unfitness on the part of other candidates." To the council, Section 18 exempted political speeches from station liability as stations had no power of censorship over political addresses.[50]

In another case, Los Angeles station KNX substituted recorded music for a fifteen-minute talk by state senator George W. Rochester when he tried to switch the copy of a speech previously approved by the station. Rochester was campaigning against Reverend Robert Shuler, formerly of KGEF, who was running as a Prohibition candidate for the U.S. Senate. The station claimed it followed a policy of not allowing anything to air that might be construed as libel. The next day, two Los Angeles Hearst papers, the *Examiner* and the *Herald-Express,* which were backing Rochester in his campaign against Shuler, announced that the reason for canceling the speech was that the state senator had been stricken with acute indigestion. At the same time, Neal Jones, editor of *Los Angeles Record,* a rival to the Hearst papers, attacked Hearst over the air as a "political boss" and "a national menace." Soon Jones found stations barring his talks as too "controversial."[51]

Stations also feared possible FRC refusal to renew licenses because of alleged defamatory speeches about candidates or those made during campaigns. They hoped disposition of the Shuler-KGEF case, then awaiting decision by the court of appeals, could provide some answers. Meanwhile, several states, including Oregon and California, enacted statutes applying libel and slander laws to radio. Broadcasters saw a need for uniform federal legislation and limits on station liability unless the station had given its consent to the broadcast of the remark considered libelous.[52]

The ACLU also wanted a national law relating to libel or slander over the air so stations would not impose gags on political speech, and Senator Clarence Dill asked Morris Ernst of the ACLU for help in drafting a bill to overcome the detrimental effects of the *Sorenson* decision.[53] In late December 1932, the National Council on Freedom from Censorship drafted a bill assigning responsibility and liability for slander by speakers and stations. Drawing analogies to cases involving telegraph companies' transmission of allegedly libelous material, the council concluded that broadcast companies could not be held responsible for messages they could not exclude. Consequently, the bill prescribed both limits to subject matter that could be prosecuted for slander and standards for placing responsibility. Truth, absence of malice, and speech having a public interest or delivered as a part of a true report of official proceedings were to be exempt. Liability was restricted to the originator and/or utterer of the speech, with station liability limited to instances where the station was an active collaborator in the dissemination of the statements. Anyone against whom a prosecution for slander by radio was sustained would be guilty of a misdemeanor. Stations would not be held responsible for ad-libbed remarks.[54] The bill, however, went nowhere, and the question of station liability in libel cases involving a political candidate remained unanswered until 1959.

The Elections of 1930: Indecency and Station KVEP

While stations feared libel actions, only one station forfeited its license over a candidate's speech, and that station lost it not for defamation but for broadcast of indecent language. In May 1930, William Schaeffer lost ownership of KVEP in Portland, Oregon, because a candidate's attacks on another candidate involved indecent language. The FRC held Schaeffer responsible for this language, even though he was not always physically present at the station during the errant broadcasts.[55]

During a bitter political primary, congressional candidate Robert Duncan vilified his opponent and, after his defeat, those whom he believed responsible for his loss. Duncan used KVEP two hours daily, beginning in February 1930. Attacks on his opponent for the Republican nomination, Congressman Franklin Korell, began almost immediately and escalated just before the primary took place on May 16. While these broadcasts covered a radius of only about twenty-five miles on KVEP's assigned power of 15 watts, the signal reached one-third of the state's population by blanketing all of Multnomah County, Portland's location.[56]

In his invectives, Duncan accused Korell of being a degenerate and a "sodomite." He also used words and phrases such as "hell" and "by God." FRC commissioners found the broadcast of May 9 particularly offensive. During it, Duncan said:

> Now, let us examine this man Korell himself. If Korell is really a man—which is a debatable proposition. Korell is a bachelor, and when he was asked why he didn't marry he says: "I don't care for women."

What do you know about that? Isn't it a strange statement for a natural man to make? I don't think a natural man ever made that statement. It must be explained thoroughly, and in ways that I can understand, to free the man who says it from the charges of practicing the vices that caused the destruction of Sodom and Gomorrah.[57]

After the biblical reference, Duncan charged Korell with fraternizing with Clarence Brazell, whom Duncan implied had been convicted on morals charges. He continued:

Now this unnatural statement from Korell takes us back to the Brazell vice case, and back to the time when Frank Korell was for nearly three years the roommate and bed-fellow of Clarence Brazell.[58]

Duncan accused Brazell of skipping the country when he was out on bond and obtaining protection from Korell:

Brazell is now a fugitive from justice, but not so much a fugitive, he returns to Portland now and then under the protection of the representative to Congress of the Third District of Oregon. A few days ago he was walking the streets of Portland and boasting that Korell was protecting him. Maybe this explains Korell's dislike for women.[59]

He called for all "natural men" listening to turn Korell out of office as a favor to their wives, mothers, and sweethearts as Oregon did not need to be represented by "a sissified Sodomite." He also threatened to broadcast the names of Korell supporters, "any of you who are proud of the fact that he slept in the same bed with Clarence Brazell three years."[60]

Korell appeared before the commission to testify that Duncan "assailed my character and maliciously vilified me" only because Duncan had lost the election by twenty-two thousand votes. Transcripts of Duncan's attacks showed that his verbal assaults on Korell continued after the election. In addition, both during and after the campaign, Duncan denigrated others, especially B. R. Irvine, associate editor of the *Portland Journal*; Paul T. Shaw, a member of the Portland school board; and those associated with banks and chain stores. Describing these individuals and other Portland business operators, Duncan used epithets such as "a dirty low-down puke," "you undiapered kid, you," "you yellow dog son-of-a-gun," "dirty, stinking, lying coward," "cock-eyed liar," and "half-brother of the skunk." He also said that "by the living God" he would shoot the next crook trying to bully him and threatened to expose over the airwaves various scandals that only he knew about. When asked if he had tried to censor these broadcasts, Schaeffer stated that Duncan had refused to submit his speeches as he believed Schaeffer could not censor his talks during the political campaign.[61]

FRC chair Ira Robinson noted the hearings were investigating not a question of stations' usage during a political campaign but rather whether Duncan used KVEP in "the right way" during the campaign. Candidates could use stations for political discussions as intended by Congress but could not move into the arena of "personal discussions." The FRC could take into account the nature of broadcasts without violating free speech or Congress's intent in passing Section 18. Broadcasters were responsible for their broadcasts' character, even those delivered by political candidates.[62]

To the commission, language broadcast over radio need not be taken in complete context if words and phrases in and of themselves were objectionable. Robinson said even a good, religious sermon containing inappropriate language would be deemed inexcusable over the airwaves. "The fact that there is good in it does not excuse the indecent part," he noted, adding the commission was investigating how many statements KVEP carried "that are unrefined and indecent . . . [and] put on the air over this licensed station."[63]

The FRC stated that the Radio Act's censorship clause, Section 29, meant that no one would be deprived of free speech over the airwaves, and while the proviso protected an expression of views, it did not protect "impolite or annoying language, or defamation," especially when the public's welfare was concerned.[64] Balancing Section 29's prohibition against censorship with application of the public interest standard in broadcast operations, the FRC decided "the right of freedom from censorship thereby becomes a qualified right subject to such reasonable control by the Commission as would be consistent with the primary consideration of the public welfare." The FRC stated that this decision was consistent with the First Amendment because "this constitutional provision has never been construed to protect obnoxious and indecent language."[65] When broadcasts exceeded acceptable bounds, preventative measures could be taken to protect society from tirades of indecency. "When unlimited discussion interferes with certain interests of the government in protecting and promoting the welfare of its citizens, it must then be balanced against freedom from censorship," the FRC wrote.[66]

As individual rights and the interests of the public were balanced, "public support" for the station could be taken into account. In this case, the FRC applied an unusual test of what "public support" meant: establishing a sound financial base through programming and advertising. This standard was new and, ironically, had not been applied to the Brinkley, Baker, and Shuler stations. All were financially stable and exceedingly popular with listeners in their respective areas. Brinkley and Baker had large followings in the Midwest, while Shuler had numerous loyal listeners throughout southern California. However, their programming, while appealing to certain listener tastes, was contrary to segments of mainstream society, including the medical profession and major religious groups. Now, with Schaeffer's financially struggling station, this new criterion could be applied to measure "public interest."

"The very bulwark of broadcasting under present day conditions is the confidence which the listener extends to advertising as well as other features of which the program consists."[67] The commissioners reasoned that when a station failed to get listener support through advertising and other programming, it might permit facilities to be used for objectionable purposes. Evidence showed that KVEP was not profitable until Duncan began broadcasting, so the FRC concluded, "[S]ince cancellation of the agreement [Duncan's contract] would leave the station financially unstable, the Commission believes that, by failing to renew the station license at this time, it was merely anticipating what would have happened of its own weight if the contract with Duncan were terminated."[68]

The commission concluded that Duncan's broadcasts were in his private interest, publicized his personal grievances, and provoked public antagonism. As owner of the station, Schaeffer should have stopped them, even though many were delivered when Duncan was a political candidate. The commissioners were amazed that Schaeffer did not fully understand references to sodomites and Sodom and Gomorrah. Schaeffer, a naturalized citizen who did not speak English as his first language, confessed he thought the words referred only to corruption and admitted he did not know what sodomy was.[69] This ignorance, however, did not help Schaeffer, because the commissioners noted he had done nothing to keep Duncan's scurrilous and indecent language from entering the home. The commission found Schaeffer responsible for everything that aired and concluded that Duncan's broadcasts maligned reputable citizens by innuendo and through direct use of indecent language.

The commission reasoned that while Schaeffer did not actively participate in the broadcasts, they were made with his knowledge.[70]

In its decision, the commission recognized the inherent vagueness in defining obscenity and indecency over radio. Each instance had to be judged on its own merits, and the FRC determined whether the words used were injurious to public morals and were "of such a nature as to create the impression that they are what Congress intended to prevent."[71] When broadcast, indecent language had a circulation far wider than through any other medium, and it reached into the home where children were far more open to influence. "The sanctity of home life is thus doubly threatened by sanctioning vivid and descriptive broadcasts of lascivious conduct," the commission stated. "It is apparent that the imputation of immorality to specific individuals and a description thereof must come within any definition of 'obscene and indecent' language whether or not it bears the earmarks of truth."[72]

In denying license renewal, the FRC noted, "A broadcasting station is public in purpose and character and any use of it as a private or individual affair is repugnant both to policy and legislation. . . . The failure to realize this obligation to the public is sufficient basis for denial of Station KVEP's application for renewal of license." The commission did not accept Schaeffer's argument that no station could censor political candidates' speech under Section 18.[73] Stations were responsible for all indecent language used by candidates.

While Schaeffer initially appealed the decision, he dropped it for lack of funds.[74] Duncan also appealed, and the ACLU offered him support. Duncan told Forrest Bailey, director of the ACLU, that the language he used could not be called profane, obscene, or indecent. He claimed the efforts were "clearly a case of stamping out free speech via radio." Duncan noted that none of the elected officials he had assailed over the radio had been reelected. He wrote Bailey that the "electorate voted a Member of Congress out of office who was back of this persecution, routed the District Attorney and wrecked the Republican machine in Oregon. I am happy to say that my campaign over the air had much to do with the results of the election."[75]

On March 9, 1931, the Ninth Federal Circuit Court of Appeals upheld Duncan's conviction and ruled that he had to serve six months in jail and pay a $500 fine for using profane language over the air. The decision upheld the right of the government to regulate the use of language in broadcasting and to impose penalties on speakers using profane, indecent, or obscene language on the air.[76]

The court stated that profanity "is usually dealt with as a branch of the common law offense of blasphemy, but in the United States particularly it has been a frequent subject of legislation." The court then cited cases from the 1800s and early 1900s that defined profane language as "language irreverent toward God or holy things" or "any words importing an imprecation of divine vengeance or implying divine condemnation." The court concluded, "Under these decisions, the indictment having alleged that the language is profane, the defendant having referred to an individual as 'damned,' having used the expression 'By God' irreverently, and having announced his intention to call down the curse of God upon certain individuals, was properly convicted of using profane language within the meaning of that term as used in the act of Congress prohibiting the use of profane language in radio broadcasting."[77]

The decision, then, upheld the right of the government to regulate the use of language in broadcasting and to impose penalties on radio speakers who employed profane, indecent, or obscene language on the air. Even though many of Duncan's utterances were made while campaigning for election as a congressional representative, running for election did not protect him.[78] This decision plus *Sorenson v. Wood* played a major role in increasing broadcasters' fears that their licenses might be revoked if they aired inappropriate material during the 1932 elections.

The Elections of 1932

In 1930, Democrats took control of the House and were one senator shy of taking over the Senate. A growing disposition among these Democratic congressional representatives and senators was to challenge Republican presidential policies through the newspapers and increasingly over radio as set usage increased.[79] By the June 1932 Democratic convention, about 17 million receivers existed, over twice the number as in 1928. Statisticians predicted that over 68 million listeners would hear the conventions, and both Democrats and Republicans aimed to please listeners. The large, oval Chicago Stadium was the site of the Democratic convention. To one side of the oval, convention planners set up a huge platform with a smaller platform jutting out for speakers. At the rear and placed slightly above the main platform, four glass-encased radio booths had a clear view of convention proceedings. NBC, CBS, and other broadcast stations occupied the carrels, and foreign nations were expected to tune in through shortwave.

Announcers in the booths had two microphones, one for immediate use and the other as emergency backup, while engineers sat at control panels to cut in microphones scattered throughout the hall. F. W. Wile and H. V. Kaltenborn were commentators for CBS, while William Hard provided observations over NBC. The newly developed parabolic microphone was installed to pick up voices from the floor, while regular mikes picked up the speakers' voices. Under the control booths were soundproof studios for use by political leaders and for interpretative talks by political commentators. Another wired system kept announcers and engineers in touch with each other. Estimated costs of CBS's coverage alone fell between $100,000 and $200,000.[80]

A corresponding setup was made for the Republican convention with CBS analysts airing four daily fifteen-minute appraisals of the convention's proceedings at 9:30 A.M., 1:45 P.M., 6:45 P.M., and 11:00 P.M. NBC carried similar assessments at 9:15 A.M., 1:00 P.M., 6:30 P.M., and 11:15 P.M. eastern standard time. Most letters from listeners indicated favorable reactions to convention coverage and praised the industry as a whole, while some complained that conventions were not carried gavel-to-gavel. Censorship charges arose and were aimed especially at commentators, who were labeled prejudiced and hostile, while some announcers were faulted for halting, hesitating delivery.[81]

During the campaign, the two major political parties consumed vast quantities of airtime, with cost estimates running into the thousands of dollars. Both President Hoover and Democratic candidate Franklin Roosevelt used radio to reach constituents, and of the two, Roosevelt had the more charismatic approach.[82] The total bill for CBS was $368,175, of which $194,624 was for Republican coverage, $167,171 for Democrats, and $6,380 for Socialists. NBC said precise figures were unavailable for their two networks but added that political revenue ran over $1 million. Senator Clarence Dill estimated that up to another $750,000 was spent over statewide and regional stations and networks, while local candidates' bills ran another $250,000.[83] Costs were high enough for Roosevelt to declare, "[T]he largest single item in our budget is to buy time over the air."[84]

Even though he could address audiences via radio, Hoover still preferred to swing around the country making speeches from auditoriums and railway car platforms. In October alone, Hoover made twenty-two speeches in fifteen hours to add "that personal touch." To find the largest possible audience, many important speeches aired at 10:00 P.M. eastern standard time so they would catch West Coast residents at home. Hoover's notification ceremony, for instance, was broadcast from 10:00 to 11:00 P.M. specifically for this reason. Plans called for four or five broadcasts by Hoover, and former President Coolidge was expected to go on the air to back Hoover.[85]

Candidates for federal offices in 1932 were also learning how to use the medium effectively, and station owners and employees running for office found their facilities useful in their own campaigns. Henry Field, owner of KFNF, defeated his opponent for the Iowa Republican senatorial nomination by more than fifty thousand votes. Radio was credited with his success, and he was expected to use radio extensively to win the general election. Dr. Frank Elliot of Davenport also used radio extensively to capture the nomination for the House from his Iowa district. As manager of WOC-WHO, Davenport–Des Moines, Elliot had learned how to use the medium to reach audiences.[86]

Over-the-air fireworks were expected from campaigns of two other broadcasters. John Brinkley, former owner of KFKB, was running for governor of Kansas as an independent candidate and used XER, his new 50,000-watt station in Acuna, Mexico, to reach not only Kansas but also a large part of the United States. Reverend Robert Shuler, former operator of KGEF, sought the nomination for U.S. senator from California. An ardent dry, he was endeavoring to run on all three tickets—Republican, Democratic, and Socialist.[87]

Other candidates began making transcription records to reach their constituencies. Every Tuesday night, Senator Arthur Capper of Kansas recorded broadcasts in a transcription studio in Washington, D.C., and sent them to his station, WIBW in Topeka. Kansas representative Harold McGugin and West Virginia representative Hugh Ike Shott also recorded messages each week for broadcast over stations they owned, KGGF in Coffeyville, Kansas, and WHIS in Bluefield, West Virginia, respectively. Although he was not running for office, W. K. Henderson was expected to use his *Hello World* station, KWKH in Shreveport, Louisiana, to attack the Democratic party's candidate for the vice presidency, John Nance Garner.[88]

Stations initiated further policies to treat candidates equitably. For example, in 1932, Wisconsin's two state-owned stations offered all political parties free time for their campaigns. WHA and WLBL did not censor the programs but did limit coverage to statewide campaigns or to campaigns for federal offices and discussion of state and national issues. Stations set aside time for all political parties, and schedules were developed after lots were drawn. Under the plan, candidates for local or district offices could be invited to discuss party issues, but stations would not be used for either local or district campaigns. Candidates and stations generally agreed that all speakers would avoid material regarded as libelous.[89]

On election night, networks planned coverage of election returns from 6:00 P.M. eastern standard time until the last ballot was counted. On CBS, announcers gave bulletins while F. W. Wile and Edwin Hill supplied commentary. On NBC, William Hard and David Lawrence furnished assessments. Between reports, networks fed musical programs with local station cutaways for local election results. As reports intensified during the evening, networks gave returns priority. Independent station WOR also presented national election coverage, with specialization in local New Jersey returns. WOR placed microphones at various New York City hotels so prominent political figures could speak to the public. The Hotel Astor hosted eyewitness accounts of events in Times Square. The few hundred television set owners also saw election news bulletins printed on their screens for the first time, presaging what the *New York Times* reported would be "the way Americans may get the election returns in the '40s." TV station W2XAB began televising still pictures of candidates and bulletins beginning at 8:00 P.M. Radio microphones were available for Hoover and Roosevelt at Palo Alto, California, and Hyde Park, New York, respectively. Announcers at these locations described events and activities as candidates and listeners heard the Democrats capture both houses and Democrat Franklin Roosevelt win the presidency.[90]

In assessing the campaign and election, broadcasters recognized that politicians still had a lot to learn about using radio effectively.

For realism, CBS sent out its returns from the studio where information was gathered via telegraph and compiled using typewriters and calculators. Some listeners later complained that the telegraph clicks sounded too much like static, while others applauded the realistic atmosphere created by the background noise. Listeners complained that candidates' ninety-minute speeches were too long. "Shorten them" was the common thread running through broadcasters' mail, and time limits mentioned ran from fifteen to thirty minutes. Shorter speeches would not only hold the audience but also save political parties money. Contending that "the rights of the listeners are paramount, especially when great public questions are under discussion," a *New York Times* article noted that listeners protested "against the effrontery of the broadcasting companies in taking candidates off the air before they complete their addresses."[91]

Often, candidates competed for airtime with members of their own political party. In addition, last-minute arrangements vexed the stations. Stations were also caught in a bind with the speeches themselves. If a speech ran long, stations dared not cut the speaker off for fear of insulting the candidate or being charged with partisanship or censorship. When stations and networks canceled favorite programming in favor of political discussions, listeners also reacted negatively. For example, when President Hoover overlapped the popular Ed Wynn program, WEAF received eight hundred phone calls protesting the president's speech, while the Red network's sixty affiliates received a total of six thousand calls.[92]

Both NBC and CBS also complained that candidates' last-minute scrambling for airtime upset their election eve plans. All political parties regarded the "last word" as crucial, so each party planned a last, hour-long appeal to the voters the night before the election. The Democratic National Committee contracted for time from 11:00 P.M. to midnight on all the networks, a move that involved more than two hundred stations. The combined NBC Red and Blue networks cost the Democrats about $17,500 for their hour of time. The Republicans reserved 10:00 to 11:00 P.M. on CBS and were expected to reserve time over NBC's networks. Republican plans were upset when President Hoover decided to go back to Palo Alto from St. Paul to vote. Republicans and broadcasters had hoped he would go to Washington, where radio facilities at the White House were easily accessible. Even the Socialist party purchased a short time period on CBS flagship station WABC. Socialist candidate Norman Thomas scheduled his last address over CBS at 9:15 P.M. on election eve.[93]

After the election, Senator Dill praised the fairness of the networks and independent stations in their overall treatment of candidates, and he congratulated stations for observing both the letter and the spirit of the law. If stations had wanted to show partiality, he said, there were numerous ways they could have done so. One way was to grant favored candidates better time slots. Stations could place a speech on the air either before or after a popular program or program it against popular shows on rival stations. Stations could also ask to "proofread" a speech before its airing. While within the letter of the law, these actions would be contrary to the law's spirit, which provided for equitable treatment.[94] For the most part, stations did not engage in these activities.

After the election, the *Christian Century* commented favorably on changes radio had brought to campaigning. No longer were nominating conventions needed, it contended, because radio gave candidates the needed publicity. The magazine also editorialized in favor of a "new type of oratory" delivered over radio that would contain a candidate's warmth and personality and that would put a premium on intelligence, not on organized, yelling crowds of enthusiastic supporters.[95] A *New York Times* editorial also lauded radio coverage and broadcast of election returns and predicted as radio news grew, broadcasting would become more important.[96]

As Roosevelt's inaugural approached, radio networks linked the world for the ceremonies. At least seven powerful shortwave transmitters along the East Coast carried the inauguration as well as other festivities on signals powerful enough to be heard in Europe, Australia, and the Far East. The NBC networks linked eighty-eight stations nationwide, while CBS linked ninety-one transmitters. Changes in microphone technology, including parabolic and lapel mikes, brought elaborate sound setups. Nearly seventy-five mikes in all were in service at one time or another during the inauguration, and ceremonies were covered from the air as well as from the ground. Listeners heard coverage from the White House, the Capitol, various D.C. hotels housing dignitaries, and the parade route along Pennsylvania Avenue. Both airborne blimps and special portable transmitters strapped to the backs of announcers in the crowds brought events into the home as political power transferred from Republicans to Democrats.

Announcers began at 9:30 A.M. eastern standard time and continued through the inaugural parade until 4:00 P.M. They returned at 10:00 that evening for coverage of the inaugural ball. Included in their daytime reports were Roosevelt's journey from his rooms at the Mayflower Hotel to the White House, his and Hoover's ride to the Capitol, the swearing-in of Vice President John Nance Garner in the Senate chambers, the presidential inauguration on the Capitol steps, Hoover's departure from Union Station, concerts by armed forces bands, and the inaugural parade in the afternoon. Announcers for both NBC and CBS aired numerous anecdotes about FDR and past inaugurations to add color to their descriptions of the day's events.[97]

By 1933, radio was clearly recognized as a way government officials could reach the public. The Democratic National Committee resolved to manage speeches of the new administration over radio. During his first year in office, FDR held press conferences every Wednesday morning at 10 o'clock and Friday afternoon at 4 o'clock with few exceptions. Over one hundred correspondents, including broadcasters, attended these conferences. By Christmas 1934, FDR had made forty-one broadcasts, twenty-three in 1934 alone. Mrs. Roosevelt had made twenty-eight broadcasts in 1934 and a total of forty-five since her husband became president. Eighty-nine members of the House spoke a total of 172 times, while fifty-three senators spoke a total of 136 times. Believing Roosevelt had used radio too often, his advisors convinced him in the fall of 1934 to curtail his broadcasts. So, Roosevelt chose to reserve his broadcasts for his "fireside chats" to the American people.[98]

Conclusion

In sum, protections for political speech were limited, even though by the 1928 election, equal opportunity for candidates was mandated under Section 18 of the Radio Act. Airtime allocation for political purposes often depended upon the ability of candidates to pay for the time, and equal opportunity did not mean free time had to be given. So long as broadcasters assessed equitable charges for airtime, they complied with the equal opportunity provision. Broadcasters effectively used the cost of airtime to keep dissidents and other undesirable speakers off the air.

In addition, the *Sorenson v. Wood* and *Duncan v. U.S.* cases created timidity as broadcasters feared liability for slanderous, libelous, profane, or indecent remarks made over the air during campaigns. Thus, political speech on radio had its limits—restrictions that would not be challenged effectively until the 1950s. These constraints and the general climate of fear of license denial led to broadcasters' oversight and sometimes censorship of political speeches. While government officials saw the public's ability to participate in the political process through radio as serving the public interest and enhancing both democracy and freedom of speech, broadcast policies and practices enhanced dominant, commercially based social norms. Broadcaster-imposed censorship protected broadcasters' rights to use the airwaves as they deemed fit. These actions were often taken to the detriment of diversity in viewpoints and entertainment.

8 ➤ SPEAK NO EVIL: THE EARLY 1930S

While censorship of political speakers occurred because station owners feared libel suits or accusations of indecency, most stations and networks censored programs ostensibly to keep indecent or inappropriate material from coming into the home. They thereby protected children and unsuspecting adults from unsuitable matter and prevented atypical religious programming from offending listeners, especially members of more conventional religions. Although the Federal Radio Commission received numerous complaints and requests to prosecute unseemly matter, the commissioners for the most part detested review of program material as unwarranted government oversight.

A widely held belief of government and civic leaders was that radio had immense power to mold minds and determine people's ideas and attitudes, and this sentiment prompted the National Association of Broadcasters' adoption of its first code of ethics during its January 26, 1928, meeting. Among the ideals endorsed were that broadcasters pay conscious attention to their audiences' different backgrounds to guard against offending any sensibilities. The code also stated that because radio came into the home as an "intimate friend" and helped mold the minds of children, all programming should reflect this reality. Station owners also should consider radio's development as a part of bettering living conditions and cultural standards.[1] After this code's adoption, radio operators often became overzealous in keeping what they considered inappropriate programming off the air and out of the home.

What *Is* Improper Programming?

Some listeners complained about racism in NBC's *Amos 'n' Andy* program, while others railed against handwriting analysts, astrologers, divine healers, numerologists, and stations playing the "Star Spangled Banner" in dance time. A few listeners claimed crime and mystery programs corrupted the susceptible, while others denounced foreign language broadcasts as detrimental to Americanization of immigrants. "Wets" and "drys" alike protested an alleged lack of coverage of their viewpoints. Religious organizations deplored commercialism on Sundays and parodies of religious subjects such as the Twenty-third Psalm. One group, the Lord's Day Alliance, even asked the FRC to limit Sunday programs solely to sermons and hymns.[2]

Special interest groups rose at the least affront to their sensibilities. Comedians came under harsh criticism for making fun of government officials, even long-dead chief executives. When congressional representative Emmanuel Celler of Brooklyn mentioned George Washington's wine drinking, listeners complained, and stations barred a comedy skit prepared for Washington's birthday because it treated Washington facetiously. The lines were saved, however, and used later with the protagonist changed to Joan of Arc. Of course, for some, that action was worse as many listeners found it difficult to forgive writers for taking liberties with a saint. People who stuttered denounced stammering characters, while magicians became angry when their secrets were revealed. Rabbit raisers objected to a skit when one character asked another where he got his rabbit sandwich. "Oh, I go out in the alley and when one meows I shoot it" was the reply. Taxi drivers wrote the FRC, objecting to portrayals of being hand-in-glove with gangsters and crooks, and laundry workers claimed slander when broadcasters aired a radio sketch about laundries pulling buttons off shirts. In May 1931, an old vaudeville gag insulted druggists. A comedian stated he couldn't become a druggist because he didn't know how to make sandwiches. *Variety* reported the offending station received over eight thousand letters of protest and added that even "Pat and Mike" jokes were out because they offended the Irish.[3]

The NBC hit nighttime program *Amos 'n' Andy* came under constant fire for its script content, with much of the criticism coming from some, but not all, African American groups. In August 1931, *Amos 'n' Andy* stars Charles Correll and Freeman Gosden attended a picnic for African American children at the invitation of the *Chicago Defender,* a leading African American weekly. Niles Trammel, general manager of NBC's Chicago station, accompanied the duo. According to *Variety,* the *Defender*'s editorial attitude toward the program was "that the blackface team hasn't resorted to any material objectionable to colored people, and opposes the petition now being circulated by the Pittsburgh *Courier,* demanding that *Amos 'n' Andy* be put off the network. [That] petition to date has over 15,000 signatures." During the appearance, the radio stars took time to plug their candy bars by distributing samples to children.[4]

Later in December, when *Amos 'n' Andy* enacted alleged third-degree police methods, Hugh Harper, president of the International Association of Chiefs of Police, protested vigorously to the program's sponsor, Pepsodent. "Such propaganda," he stated, "cannot help but seriously handicap law enforcement officers in the prosecution of crime. No up-to-date officer ever uses the methods as exemplified in your radio program."[5] These complaints and others reached the FRC.

Clearly, the commissioners wanted no part in restricting programs, and they often told critics that the commission could not censor shows under Section 29 of the Radio Act of 1927. They added that the Radio Act prohibited only utterances of obscene, indecent, or profane language over the air, and no one had complained about this forbidden speech. Complaints of indecency did materialize with proposed coverage of sex and birth control and with "immoral" or "lewd" song lyrics and suggestive dialogue. For these specific complaints, the commissioners usually suggested protesters contact stations, networks, or advertisers responsible for the programming. The FRC also warned it would take any improper programming into consideration at license renewal time, a potential FRC action that prompted broadcasters to watch closely the topics and issues covered in their programs.[6]

Among issues broadcasters considered inappropriate were pacifism, socialism, and discussion of eliminating Prohibition. Speakers attacking newspapers and journalistic integrity in covering the

Snyder-Gray murder case also found no airtime. This scandalous, celebrated case involved the murder of Albert Snyder by his wife, Ruth, and her lover, Henry Judd Gray. The pair was convicted of murder in May 1927 and sentenced to death in Sing Sing's electric chair. On January 12, 1928, the sentences were carried out. Of course, cameras had been banned from the death chamber, but a persistent photographer for the *New York Daily News,* Thomas Howard, fastened a small camera to his ankle under his trousers, and he took a photograph of Snyder as current surged through her. The next morning, the *Daily News* published the photo on its entire front page.[7] When Representative Carrol L. Beedy of Maine criticized the publication of such lurid details during WNYC's live coverage of the 1928 American Newspaper Publishers Association annual convention, WNYC's station manager cut Beedy off the air because his criticism of the press was "controversial" and not fit to broadcast.[8]

KOA in Denver barred a speech by Eamon de Valera, president of Ireland, for his "propaganda against the British government," and when Hudson Maxim opposed Prohibition, he was left talking into a dead microphone. Four stations in Los Angeles refused to carry a speech favoring home rule in India, while former presidential candidate and one-time secretary of the treasury William McAdoo was refused airtime unless he submitted his remarks for prior approval. In Los Angeles, John R. Haynes was denied a request for free time over L.A. stations to present views on municipal ownership of electrical power, a topic considered too controversial at the time. Haynes was hardly an irresponsible person as he was on the Municipal Water and Power Bureau. While he could afford to buy time, stations refused him time under any circumstances. Paul Hutchinson, writing for the *Christian Century,* rightly believed the topic killed Haynes's speech.[9]

Other stations also curtailed speakers, and ridicule or questioning actions, theories, or attitudes of government and its officials found little radio voice during these Depression years. In late 1932, WOR canceled its efforts to get Soviet leader Joseph Stalin to talk from Moscow when the station heard "unofficially" of the government's displeasure over the plan.[10] In Iowa in November 1933, a review of Hitler's *Mein Kampf* was quietly kept off WOI for fear of offending Jewish groups.[11]

In mid-April 1934, WBNX in New York City took two anti-

Nazi, pro-Jewish radio programs off the air, saying erroneously that cancellation was "due to specific instructions from the Federal Radio Commission in regard to the broadcasting of subjects of controversial or argumentative nature."[12] Both programs were highly critical of Nazi and Fascist rule in Germany and Italy, respectively, and called for extermination of Fascist elements in the United States.

The FRC, of course, had not sent any instructions to WBNX on its programming. Later, the station's general manager, W. C. Alcorn, refuted the statements when they were made public in a *New York Post* article as "one of those unfortunate things on which the wrong interpretation can be placed." He stated the station had never received censorship instructions and added that WBNX was trying to comply with what it interpreted as FRC general policies on balanced programming. WBNX carried about thirty-three Jewish programs and no Nazi programs during its broadcast week. He also mentioned WBNX had an application for greater power before the commission. Fears of not being granted the increase in power led to cancellation of programs the station considered too controversial.[13]

Another New York station, WRNY, cut off a speech on "Moral Issues Confronting the City [of New York]" when it determined the speaker was attacking New York City mayor Jimmy Walker's administration.[14] WGL cut off Mrs. Mary Alford's speech at an "All Nations' Association" dinner honoring Mrs. Millie Gade Corson, who was sailing to start practice for her English Channel swim. WGL halted coverage when Alford began extolling Denmark as an ideal of peace, "a country which said to an enemy, 'If you must cut through our country, even if you must cut through our women and children—'" The next day the station manager stated, "We believe in free speech and I have always been willing to extend the use of our station to anyone to express his views, but there are certain things which are dictated by good taste. This was not the time nor the occasion for such a speech." The American Legion applauded his action.[15]

Later, the same station refused to broadcast a pacifist play, *Spread Eagle*. WGL's president, Louis Landes, said action was taken after veteran organizations criticized the play. Most station employees were veterans, he added, and WGL would "under no circumstances broadcast anything that has not the full endorsement of veteran and patriotic organizations." WGL did broadcast a speech on "trout fishing," a sport Calvin Coolidge loved, that CBS station WABC had canceled as "more or less propaganda" for conservative causes.[16]

Speakers were also censored if they questioned the status quo in race relations. In September 1932, Paulist priest James Gillis condemned injustices against African Americans in an address over the NBC networks titled "The Catholic Church and the Negro Question." Memphis station WMC cut him off in midsentence and substituted a phonograph record. Reportedly, the station received numerous calls protesting the talk, and during the week after, the Catholic Church received "indignant" calls "from irate southern Catholics objecting to the address."[17]

As the Depression worsened, more and more speakers found their evaluation of economic conditions censored. In April 1930, Heywood Broun stated during a march of the unemployed on Washington that "the only mistake that starving unemployed in this country have made is that they did not march to Washington and under the windows of Mr. Hoover in the White House display banners reading 'We Are Belgians,'" a reference to Hoover's brilliant organization of food relief for that nation in postwar Europe. The next day, station officials received "grapevine information" that they were airing too many liberal opinions.[18] When Broun later proposed asking listeners to contribute a nickel for the benefit of the unemployed if they liked a program, his idea was turned down because stations said the Hoover administration did not want to emphasize the seriousness of the Depression.[19]

On October 2, 1931, both NBC and CBS refused to carry New York senator Robert Wagner's speech on unemployment. Originally, Wagner was to have addressed organized labor groups gathered at Cooper Union Square to celebrate the thirty-fifth anniversary of the founding of the *Evening Journal,* a labor paper, in person, but he was unexpectedly called to Washington. When his staff attempted to set up a broadcast, they were turned down. In similar fashion, Wagner was refused a national hookup for a Labor Day address.[20]

Newspapers reported that CBS was "withholding its facilities from incidental discussions of employment of the economic depression pending completion of the program being worked out by the committee on radio of the President's Organization on Unemployment Relief." The committee had "just been organized . . . with a view to setting a correct picture of the situation before the public in a sensible and reasonable manner." NBC publicly stated that it had not been offered Wagner's speech, but other records indicate that NBC had refused the speech on the grounds that the network worked solely with President Hoover's commission on overcoming the Depression. NBC president Merlin Aylesworth issued a press release stating that Wagner had always been a welcome guest and could speak over NBC anytime he desired.[21] Later, after receiving letters of inquiry from the ACLU, both CBS and NBC claimed the ACLU had been misinformed as to reasons for not giving Wagner airtime. After checking the situation out, the ACLU dropped the matter, but later editorials condemned the networks' actions.[22]

Protests against censorship again arose in early March 1933 when WGY banned an address entitled "A New Philosophy for a New Age" as WGY officials believed it would "undermine confidence and faith" in American principles, especially economic assumptions and expected recovery under the new president, Franklin Roosevelt.[23] When contacted, the ACLU stated it would protest actions to the station involved, but not much else could be done as "radio stations are the sole judges of what they will broadcast."[24] Later that month, former FRC commissioner Henry Bellows, now a CBS vice president and representative for the NAB, summed up the approach taken by most broadcasters in coverage of the current economic situation when he told the *New York Times* that "as a matter of public policy during the present [economic] emergency, we limit discussions of public questions by ascertaining that such programs are not contrary to the policies of the U.S. Government."[25]

In January 1934, CBS canceled a speech it considered detrimental to recovery efforts. The network barred Frederick Schlink, president of Consumers Research Inc., from presenting a talk titled "The Consumer in the National Recovery Program" because a CBS official believed he was critical of the Roosevelt administration. He was later put back on the air, and CBS head William Paley denied curbs by the administration.[26] A few days later, a speech by Senator David Reed of Pennsylvania critical of Roosevelt and the National Recovery Administration was cut short. The radio station involved seemed fearful for its license if it allowed the criticism, according to several editorials, and *Editor and Publisher* called such censorship "shameful" and added, "[W]e hope to see the day when radio will come into its right as a free instrument."[27]

These orthodox views of radio's role in assisting recovery from the Depression were expressed succinctly by Merlin Aylesworth in his 1930 report to the NBC Advisory Council. Under current economic pressures, he noted radio became essential for "we must know and honor the same heroes, love the same songs, enjoy the same sports, realize our common interest in our national problems." After this view was published, one liberal author retorted, "If we are to honor the same heroes, sing the same songs, enjoy the same sports, are we also to think the same thoughts? And are those thoughts to be dictated by NBC?"[28] Overall, however, government and broadcast industry leaders saw radio as a unifying force, one that was not to upset the status quo, and they worked together to present a limited view of the economic downturn over the airwaves.

Songs, Skits, and Protecting the American Home

The FRC engaged in indirect censorship because its exercise of the "public interest, convenience, or necessity" standard in determining licenses carried with it implicit censorship powers. The character of station program services could be reviewed, and the FRC as the licensing authority had power to decide on the appropriateness of programs in the public interest. Because KTNT, KFKB, KGEF, and KVEP had lost their licenses for not serving the public interest and the FRC was examining other stations' applications, radio operators were understandably nervous and reluctant when it came to presenting material that station owners deemed unfit for entry into the American home.

Churches and organized groups of mothers often led the assault against immorality through their attacks on offensive radio programs and immoral motion pictures. At times, these rebukes led to unexpected clashes. For instance, in January 1931, Father James Delaney denounced "salacious movies" over KDKA, and station management took him off the air after theater owners complained. When protests over KDKA's action reached the ACLU, director Forrest Bailey noted that complaints raised an odd situation for the ACLU because the organization opposed all censorship, including movie censorship advocated by Delaney.[29] In this case, Bailey and others reasoned that Delaney was promoting a boycott, not outright censorship, of movies he disliked; therefore, Delaney was the victim of censorship, not the perpetrator thereof.[30]

In March 1933, a group of New York mothers complained that radio programs were too bloodcurdling; they organized to combat "radio horrors." Complaints ranged from poor grammar usage to programs that were "pure trash, just the combination of affectation and sophistication that some girls of junior high-school age love to adopt." One mother noted that "some of the programs we consider the worst are the ones children like the best. We object to the mystery thriller, usually not because of its individual content, but because it is a serial. The children don't just hear it and forget it, but they carry the story in their minds from day to day, or week to week."[31]

In a sermon that same month, Reverend Dr. Minot Simons of the All Souls' Unitarian Church in New York urged mothers to unite against indecent songs on radio. He said, "Some of these songs are obscene. There is almost no limit to their immoral suggestiveness." Simons predicted that parents would unite in protest against "indecent" songs as they had "lurid" bedtime stories.[32]

Indeed, a survey conducted by the Child Study Association showed that parents did not think much of radio's influence on their children's lives. The study revealed that some children spent from five to fifteen hours per day listening to radio and that drama programs and comedy shows were more popular with children than music and jazz programs. While a number of mothers found radio to be an educational influence, nearly one-fourth denounced their children's interest in the medium.[33]

To ward off any church or mothers' crusades against indecent radio programming, station and network censors modified songs and skits. While some songs were banned outright, words to objectionable songs or questionable song titles were often modified to keep offensive language off the air. Cole Porter's "Love for Sale" was barred in 1932, and the song title "Let's Put Out the Lights and Go to Bed," was revised to "Let's Put Out the Lights and Go to Sleep." In another popular song, "I Love Louisa," a bothersome phrase was "Ach! when I choose 'em, I love a great big bosom." When sung over NBC, the Cliquot Club modified the offending line to "Ach! when I choose 'em, I always hate to lose 'em." In April 1933, CBS chastised band leader Ted Fiorita when one of his vocalists sang "42nd Street" from the musical as written instead of substituting CBS's sanitized version. His singer used the lines "Sexy ladies of the eighties who are indiscreet" instead of the CBS rewrite, "Lovely ladies of the eighties give your eyes a treat." Another song from *42nd Street* was banned completely from the airwaves—

"Young and Healthy." Advertisers also had problems with recognizable song titles or lyrics. In March 1932, a watch company wanted to use a tune entitled "Every Little Movement Has a Meaning All Its Own," only to be told it was "too suggestive."[34]

By June 1933, humming often replaced words deemed indecent for radio. One song, "Pettin' in the Park," contained lyrics, "Pettin' in the park . . . bad boy . . . pettin' in the park . . . bad girl," and it was allowed on the air only if humming replaced the "bad boy/girl" phrases. Ironically, radio censors prohibited completely the song "Hold Your Man" from the movie by the same title, while movie censors had approved both movie and song.[35]

In reaction to concerns, well-known orchestra leaders and radio broadcasters formed a committee shortly after the Communications Act was passed in June 1934 to self-censor suggestive songs and titles. The committee comprised Richard Himber, Rudy Vallee, Paul Whiteman, Guy Lombardo, and Abe Lyman. It met weekly to pass judgment on all songs published during the week. When a song was found objectionable, in title or lyrics, the publisher was asked to revise it. If the request was denied, the song was placed on a list of banned songs mailed weekly to orchestra leaders, many of whom had agreed not to play any prohibited song over the air.[36]

Much of the industry lauded the board's activities, although NBC's vice president in charge of programs hailed the move as "amusing." He noted that "certain dance conductors, odd as it may seem, have been the worst offenders. We have always maintained a censorship of songs. We have condemned many and have caused many to be rewritten. Every new song we look over and if any suggestive lines are found they are killed or changed. We have often warned that dance band leaders have used too many double meaning titles and songs. We are pleased to see that they are beginning to see the light." CBS also banned "off-color" songs, as did large, independent stations such as WOR.[37]

After the committee's second meeting, the members announced that no major networks were broadcasting indecent song lyrics, nor was the committee trying to censor the networks. Smaller stations, not networks, were primary offenders in presenting unsuitable songs. Spokesman Paul Whiteman said the committee was trying to discourage off-color songs because, unlike stage shows where customers paid money to see the production, radio came into the home whether a show was good or questionable. He stated that several dozen orchestra leaders had allied themselves with the movement and added that the only comments the committee had received were from people who were in complete accord with the work of the committee.[38]

For the most part, network censors were good at keeping "blue material" off the air, whether it was song or skit. Sometimes skits aired, though, without station or network sanction when the censors who approved programs did not "get" the suggestive gags or lines.[39] At other times, complaints brought changes. For example, in its *Retold Tales* series, NBC dropped references to the Mormon Church and substituted a "cult" known as "Sons of Eli" in its second airing of Arthur Conan Doyle's Sherlock Holmes story "A Study in Scarlet." The first broadcast had resulted in complaints from the Mormon Church for negative references to the church. NBC apologized and changed the references in later broadcasts.[40]

In other situations, advertisers wanted no mention of groups or nationalities that might offend some listeners in programs. For instance, in mid-November 1931, Italian Campagna Cold Cream sponsored NBC's broadcast of a play, *The First Nighter.* As the program began, the agency called, frantically demanding references to "German" and "boche" be deleted as offensive. And, they were— while the program was in progress. NBC's production executive Clarence Mesner whispered to the actors to make the deletions, and as luck would have it, the mike picked up his words.[41]

In mid-May 1933, advertisers spread an unfounded rumor that President Roosevelt was personally campaigning against "shady gags" over radio. Supposedly, he had warned networks of strict censorship unless they tamed their comedians. The rumor began when an advertising executive told comedienne Fanny Brice that her material was a little too risqué for the home. When she declared that her act was not offensive, he told her of Roosevelt's supposed threat. This story soon spread, and fiction was perpetuated as fact. Advertising executives as well as network officials began cutting potentially questionable material and speakers.[42]

Editing Speakers?

One of the most celebrated incidents of cutting speakers off the air occurred in 1931, when a Philadelphia station owner abruptly cut General Smedley Butler off the air when the general used the word "hell" in describing the capture of Fort Riviera in Haiti, for which he received the Congressional Medal of Honor. A sergeant, a private, and Butler were about to enter the fort by way of a drain hole through which the enemy was firing. In telling the story, Butler said, "Then I saw Sergeant Russell L. Iams looking at me as if saying to himself, 'Hell, if you're not going through, get out of the way and let me go on.'" He was immediately cut off the air for the offensive "hell." Howard Miller, station owner and announcer, took action because the word "wasn't fit for a child to hear."[43]

After receiving complaints from listeners for this action, the FRC upheld the station, since "profane language" was forbidden in radio, and FRC officials told Miller he was within his rights, noting broadcasters were responsible for what went out over their airwaves.[44] Shortly after this episode, KOIL of Omaha booked Butler for fifteen minutes, and he again "let loose with more cusswords than have been heard over the air here in three years," according to a correspondent for *Variety*.[45] Later in 1934, Butler was again cut off the air for using inappropriate language over WAVE in Louisville.[46]

Official network policies existed for such "profane" language. In late 1931, NBC policy permitted one accidental "hell" or "damn," while the more liberal CBS allowed "exactly three damns and two hells." As for programs themselves, NBC stated that it selected "balanced programs which will not bore, insult or outrage the listening public," while Anne Honeycutt of CBS stated that "no gossip, announcement of prices, appeals for funds, fortune telling, lottery promoting or direct salesmanship may be mentioned over CBS stations." She added CBS did not want speakers to believe they were being censored and cited a case involving Father Charles Coughlin. "For some reason, he said he was being curbed and in one week's time we were struggling with 498,000 letters denouncing us for censoring a clergyman. I think we merely declined to permit him to solicit funds."[47]

The ACLU disputed this position and asked, in a formal statement, how the networks could state that these were their policies when they refused anything of a controversial nature or that attacked government policy. They then cited the inability of birth control advocates, speakers against Prohibition, and Puerto Rican nationalist Dr. Antonio Barcelo to get airtime.[48]

In October 1931, CBS and WMCA refused to carry the speech of Dr. Antonio Barcelo, former president of the Puerto Rican Senate, on Puerto Rican independence on the grounds that the speech interfered with policies of the State Department and the FRC. The speech protested American rule and Congress's failure to fulfill promises made to Puerto Ricans. Barcelo called for justice and compared Puerto Ricans to "the abject servants of the feudal states." He charged corporations and landowners with political slavery and called for Puerto Rican self-determination.[49]

Protests to the FRC, WMCA, and CBS over cancellation were to no avail. FRC secretary James Baldwin denied that the FRC had power of censorship over programs, while the station said the talk violated FRC principles.[50] In both letter and press release, Professor Hatcher Hughes, chairman of the National Council on Freedom from Censorship, noted this instance was another evasion of responsibility for censorship on the part of both station and the commission. He added it would be used as "evidence in support of a much needed amendment to the radio law this winter to end the present indirect censorship and to give the radio the same immunities and responsibilities now attached to the press." Several newspapers endorsed the proposed amendment.[51]

After assessing the situation and lodging complaints with the station and FRC, Baldwin wrote Barcelo that controversial broadcasts often resulted in injured parties charging stations with failure to operate in the public interest. Baldwin conceded that the definition of "public interest, convenience, and necessity" was extremely vague and added that "provoking political or religious strife, attacking institutions and individuals in a manner calculated to stir up antagonism, or in fact, engaging vigorously in any controversy of a kind likely to arouse great public feeling, have been reason enough in some cases to justify withholding a station's license." Fear of reprisals that could lead to license loss made stations afraid to sell time.[52]

The ACLU had long been involved in trying to get more liberal viewpoints, such as Dr. Barcelo's, on the air. In January 1930, Roger Baldwin of the ACLU's board of directors asked NBC to allocate one hour of airtime per week to the presentation of liberal viewpoints after a conservative group, the National Security League, was given free time for educational programs on patriotism intended for schoolchildren. NBC president Merlin Aylesworth wrote back, saying that he was looking into NBC's presentation of "so-called liberal programs" already on air. Both Baldwin and Oswald Villard of the ACLU thought Aylesworth was stalling, and they were right. Aylesworth did not reply to the prodding letters received over the summer of 1930.[53]

In early 1931, the ACLU surveyed radio stations as part of study of free expression in all media: broadcasting, movies, school textbooks, and print publications, including post office interference with their distribution.[54] The survey was sent to radio stations the ACLU labeled "liberal" and "conservative" to discern free speech on radio, especially as it related to coverage of a variety viewpoints on controversial issues. While no evidence exists of how the stations were labeled or selected, sixty-seven letters of reply—twenty-six from liberal stations and forty-one from conservative—are found in the ACLU files. Most stations, liberal and conservative, stated that when they covered issues, they did not discriminate and knew of no instances of bias or favoritism. Conservative stations were more likely than liberal stations not to cover controversial issues at all, however, and to have no "open door" policy when it came to broadcast of issues.[55]

In the survey, Stanley Hubbard of KSTP replied that the Minnesota legislature was considering legislation that would virtually squelch discussion over radio. "Under this bill, the manager of a station would be subject to fine or imprisonment should any matter be broadcast which could injure anyone," he claimed.[56] The bill did not pass, but the threat of legislative intervention in radio speech remained.

Although liberal causes had more difficulty getting airtime, occasionally even conservative groups suffered discrimination. For instance, when NBC and CBS refused airtime to the National Security League for one of its talks in a series of patriotic speeches the networks deemed "jingoistic," the organization turned to WNYC, a station owned and operated by New York City. Phil Strong of the *New York World* noted the speech was carried at taxpayer expense since the city owned the station. He questioned if tax dollars should be spent in this fashion, while others argued that all viewpoints should be aired on stations funded with public monies.[57]

Conclusion

During this time, much censorship revolved around protecting the home from inappropriate material. Battles unfolded over both moral values of numerous groups and the sanctity of the home and parental control over media entering home. Broadcasters interpreted listeners as wanting inoffensive material via radio and nothing else. In addition, broadcasters were reluctant to broadcast material that might put their licenses in jeopardy. As such, broadcasters were averse to pursuing controversial issues.

"Improper" programming became the focus of celebrated incidents involving freedom of the air and the public interest. Among issues considered inappropriate were pacifism, socialism, and discussion of eliminating Prohibition. Speakers were also not to question the prevailing views on Prohibition, race relations, or birth control. Overall, conservative stations were more likely than liberal stations to ignore controversial issues and to have no "open door" policy for issues with which the owners did not agree.

As the Depression worsened, more and more speakers found their evaluation of economic conditions censored. Little discussion occurred via radio on unemployment or food relief efforts, and records indicate that NBC and CBS networks refused time on the grounds that speeches were contrary to government policies trying to overcome economic hardship. Programs undermining confidence and faith in American principles were not allowed. Behind these censorship efforts was the remote fear of losing licenses. The FRC had warned that the character of station program services could be reviewed, and that as the licensing authority, it had power to decide the appropriateness of programs in the public interest. The application was in the negative. That is, programs were deemed not to be in the public interest if they provoked political or religious strife or attacked institutions and individuals in an antagonistic manner or in ways likely to arouse great public passions. Fear of reprisals that could lead to license loss made stations afraid to sell time to any programming that was slightly controversial.

Protecting the home from improper programs was another role broadcasters adopted. To ward off any church or mothers' crusades against indecent radio programming, station and network censors modified songs and skits. Off-color radio material was unlike stage shows where customers entered the theater and paid to see productions. Because radio came into the home unannounced, broadcasters believed the medium should consider itself a well-mannered guest. Listeners, especially children, had to be protected from unsuitable matter, and station actions prevented programming from offending listeners. Among the most controversial programs were programs that dealt with issues of birth control, unorthodox religious views, and entry of evangelists and other clergy into discussions of social issues in the midst of an ever-widening Depression.

9 ⇒ GIMME THAT OL' TIME RELIGION: RELIGIOUS ISSUES ON RADIO TO 1934

When clergy appeared on radio, their speech was often controlled, and issues deemed too controversial because they offended social or religious groups found no pulpit on radio. Listeners in the early 1930s were especially irritated or inflamed by speakers such as Father Charles Coughlin and Reverend Herman J. Hahn, who challenged cultural or social standards of social justice. While both men found themselves running afoul station and network policies and drawing pointed denunciations from those who did not agree with their views, the more conservative Coughlin found an easier time getting on the air than did the more liberal Hahn. This bias reflected and emphasized a propensity for airing conservative causes over more liberal ones.

As with more secular programming, the FRC received complaints from listeners about religious broadcasters. While Reverend Robert Shuler's attacks on others cost him his license, Coughlin, Hahn, and other religious speakers did not own stations, so the FRC believed it could do little to curb them. Those who owned stations or networks, though, did not often like airing opinions that antagonized reigning social and political forces or the religious views held by the majority of Americans. They chose either to cancel speakers or not to sell them time.

Nor did religiously orthodox conservatives like discussions of any kind on subjects they found abhorrent, including atheism, evolution, and birth control. Advocates of these issues had little success getting on the airwaves. Throughout the 1920s and 1930s, religious fundamentalists openly fought these doctrines within American society as a whole, and their battles spilled into requests for radio time to cover conventions of birth control advocates and to discuss the teaching of evolution in schools. Struggles over possible radio coverage of these topics as well as controversies ignited by Coughlin and Hahn illustrated most vividly the clash between conservative religious fundamentalists and liberal modernists over religious issues and concurrent free speech/public interest concerns in the late 1920s and early 1930s. As with other radio coverage, conservative views found voice more often than did liberal perspectives.

Father Charles Coughlin

Father Charles Coughlin, pastor of the Shrine of the Little Flower in Royal Oak, Michigan, originally began his broadcasts to break down intolerance aimed at Catholics, but he soon began broadcasting question-and-answer sessions covering many social issues. His endorsement of workers' welfare and attacks on socialism, communism, and industrial problems met with warm listener response in the early Depression years, which sometimes alarmed industry leaders and government officials.

At first, only three stations—one each in Detroit, Chicago, and Cincinnati—carried Father Coughlin's weekly sermons, but by October 1930, the broadcasts went nationwide. By year's end, mail for his *Golden Hour of the Little Flower* averaged more than fifty thousand letters per week, with over seventy-five thousand coming in the Sunday before Christmas. Coughlin employed fifty-two clerical assistants to handle the mail. A printing plant in Detroit printed and mailed out fifty thousand copies of his weekly sermons to those requesting them. Father Coughlin did not mention money over the air, and fund-raising was left to the Radio League of the Little Flower. By using the method then employed by broadcasters to calculate listenership—one letter writer equaling two hundred listeners—the audience was estimated to be over ten million. More than half the writers were Protestant or Jewish. Even though Coughlin was later accused of anti-Semitism, in 1930 he received little adverse criticism—about two letters in a thousand—and most criticism came from Catholics. Complaints were filed with the FRC or Coughlin's bishop, the Right Reverend Michael Gallagher of Detroit. Father Coughlin paid little heed to his critics as he had Gallagher's approval and a letter from the pope thanking him for his efforts, controversial though they were.[1]

One contentious Coughlin sermon, "Prosperity," was initially banned from broadcast over CBS on January 4, 1931. The speech attacked unemployment and economic issues, especially President Hoover's policies, and CBS asked him "to moderate his expressions as to avoid objections." Coughlin announced that CBS forbade the broadcast as an inflammatory attack on government officials, big business, and international banking. CBS denied the charges, stating they had not barred Coughlin from talking, yet admitted they had asked him to moderate his criticisms of government policy.[2]

Among those denouncing CBS's action was Socialist Norman Thomas, who had been denied time when Coughlin attacked socialism over Detroit station WJR. In that instance, the FRC had endorsed WJR's actions against Thomas and replied that WJR had shown its devotion to the public interest in "preventing speakers from indulging in personalities" over their facilities. Now, Thomas protested "gagging" Coughlin, even though he disagreed with the priest's views.[3] After a week of criticism, including negative newspaper coverage and an estimated 200,000 protest letters, CBS allowed Coughlin to preach "Prosperity" over the network, but later that fall, CBS did not renew Coughlin's contract. Understandably, censorship charges reemerged.[4]

After his cancellation, an editorial in the *Christian Century* decried sanctions, to which a CBS spokeswoman replied:

> In connection with the recent editorial . . . inferring that freedom of speech over the radio is being denied American clergymen and citing Father Coughlin as an example of so-called censorship, we take the liberty of quoting from a telegram we have received from Father Coughlin: "You have full liberty to state that the Columbia broadcasting system [*sic*] has at no time attempted to censure my discourse nor in any way did the Columbia broadcasting system [*sic*] try to have me removed from the air. You are free to convey this message to *The Christian Century* magazine."[5]

Coughlin did denounce CBS on air, however, and then set up his own network through WJR. Meanwhile, CBS issued a new policy regarding religious broadcasting: "Columbia believes that religious broadcasting should be a public service, without remuneration . . . and has turned to the authorities of the various denominations and others apparently most competent to nominate the preachers to fill the ever-changing pulpit of the *Church of the Air.*" CBS asked various Catholic dioceses to select speakers to appear on the program. Thus, CBS had rid itself of the vexatious Coughlin.[6]

The ACLU board directed Forrest Bailey to write the FRC in connection with censorship of Father Coughlin's broadcasts,[7] yet nothing official came of these protests as the FRC stated it had no jurisdiction. During 1932, the commission received nearly three dozen complaints about Father Coughlin's speeches and his attacks on President Hoover, but an FRC investigator found no statement to justify the commission setting any station for license renewal hearing because of Coughlin's speeches. "Most of the Rev. Coughlin's remarks do not name any particular person or group and are aimed more at our national or financial system, and the principal subject discussed in all of them is revaluation of the gold standard," the investigator concluded.[8]

In April 1932, Cardinal William Henry O'Connell of Boston issued a thinly veiled denunciation of Coughlin, condemning "hysterical addresses from ecclesiastics" and adding it was wrong for individual priests to address the whole world. Father Coughlin asserted that he would continue his weekly addresses despite the cardinal's criticism because his bishop approved them. Coughlin said that he showed the bishop his speeches on Saturday, the day before broadcast, for approval, adding that his talks on economic and social problems were based on the writings of Popes Leo XIII and Pius XI. Meanwhile, Coughlin's popularity grew. The *New York Times* reported that during the 1931 broadcast season, Coughlin received over 2.5 million letters and added that although his parish comprised only forty-two families, ten thousand persons attended his church every Sunday.[9]

In short, Coughlin's attacks on President Hoover and economic issues cost him his time slot at CBS. As a result of its battles over Coughlin, CBS changed its policy on religious programming to confine sermons to officially chosen representatives of mainstream Catholic, Jewish, and Protestant thought. Such conventional speakers would not present controversial ideas that would alienate listeners—and advertisers. During the decade, Coughlin's attacks became far more pronounced and embarrassing to stations and church leaders. He remained on the air until 1940, when his vilification of groups he disliked became so flagrant that major networks denied him time and stations took him off the air.[10]

Reverend Herman J. Hahn

Another major case of censorship involving a cleric evolved in early January 1932 when station WGR of Buffalo, New York, barred an address, "Jesus' Way Out," by Reverend Herman J. Hahn, the liberal pastor of Salem Evangelical Church in Buffalo, New York. Hahn's speech likened the early 1930s to Christ's lifetime, when Christ "predicted the crash of their boasted civilization. To avert it, He urged his way of brotherhood, teamwork, cooperation, collectivism." The ruling class then "put Him to death to silence His protest. They refused His way and continued on their stupid course down the road to destruction, that has been traveled by every great civilization of the past." Capitalism's "every man for himself" scramble led to chaos, Hahn's speech continued, adding that if one protested, "you are forthwith branded as un-American and cynically told to go to Russia." After decrying the accumulation of wealth, taxation of the poor, and relief measures freeing the rich from responsibility for responding to poverty, Hahn concluded, "The New Year brings the challenge to venture the new social experiment of brotherhood, cooperation and collectivism. It alone holds forth hope and promise. It is Jesus' way. Have we the courage, initiative and vision to follow?"[11]

Hahn had sent the talk, which was seventeenth in a series of radio addresses on "The Social Implications of Christianity," to WGR in accordance with the station's policy of requiring submission of speeches two days in advance. The next day, Robert Striegl, the station program director, notified Hahn that the tone and subject of his speech was objectionable, and Hahn was urged to preach a more conventional type of religion, not stressing economic or social problems. Otherwise, WGR would reject his future broadcasts. The station objected specifically to two passages: where Hahn called for taxation of higher income Americans and where he stated that charity and relief were not enough to combat the Depression's consequences. Hahn's speech noted that what was needed was "increasing the purchasing power of the workers." WGR feared the alleged radicalism of the preacher's social ideas of justice and equality and wanted Hahn to confine his remarks to "conventional religion."[12]

Hahn's supporters stated that WGR objected to discussion of questions of public policy when the speaker's views differed from the station or the president and his administration. The ACLU, the Federal Council of the Churches of Christ in America, the Methodist Social Service Commission, the Socialist Party of America, and the League for Industrial Democracy, among others, protested Hahn's situation.[13]

The ACLU especially took up Hahn's cause and notified press services about the censorship. As articles and editorials decrying WGR's action appeared,[14] the ACLU sent a telegram to WGR, asking it to restore Hahn's program "without discrimination because of his political or economic views." Hahn wanted to broadcast the same speech the next week from WGR, and if he failed to do so, he would approach rival station WBEN, owned by the *Buffalo Evening News*.[15] Word came the next day from Irine J. Kittinger, president of Buffalo Broadcasting Company, WGR's parent operation, that WGR was canceling Hahn's contract unless his broadcasts became, in Hahn's interpretation, "inoffensive 'conventional' religious messages with little or no stress on economic, social or political problems." The church's Salem Brotherhood asked the ACLU's advice on pursuing the issue before the Federal Radio Commission, and the ACLU's Roger Baldwin began pursuing the matter.[16]

An attorney for the station, Edward Letchworth, wrote Roger Baldwin that the station was justified in its refusal to air the sermon as the broadcast would "tend to disgust and alienate many of [its] listeners and so seriously damage [its] good will and the advertising value of [the] station." Hahn could deliver his speech in a public hall, but use of broadcasting facilities was a different matter. "A broadcasting corporation is dependent on its advertisers for its maintenance and support, and this in turn requires it to guard its good will," he wrote. Likening refusal to carry Hahn's speech to declining to broadcast a discordant orchestra, Letchworth restated the station's right to refuse Hahn access.[17] His letter was forwarded to the radio committee of the Salem Brotherhood,[18] and the dispute was carried to Capitol Hill and became part of an ongoing discussion of extending protections for political candidates to include discussions of controversial issues of public importance.

On January 18, 1932, Representative Thomas Amlie of Wisconsin, a LaFollette Progressive, introduced a resolution requiring the FRC to ensure Hahn's right of free speech over WGR. Referred to the House Committee on Merchant Marine, Radio, and Fisheries, the measure went nowhere.[19] Meanwhile, the Salem Brotherhood sought Senator Robert Wagner's support of a similar measure in the Senate.[20] In addition, Morris Ernst and Roger Baldwin of the ACLU suggested that the Salem Brotherhood petition the FRC to revoke the station's license "even if it gets no action by the commission." In a letter to Hoffman, ACLU secretary Gordon Moss stressed the ease of initiating such a petition because of the public's interest aroused in the situation. He added that one point to stress in the petition was "that [the regulatory phrase] 'public interest, convenience, and/or necessity' has two sides to it."[21] In controversial issues, both sides of an issue needed to be heard to serve the public interest. For stations to serve the public interest and free speech, all points of view needed to be presented.

The ACLU through its National Council on Freedom from Censorship also approached Bethuel Webster, former counsel to the FRC and now counsel to WGR for his insight. Webster told Gordon Moss, the council's secretary, that WGR was "considerably worried about the whole affair" and did not like the poor publicity being generated for the station.[22] In part because of the Hahn situation, the ACLU also discussed alternatives in radio legislation regarding freedom of expression with Webster. One option was an amendment to the Radio Act, extending the clause that required equitable treatment of candidates to include equitable coverage of controversial issues of public importance. Another was a resolution defining the term "public interest, convenience and/or necessity" as it might apply to freedom of expression.[23] These efforts are presented fully in chapter 12.

Conventional religion considered discussions advocating atheism, evolution, or birth control even more controversial than those speeches promoting social change as these advocates challenged established religious teachings and traditional values. The American Association for the Advancement of Atheism, for example, applied for a station license for New York City in October 1928 only to be told that too many stations were operating in New York. In refusing the license, the FRC counseled the association to buy time from an existing station. That was impossible, as no station would sell time to atheists.[24] Proponents of evolution and birth control also had difficulty locating stations willing to carry their messages, and stations and networks found themselves refuting charges of censorship in debates on these issues.

Free Speech and Birth Control

In the late 1920s and early 1930s, sex, including honest references to reproduction, was an absolutely taboo radio subject. One station rejected an entire series of talks on child welfare because it included a discussion of illegitimacy under the title "Children Born Out of Wedlock." CBS barred any reference to "syphilis control" in a speech by Dr. Thomas Parran Jr., New York state commissioner of health. In protest, Parran resigned from the public health committee of the National Advisory Council on Radio in Education. Other broadcasters censored a speech on Malthusian economics by noted economist Gustav Peck in October 1930. The speech, "An Essay on the Principle of Population," contained references to food reserves, population growth and control, and persistent poverty in the world, and CBS cut the sentence "Thomas Robert Malthus, arguing against his father, made some startling remarks about human nature and especially the strength of the sex impulse, which led people to marry as soon as they were able." The company explained that it was not permitted to mention sex over the radio, because the talk was going into the homes of America.[25]

Signals coming uninvited into the home became the primary reason for "editing" radio speeches about sex. In 1931, in his article "The Impending Radio War" for *Harper's Monthly Magazine,* James Rorty contended radio could never be as free as the soapbox or even newsprint because of radio's intrusion into the home and recounted a censorship incident he had personally experienced: "In rehearsing a program of poetry for broadcasting over station WJZ, the writer was counseled by the program director to omit certain poems dealing with sex and religion on the entirely justifiable ground that to have broadcast those particular poems would have endangered the continuation of a valuable sustaining program. I accepted this censorship cheerfully. The same sort of thing happens all the time in relations with magazine editors and is nothing to get especially exited about."[26] The American Birth Control League, however, did get excited about station and network censorship of its message.

From its beginning, NBC refused to give or sell time to the American Birth Control League, a leading organization promoting birth control, because birth control was a religious issue upon which Jews, Catholics, and Protestants did not agree. NBC said that it was willing to enter controversy when the public demanded it, as in political campaigns, but no sufficient public demand for coverage of birth control was evident.[27]

By far, the most celebrated and public of these cases came with the American Birth Control League's request for NBC network coverage of its 1929 three-day convention and subsequent debate of all sides of the birth control issue. When NBC refused to carry the convention, the league complained to NBC's Advisory Council. In its decision, the council dealt for the first time with the issue of freedom of the air and had to determine if the information a group wanted to broadcast was in the public interest. The council had to reconcile concerns of traditionalist and modernist attitudes toward a contentious issue, birth control, and freedom of expression with its discussion on radio. In doing so, the Advisory Council defined parameters of free speech regarding a controversial issue of public importance. Of course, central to discussions of birth control were religious values.[28]

Joining the American Birth Control League in protest to the Advisory Council was the ACLU. Forrest Bailey of the ACLU declared that, as licensees using a public resource, radio stations were obligated to transmit all sides of controversial subjects of public importance.[29] The ACLU appealed NBC's decision on behalf of the American Birth Control League, first to NBC officials and then to both the FRC and NBC's Advisory Council. In writing to John Elwood, vice president for NBC, the ACLU officials stated that "an objection to a particular broadcasting subject on the ground of its controversial character necessarily disregards the right of the public to be fully informed on all matters of public interest." The letter noted that New York newspapers covered the conference and questioned whether NBC acted in the public's interest, convenience, or necessity as mandated in the Radio Act in refusing coverage. The complaint concluded that in declining to broadcast the addresses of the conference, NBC "neglected the performance of a public service which it was under a sort of moral obligation to perform." The ACLU said it was improper for a public service organization such as NBC to censor material.[30] Copies of the letter to

Elwood were forwarded to members of the FRC and NBC's Advisory Council.[31]

The FRC wanted to avoid the issue. Frank Lovette, acting secretary of the FRC, wrote the ACLU's Harry Ward that the commission would act only upon protests in affidavit form that were made through oral testimony taken under oath.[32] FRC chairman Ira Robinson also wrote Ward, stating that the commission's jurisdiction in the matter was limited as it "extended only to individual broadcasting stations and [the commission] has made no regulations with reference to chain broadcasting." He added that with the absence of a specific request to revoke the license of a broadcast station or to refuse a renewal of a station, the commission could take no action.[33] A station was within its rights to refuse any type of broadcast material, so the matter was solely in the hands of NBC and its Advisory Council, as far as the FRC was concerned.[34] All council members received copies of the NBC-ACLU correspondence. Of council members, most acknowledged receipt and noted that, if NBC did not resolve the situation, they would review charges in the next council meeting.[35]

Only GE and RCA chief and NBC Advisory Council member Owen Young replied in depth to Ward's allegations of censorship, stating that he would put the matter before the council "because it is certainly the object and ambition of the Broadcasting Company to use its facilities wisely and in the public interest." Young noted that among NBC's duties as a public trustee of broadcasting was an obligation to carry programs that listeners would welcome. These included both revenue-producing programs to defray broadcasting costs and sustaining programs offered as a public service. Classifying the American Birth Control League in the latter category, Young noted that key in deciding what to carry was rendering "something welcome to the majority of listeners, otherwise the broadcasting station loses its audience, and its efforts, however well-intentioned, will be fruitless." He added that more groups wanted more sustaining time than was available, and consequently, programs had to be selected. Decisions were made "not in any spirit of censorship of materials, but in the conscientious exercise of judgment" as to how listeners would want facilities used.[36]

Young added that the birth control conference had been a competitor for the scant sustaining time available and that the "question before the Broadcasting Company was whether the interest of its listeners required that to be broadcast in preference to something else." He said that, even though he was in sympathy with the league, NBC was correct in deciding not to broadcast the conference. Young wrote:

> . . . I feel sure that a referendum vote of listeners would have demonstrated overwhelmingly that it was the kind of subject which was not yet ripe for introduction through the radio to the homes of America, available for any member of the family, of any age or condition, to turn on. The mass view may be wrong about this, but it merely means, if I am right, that your movement has not progressed far enough in public interest and good-will to warrant its broadcast by such a trustee of wave-lengths as the National Broadcasting Company.[37]

He added that NBC was under no obligation to circulate any cause until listeners wanted to hear it. In other words, while the issue was controversial, it had not reached an acceptable level of public interest.

Young noted NBC carried other controversial subjects such as politics because the audience wanted to hear them. In such coverage, NBC selected broadcast times carefully so that an absolutely fair and full presentation of both parties' positions could be made. He added, even though NBC refused to air the league's speeches, other stations might be glad to carry the conference. He then invited Ward to lay the matter before the Advisory Council and to state his claim as to why the birth control conference was entitled to time "to the exclusion" of other public interest material.[38]

Ward responded that the ACLU was not interested per se in promoting birth control; it functioned to protect civil rights, especially freedom of thought and freedom of expression. He added, while the ACLU recognized NBC's responsibility in choosing what to air, the "feeling that the Conference program was of a character that made it unfit to be introduced into American homes . . . is based, we suspect, on a misapprehension." Conference discussions did not explain contraceptive methods, nor were they intended to promote the birth control movement. Instead, the conference presented scientific authorities on all sides of a "much misunderstood subject." Ward compared NBC's lack of coverage to newspaper reports and asked, since the press also came into the American home and yet reported discussions fully, why NBC adopted a different standard for radio.[39]

Ward disagreed with Young's assessment that birth control issues had not progressed far enough in public interest to warrant broadcast coverage. He noted that opposition to the birth control movement made the issue controversial and that this controversy made the subject interesting and important. He said: "We cannot see the wisdom in a policy which holds away from the public all subject-matters except those about which there is no considerable difference of opinion. The tendency toward flat uniformity of public opinion under modern conditions is a thing to be deplored and resisted."[40]

He asked whether NBC's decision was made to please the anti–birth control audience, contrary to claims that NBC did not censor in selecting material. "We gathered from the remarks of Mr. Elwood printed in the press that there was a body of public opinion opposed to the discussion of birth control which the company preferred not to antagonize," he wrote. "If this is true, we see in the rejection of the Conference program a form of virtual censorship. The fact that the section of the public to which favor was shown is respectable and strongly entrenched in its preconceptions does not alter the nature of the discrimination." In closing, he chided NBC for not risking disapproval of part of its audience.[41]

When the council met in January 1930, it reviewed the complaint and related correspondence. While published committee reports contain scant reference to the council's decision,[42] Owen Young's papers contain a much more detailed account. Outlining the complete discussion and retained solely for later reference by the council's members, a four-page memo provides a confidential look at the council's handling of this issue of free speech and the public interest.[43]

NBC president Merlin Aylesworth began the meeting with a review of the letters and a public statement made November 19, 1929, that explained NBC's reasons for rejecting the program. In part it read: "The subject of Birth Control is not only of a moral and a social nature, but it is of significance in the religious world. Propaganda for birth control is objectionable to a number of persons because of their religious faith. In this circumstance, the National Broadcasting Company does not feel that it should undertake the presentation of any material on this subject."[44] To Ward's December 10 letter asking why NBC did not carry the conference addresses when newspapers did, Aylesworth replied that radio differed from print in that the press could edit its material and report only those portions of a meeting that editors wanted. With radio, once NBC said it would offer complete coverage of a conference, its discretionary powers were gone; it carried the whole meeting, not just portions of it. He added that NBC "must, therefore, exercise discretion in deciding what programs are appropriate for transmission into the home."[45]

Charles Evans Hughes, soon to be nominated as chief justice of the United States Supreme Court, added that two kinds of broadcast programs existed: controversial ones and noncontroversial ones. NBC did not have to air a program just because a subject was controversial. On the contrary, he added, NBC had to be mindful of audience needs and desires and, consequently, had to transmit primarily noncontroversial programs. Furthermore, controversial shows could be divided into two classes. The first class involved controversy for controversy's sake. Programs in this category, he stated, usually pleased only those with special interest in the subject and might be unpalatable or offensive to larger audiences. The second type was exemplified by important political campaigns in which the public demanded presentation of both sides. To Hughes, NBC had to set policies to avoid the former and to encourage the latter.[46]

In applying this principle to the American Birth Control League controversy, Hughes classified birth control in the first category as it had not reached a point where there was a general demand for its presentation. He added that if in five years such a demand existed, birth control might be an appropriate subject for broadcasting. When asked how he would respond to a question such as "Shall we give the public what it wants or what it ought to want?," Hughes suggested that broadcasters often do both, and in the "narrow field of controversy we must have the check of public demand lest we set ourselves up as a propagandist organization agitating for special interests."[47]

The other senior member of the Advisory Council, Elihu Root, agreed with Hughes. Root was a former United States senator, secretary of state under Theodore Roosevelt, and winner of the Nobel Peace Prize for settling problems of Japanese immigration to California and organizing the Central American Peace Conference. He reasoned a vast number of people had ideas they considered of great value and wanted widely distributed. In time, some of these views would prevail, and the public would demand their dissemination.

The criterion for presentation should be whether such a subject had reached a point where the public would regard its transmission as a service. When that point was reached, NBC would afford coverage. To Root, discussion of birth control had not reached that point, and NBC had acted properly in not covering the conference. The council's members agreed with both men's assessments and recommended no change in NBC's policies.[48]

With this decision, the council's secretary, Everett Case, answered Ward's letter of December 10 for the council. Access to the medium by groups espousing controversial views was different for radio than for the printed press, Case wrote, because radio came directly into the home. He then outlined the council's views, which paralleled statements by Root and Hughes. When a controversial subject reached the point of general public recognition that such a topic warranted coverage, radio would present the matter to the public as a public service. Until that point was reached—and it had not been reached in the controversy surrounding birth control—NBC would decline to broadcast the issue. Obviously, Case wrote, this principle's application was a matter of judgment. In this case, the judgment of the Advisory Council was extraordinary because of its preeminent makeup. When NBC did decide to cover an issue, it would do so fairly, with the council's aid, so that all sides would be presented adequately. For now, the matter was closed.[49]

Letters exchanged on the council's birth control ruling as well as the council's formal report made the *New York Times*. NBC held that birth control was "a religious issue upon which the three great denominations did not agree" and based its ban on that ground. Harry Ward's public reply reiterated his private letter, stating that NBC "neglected the performance of a public service which it was under a moral obligation to perform." Ward contended that controversial subjects needed airing so that the public could form its opinions intelligently. Refusal to do so violated the mandate to public interest.[50]

Attempts to get airtime did not end with this decision. The American Birth Control League approached 115 leading broadcast stations, including 29 run by universities or colleges, to request time for either a speech or a debate on the broader aspects of family planning. Neither format would provide information on contraception. To these requests, only twenty-seven stations bothered to reply, and of these, only two replied that they would be willing to host either speakers or a debate. The Buffalo Broadcasting Company, consisting of four stations (WKBW, WGR, WMAK, and WKEN), agreed to use a series of four speakers already addressing the topic in Buffalo. In the other reply, the University of Minnesota agreed to host a student debate on birth control. CBS and four other stations also showed interest but asked to see speeches before coming to a decision. Other stations claimed that either their schedules were full for the next several months or that they were simply "not interested" in speeches on birth control.[51] In fact, during this time only Socialist station WEVD was willing to air speeches on birth control without imposing conditions.[52]

During the next few years, birth control advocates continued to seek other ways to get publicity. In October 1930, Morris Ernst of the ACLU suggested that a friend or member of the league obtain fifteen minutes at an undesirable hour (around 10:00 A.M. was suggested) from CBS without revealing the purpose of the talk. He also proposed that the league try to get time from a Catholic-owned station by arguing that the league wanted to present the other side of a controversial issue. Of course, he realized that the league would get nowhere with either request, but the attempts would generate publicity that would benefit the issue.[53]

Catholics were not the only denomination to decry birth control coverage on radio. In May 1931, Bishop W. N. Ainsworth, president of the College of Bishops of the Methodist Episcopal Church, South, protested the action of a committee on the Federal Council of the Churches of Christ in speaking in favor of birth control. "Such officious invasion of the sacred realm of the home is dangerous in the extreme and in the end will promote more promiscuous sex relations. It is blasting at the foundations of the home, which is the bulwark of civilization and society whether it is so intended or not."[54]

In another instance, a veiled reference to birth control in November 1931 resulted in the curator of comparative and human anatomy of New York's American Museum of Natural History being cut off in midstatement. Dr. William Gregory began broadcasting the offending sentences—"We have reckless overproduction of goods and reckless overproduction of people. We are a beehive choked with honey, yet full of starving bees"—when a station employee cut him off. He was returned to the air only after the offensive lines were said into a dead microphone. Later, station managers sent Gregory an apology, stating the overzealous employee over-stepped his authority. Gregory blamed himself in part for the censorship as he had revised his manuscript after its approval by the station's censors.[55]

Another incident involving Gregory occurred in the fall of 1933, when he ran up against censorship during an interview on "Evolution and the Depression." Unbeknownst to Gregory, he was abruptly cut off the air by a control room employee when he uttered the sentence "We are still in a transitional stage of evolution, in which the aggressive selfishness of the solitary animal has led to unlimited cutthroat competition—" The interviewer then asked him if he favored "the Russian remedy," referring to adoption of communism. When Gregory replied, "Of course not," and as he elaborated upon the better qualities of the American system, the connection was restored. Gregory knew none of this until one of his museum colleagues asked why silence came in the middle of the broadcast. Again, station management apologized for the actions of an over-zealous control room engineer.[56]

Other restraints on speakers often succeeded because they were disguised as choices. For instance, speakers could "choose" to submit speeches for approval or not appear on the air, or advertisers could "choose" which entertainers, programs, or speakers they would sponsor. Those without sponsors lost their time slots, and none wanted to sponsor controversial programs on birth control. In the early 1930s, as noted contemporary media critic James Rorty succinctly observed, "for all practical purposes, radio in America is business-owned, business-administered and business-censored."[57] Advertisers as well as the radio industry did not support coverage of controversial issues such as birth control.

Conclusion

Religious issues, public interest, free speech, and protecting the American home were inexorably linked in discussions focusing on atheism, evolution, and birth control. Preachers who spoke on secular issues such as economic conditions were counseled to confine their remarks to more conventional religious approaches. Stations did not want to alienate listeners and thereby damage the goodwill they had established with advertisers wanting to reach those listeners. In covering religious issues, stations wanted inoffensive messages with little or no stress on current economic, social, or political problems. Clergy such as Reverend Charles Coughlin and Reverend Herman Hahn faced adversity and challenges when they broadcast, while proponents of issues such as evolution and birth control found little access to radio.

The desire for inoffensive material plus a need to protect listeners from unwanted material coming into the home kept stations and networks from carrying discussions on controversial issues such as birth control. Because major religious denominations did not agree on the issue of birth control, NBC refused to carry the American Birth Control League's conventions. NBC said no evidence existed of sufficient public demand for coverage of the issue, unlike political campaigns where the public demanded coverage. As NBC's Advisory Council dealt with programming covering birth control, it had to determine the public interest in the topic and to reconcile traditionalist and modernist attitudes toward the issue. Key to their ruling was deciding if the subject matter was welcomed by the majority of listeners. They determined it had not reached the level where the public demanded coverage, especially of material that might not be appropriate for transmission into the home. In the eyes of the council, birth control involved controversy for controversy's sake, and the council deemed the subject as pleasing to only those with an interest in the subject. In airing controversial issues, NBC did not want to be perceived as an agitator for special interests, especially if those special interests could cost them listeners or advertisers. This concern over advertising also precipitated a battle between radio and the print media as radio grew to rival print as both a presenter of news and a competitor for ad dollars that had formerly gone to newspapers and magazines.

10 ➜ FREEDOM OF THE (RADIO) PRESS?

When it came to the dissemination of news and information, distinctions between press and speech began to blur with radio. Radio obviously was "speech," but was it "the press" when it distributed news bulletins, commentary, or newscasts? In other words, could radio news be deemed a part of "the press"? Newspapers often contended that radio was not the same as the press, and within both industries, confrontations arose over who were appropriate disseminators of news and information. Newspapers espoused controls on radio news and information flow, ostensibly to protect the public welfare and the public interest in receipt of accurate information. Because radio was an entertainment medium and could also be a stiff competitor for breaking news, newspapers saw little irony in stifling radio's freedom of expression while promoting their own First Amendment rights.

Free Speech, Free Press, and News Broadcast Coverage

As early as 1922, the Associated Press (AP) warned its member newspapers not to broadcast news or permit others to do so because of unnecessary competition with newspapers, and in 1923 the American Newspaper Publishers Association formed a committee on radio to keep tabs on radio's impact upon papers.[1] Radio news commentary and occasional news bulletins had been staples of early radio. Election returns, for example, were disseminated by radio in 1920. Sports events and scores soon followed, as did coverage of special news events, such as Charles Lindbergh's solo flight across the Atlantic in 1927. By 1928, some stations had begun regular news reports. For example, WMAQ broadcast news "flashes" twice daily except on the weekends. The news programs were carried at 12:15 P.M. and 3:30 P.M. weekdays and Saturday at 12:15 P.M. No reports were issued on Sunday.[2]

Concerns over "appropriate dissemination" of news, plus threats to advertising income, caused consternation among newspapers and ultimately resulted in what became known as the "Press-Radio War." Some of the first salvos fired in that war came at a meeting of the New Jersey Press Association in October 1929, when M. V. Atwood, associate editor of the Gannett newspapers, assailed news broadcasts sponsored by "lipstick factories, orange juice stands, iron foundries, and microscope manufacturers." He said disseminating news belonged to newspapers and warned that radio was claiming too much reader time and attention.[3] That attitude typified those newspaper owners who wanted to curb radio's speech rights to protect their business enterprises.

When attempts to minimize radio news broadcasts began, newspaper ownership of or alliances with radio stations muddled the situation. In 1927, over half of the prominent stations had some newspaper affiliation; some newspapers owned stations outright or had entered contractual arrangements with stations for news or other information.[4] This figure remained stable to the early 1930s. In February 1932, *Editor and Publisher* noted that out of over 600 licensed stations, 104 had some newspaper connection—40 owned outright and the rest affiliated with papers.[5]

Spot news broadcasts continued growing throughout the early 1930s, and radio became a major source of breaking news. In March 1932, for example, reports of the kidnapping and death of Charles and Anne Lindbergh's son engrossed audiences, and broadcasters realized that nothing before had attracted such large numbers. News bulletins, announcers' recitations of the Lindberghs' written entreaties to their son's kidnappers, and pleas of clergy and public officials to release the two-year-old captivated the public.[6] NBC network coverage cost a reported $2,800 daily with overnight coverage from 1:00 A.M. to 6:00 A.M. alone costing $1,600. Additional expenses were incurred for maintaining announcers and engineers in New Jersey, the site of the kidnapping. CBS noted its expenses for the first week's coverage totaled $15,000. While other stations mounted their own coverage, by the end of the first week some smaller broadcasters wondered if they should abandon their self-originated costly coverage in favor of reading print press bulletins over the air. The Lindbergh situation also taught radio that it had to be extra careful in presenting bulletins to prevent broadcast of rumors, false reports, and inappropriate commentary, dangerous to the child if misconstrued by the kidnappers.[7]

During the early 1930s, an unprecedented amount of news broadcasting occurred. Topics covered ranged from national recovery to local disasters. Some coverage brought protests to newspapers in the form of letters to the editor from people outraged over radio inaccuracies. An ANPA report on the increase of these letters noted that the writers "unhesitatingly accept the newspaper version as true, and assume the radio accounts to have been inaccurate."[8] Some newspapers saw radio's inaccurate reporting as adding an additional burden upon newspapers "to reconstruct the true facts in the minds of the people." Consequently, newspaper publishers thought that "in the face of many national difficulties, the responsibility of giving the correct facts to the public should be restricted to the legitimate purveyors of news, namely, the newspapers. Radio primarily is a means of entertainment and it is accepted as such by the public."[9] In other words, radio had no business disseminating information, especially during the Depression, and newspapers actively sought to control radio's "freedom of the press."

Typifying newspaper concerns was alarm over Walter Winchell's broadcasts. The Broadway columnist began a news and commentary program in early 1933. Sponsored by Jergens Lotion and titled *Tomorrow's News Today,* the program went on the air each Sunday evening about the same time that three major New York papers were getting their first Monday editions on the street and several hours ahead of the first edition of many other morning newspapers. Using news services, Winchell summarized news since the Sunday morning editions and before it appeared in Monday newspapers.[10] ANPA members seethed over such rapid news dissemination and feared a decline in subscriptions.

At ANPA annual meetings from 1930 to 1933, lengthy deliberations ensued over ways to combat radio's growing coverage of news events. Citing an article written by Ray Launder in *Broadcast Reporter,* the ANPA in 1933 noted Launder's prediction that radio stations would greatly increase their dissemination of the news in the future:

> The day is coming when the American people will look to their broadcasting stations to bring them authentic news daily, not just occasional outbursts during presidential campaigns and the like. They will look to the stations not as a means of replacing the newspapers, but as the source of news highlights—fast, factual flashes to reach them when it is still news. In these days speed is the essential, and only radio can overcome the mechanical delays in bringing momentary news to the public.[11]

Launder concluded that the public would come to expect these reports as a part of a station's obligation to serve the public interest.[12]

By the presidential elections of 1932, tensions between newspapers and radio reached a peak. While the Associated Press furnished radio networks presidential election returns, their action hastened adoption of ANPA recommendations limiting release of press association news to radio stations. Emphasizing their property rights to news, the ANPA recommended that associations neither sell nor give away news in advance of newspaper publication. News broadcasts would merely be brief bulletins designed to encourage newspaper readership and credit newspapers for collecting the news.[13]

ANPA members had clashed for years with radio over property rights in news dissemination, even though the Associated Press had given its permission to broadcast AP news items beginning in 1927. At the ANPA's forty-second annual meeting in April 1929, arguments exploded over the policy's continuance, and members split fifty-fifty over allowing radio to broadcast news dispatches. By the meeting's end, the organization asked its directors to study the problem further and report their findings at the 1930 meeting.[14] Other state newspaper associations also believed radio was moving needlessly into news distribution. In January 1931, the Minnesota Editorial Association warned radio to "stay in its own field" of entertainment programming, or member newspapers would cease publishing radio program schedules and take other action. The resolution also called upon all Minnesota newspapers to stop supplying radio stations with news bulletins and to halt free publicity such as program listings. As an open competitor to newspapers in both news and advertising, newspapers believed radio should confine itself to "radio features," primarily entertainment programming. The association believed that the two industries were distinct and could help each other only "if each respects the other's field."[15]

Some newspaper editors believed these views were shortsighted. In speaking to the American Society of Newspaper Editors in April 1931, Volney Hurd, president of the Newspaper Radio Editors Association, appealed for wider recognition and support of radio. He noted that the press failed to grasp radio's importance in the 1920s, and he regretted newspapers had not taken over radio then. "In the early days," he noted, "when broadcasting stations were mostly liabilities, they could be purchased for a song. Today, they are of prohibitive value. . . . If the press had taken over broadcasting, it would then have been sitting at the controls of radio, a subject of such potentialities that it should be most carefully governed." He then correctly identified advertising as the reason for tensions between the media. "Radio advertising would have then paid its profits into the press and the question of the press versus radio advertising would not assume the proportion it has today. Radio production would have been governed by men trained in the problems of serving the public and maintaining its interests." Hurd called for a special study of radio program advertising, adding that he regretted the tendency to cut radio newspaper listings to a minimum. He warned that broadcasters might even publish their own listings, which would probably carry advertising and further damage newspaper profits.[16]

To protect those advertising revenues during the growing Depression, the ANPA adopted a resolution in December 1932 that press associations not give or sell dispatches for broadcast, rationalizing that radio should not impinge upon publishers' property rights in news. They also set up a committee to report on the situation for the association's annual meeting in April 1933.[17] In early March, United Press (UP) president Karl Bickel told the ANPA that the UP was ready to prohibit broadcasting of its news dispatches at any time the ANPA membership voted to support that policy, provided the other two major news services, AP and International News Service (INS), also banned broadcast of their releases.[18]

During the 1933 ANPA annual conference, the focus of discussion was property rights to news gathered by various press associations and possible prohibitions on broadcasts. The ANPA Committee on Radio noted three general attitudes of publishers toward broadcasting. First were those publishers who believed news broadcasting served no particular public good and was seriously damaging the newspaper industry. Some went so far as to call radio "a dangerous and parasitic competitor" for both news and advertising revenue. Second were those who believed that the public was entitled to news bulletins so long as they were not aired prior to print publication and were worded to whet listeners' appetites for amplified newspaper accounts. Third was "a very small group of publishers that feels that the newspapers should take no hand either in the regulation or the restriction of the broadcasting of news." The committee noted, "[T]hese publishers, however, are so few in number that little consideration has been given to their viewpoint," and in the eyes of radio's opponents, they offered no workable solution to handling growing radio news programming.[19]

Among this third group was Alfred Ochs of the powerful *New York Times*. At the annual meeting of the Associated Press a few days earlier, he warned newspapers not to bury their heads in the sand because radio would find a way to carry news of extraordinary importance regardless of what the AP decided to do. He agreed news broadcasts stimulated a public appetite for news and helped newspaper circulation and added that members should be able to use news as they saw fit, so newspaper owners of stations should be able to broadcast "brief" news items.[20] When the question of the AP permitting broadcast of any AP news by radio chains with an extra charge to AP members who both published and broadcast "brief" news bulletins, members voted more than two to one against the proposal. The AP wanted the ANPA board of directors to set rules defining "brief bulletins," governing hours of broadcasts, and protecting AP news reports "from pilfering or such other illegal use by radio news commentators or others."[21]

Because an outright ban met stiff opposition, the ANPA board set rules and prescribed that bulletins could not be more than thirty words each and that one bulletin could cover only one subject. The only exemption was sports coverage. Bulletins had to be broadcast during newspaper publication hours and could not be connected with commercial programs. Local news broadcasts were stopped, except for brief bulletins of major local events over stations at or near an individual newspaper's place of publication. The committee also urged members to cease selling or giving away news before publication, to keep news bulletins short, to concentrate on local news, and to take legal action in news piracy cases, where radio stations used information gathered by newspapers without paying for it.[22]

News Piracy

The first such piracy case began February 25, 1933, when the Associated Press filed suit in the federal district court for Sioux Falls, South Dakota, against the Sioux Falls Broadcast Association, which operated station KSOO. Judge James Elliot signed a temporary restraining order against the station to prevent it from pirating or appropriating news gathered by the AP and its local member, the *Daily Argus-Leader*. Citing a property value present in the news story, the judge stated that the station could carry news only if the stories were at least twenty-four hours old.[23]

The AP argued that unauthorized use of its news greatly impaired its value and caused irreparable injury to the AP and its members. The complaint added that KSOO did not maintain any organization for gathering the news itself and used the AP's dispatches to popularize itself and to make advertising time more valuable. The AP contended that the latter practice constituted unfair competition. Judge Elliot found that the AP's expense of gathering and transmitting news to its members amounted to millions of dollars each year. KSOO immediately countered with a motion attacking AP bylaws as an unreasonable restraint on interstate movement of news. Elliot dismissed the contention, holding that the bylaws were proper and constituted a "reasonable and legitimate safeguard" of its news reports. Unauthorized use of AP dispatches by the radio station constituted unfair competition.[24]

KSOO asserted it should not be barred from using news while other stations owned, controlled, leased, or operated by or otherwise affiliated with newspapers were permitted to broadcast this information. The court did not agree, and the AP won. The judge's order would remain in effect until a final hearing was held or until the radio station appealed. KSOO appealed but soon dropped the petition because of the outcome of another news piracy case in Louisiana.[25]

In June 1933, New Orleans station WDSU admitted that it wrote "news commentaries" based on news in the papers, but station operator Joseph Uhalt denied that the news was pirated as news items were not quoted directly and were rewritten before being put on the air. During the suit, WDSU assailed newspapers in a series of broadcasts "for trying to obtain a monopoly in news." Listeners were told the station was fighting the people's battle against selfish newspapers. The tactic did not work, and the courts ordered WDSU to halt use of items taken from local newspapers and enjoined the station's use of news for a period of twenty-four hours after first publication.[26]

After the decision, four New Orleans stations turned to a newly formed New Orleans City News Service for their reports. Teletype machines were installed in the stations for local news, and a five-thousand-word daily national news summary was received from Washington. Each station broadcast the news on a regular schedule, and important news items were presented as bulletins between scheduled broadcasts.[27] Radio was beginning to develop its own news-gathering operations.

Noting charges of piracy against stations and the resulting AP-ANPA resolutions, *Broadcasting* magazine editorialized in May 1933 that print journalists had declared war on radio. The magazine reported that individual stations owned by or affiliated with newspapers were still broadcasting news: "Those that have connections with A.P. newspapers are limiting news to the regulation 30-word bulletins, but this has simply meant that more news bulletins are being used to fill in the news periods. Those connected with newspapers taking U.P. and I.N.S. services are broadcasting news in about the same manner as usual."[28]

Martin Codel, *Broadcasting*'s editor, wrote that these decisions established that a radio station could not broadcast press association news without permission and said broadcasters should organize their own news-gathering operations. Because broadcasters had established wire interconnections and had hired station staffs often comprised of ex-newspaper personnel, skeleton organizations could be formed without great expense. Expenses could also be controlled if stations gathered and shared only those stories of national importance in their listening areas. In addition, if radio controlled its own news-gathering organization, stations could use news on commercial programs instead of sustaining programs to which agreements usually limited them.[29]

By fall 1933, the AP had set extra rates for broadcasting messages: for one news period, the charge was 2.5 percent of the member's first wire plus general charges; for two or more periods, the charge was 5 percent.[30] Meanwhile, in October, Western Union and the Postal Telegraph Company changed their regulations to permit news dispatches intended for broadcast to be transmitted at the lower press rates. The new policy was decidedly beneficial to development of CBS's Columbia News Service as an independent news-gathering operation.[31]

On September 16, 1933, the Columbia News Service was incorporated to gather and disseminate radio news. CBS added two five-minute news broadcasts to supplement its early evening fifteen-minute broadcast sponsored by Philco. The added news programs, sponsored by General Mills, aired at 12:30 and 4:30 P.M. EST. At the same time, another fifteen-minute newscast was added at 11:15 P.M. CBS's embryonic news-gathering staff was augmented by stations sharing news, by stations' reliance on newspaper-trained members on their publicity and spot news broadcasting staffs, and through hiring former newspaper reporters as correspondents.[32]

No sooner had the news service gone on the air than it was embroiled in a controversy over an affiliate's faking a news report. CBS affiliate WIND in Gary, Indiana, contrived and aired a shoot-out between police and escaped convicts in a wooded area on a rural Indiana farm. Supposedly the convicts made a desperate stand. In reality, no such incident took place. Indiana State Police investigated and ultimately released station personnel involved on the promise of a retraction. While a retraction was not made, the station released a statement denying that the broadcast had been deliberately faked. The statement explained that off-duty police taking part in the broadcast as amateur actors had fired their revolvers "spontaneously in their enthusiasm." The state police then filed formal complaints with the FRC, alleging that the false report had interfered with police work and needlessly alarmed citizens. The employees responsible for the broadcast were fired, and no other formal action was taken.[33]

Newspapers used this incident to highlight their charges of radio's irresponsible news-gathering practices and continued trying to control radio's access to information. On November 7, 1933, the Standing Committee of Correspondents of the congressional press galleries rejected the Columbia News Service's application for admission to the galleries. Citing Senate and House gallery rules, Samuel Bell, chairman of the committee, noted that admission was limited to daily newspapers and press associations furnishing a daily telegraphic service. CBS vice president Henry Bellows asserted that the rules should be amended to admit radio correspondents. The ANPA disagreed. Stating that radio stations could not present unbiased information because stations needed a government license, ANPA Committee on Radio chairman E. H. Harris sent a telegram to the Standing Committee of Correspondents: "The radio, under its present control, operating under government license which is issued by a partisan board, is not a free institution. Official recognition of radio broadcasting as a medium of disseminating news would be an official sanction of the censorship of news. If proof of the above statement is necessary, we will have our attorney appear before the committee with formal protest."[34] Papers feared radio would be on an even footing with print if it entered "their" press gallery,[35] and Harris's telegram reflects not only this animosity toward radio news coverage but also the hostility of much of the newspaper industry toward the Roosevelt administration. In great part, the largely Republican-owned newspapers feared Roosevelt's power during these early months of his administration and saw radio, which Roosevelt effectively used to circumvent the papers in reaching the public, as part of his power base.[36]

Henry Bellows argued that the CBS news service was a "news association" as defined in congressional rules because over ninety stations associated with CBS received the service. Bellows conceded that rules might bar individual radio broadcasters but should not bar correspondents of the newly formed radio news service from reporting on congressional proceedings.[37]

This sentiment against radio's news coverage received a further blow when the AP won an appeal in the Ninth Circuit Court against a radio station in Bellingham, Washington, that had been pirating its news reports. Judge William Denman declared that taking news gathered by the Associated Press and broadcasting it without prior permission in commercial programs constituted unfair competition. The opinion connected First Amendment rights of freedom of press with protection of the business aspects of gathering and disseminating news. The court noted that "the public function in the gathering and dissemination of news is presumed by the Constitution to be in private hands." Under the American capitalistic system, this meant "that news distribution as a public function will be in large part by businessmen acting under the inducement of the profit motive." Recipients of news—the public—had a self-interest in protecting the news-gathering business from a misappropriation of news.[38]

The Press-Radio War

Such battles continued over news presentation, and finally a committee of publishers, radio networks, press associations, and broadcast associations announced a ten-point plan under which newspapers would supply news bulletins through press associations to radio stations. Because representatives met in New York City's Biltmore Hotel in December 1933, the accord became known as the Biltmore Agreement. The informal, two-day conference featured representatives of three major press associations, two national broadcasting chains, the National Association of Broadcasters, and the ANPA Committee on Radio. They agreed to limit radio's dissemination of news as of March 1, 1934.[39]

The agreement allowed news broadcasts only twice a day, for five minutes in the morning and five minutes in the evening, after newspapers had been published. A committee controlled editorial procedures and supervised the Press-Radio Bureau furnishing radio broadcasters with specially written daily news broadcasts consisting of stories of thirty words or less. Occasional news bulletins of transcendent importance were also furnished. Most importantly, broadcasts could not be sold for commercial purposes, and broadcasters would pay all bureau expenses. Decisions about publishing radio program listings were left to individual publishers.[40]

In accordance with the plan, NBC and CBS announced they would discontinue spot news broadcasts on March 1 and would carry the bureau's daily news accounts. News would come via AT&T teletype machines and would consist of two five-minute reports, one for air no earlier than 9:30 A.M. and the other no earlier than 9:00 P.M. local time. Each report would comprise about six hundred words, which had to be aired in full and without comment. From then on, radio commentators would have to keep their broadcasts to "background material," not current news. James Barrett, former city editor of the *New York American,* was appointed head of the bureau.[41] The plan ostensibly was designed to give the stations and listeners "the benefit of careful résumés of the day's events and at the same time to protect newspapers from the unauthorized use of their news" and did not affect use of local news by individual stations.[42]

The Press-Radio Bureau began operating in March 1934. The first day, twenty-six items were provided, and they varied from reports on the Roosevelt administration to the postponement of the Carnera-Loughran prize fight.[43] The ANPA discussed its operation a month later at its annual meeting. Its radio committee urged continuation of the bureau as it served the public through its broadcast of news items while it protected newspaper property rights to news items and prevented broadcast news advertising. The ANPA also hoped that reliable bulletins would contribute to increased readership.[44] While bureau policies hampered radio, news broadcasting could not be so easily limited.

A few months into the agreement, Senator Clarence Dill called for stations to form their own news-gathering agencies—which stations soon did—if press associations failed to supply stations with more up-to-the-minute news. He declared the Biltmore Agreement a failure as radio stations should be "just as free to broadcast any and all news as newspapers are to print any and all news." Operating their own agencies would give broadcasters editorial control and serve the public. ANPA radio committee chairman E. H. Harris criticized Dill's suggestion as "a bid for public support of a potential semi-official government news agency, similar to the ones existing in certain European countries," alluding to Germany and Italy. With broadcasters receiving the cream of news, he said, "Senator Dill's proposal can only be interpreted as an attempt to build a news-gathering organization that will be under the direction of agencies licensed by the government," adding that "when the chairman of the Senate committee, that wrote the Communications Bill and recommended its passage to Congress, advocates the organization of a national news gathering organization, under government license, he in effect is proposing a potential censorship of radio news and the building of a news machine for propaganda purposes."[45]

To Harris, newspapers and existing news-gathering organizations faced no such government supervision, license, or restriction, and consequently, no government censorship or control existed over newspapers. Harris contended that if broadcasters did as Dill suggested, free and uncensored press agencies could be destroyed or hampered. He predicted then that the decline of democracy would soon follow.[46] Senator Thomas Schall of Minnesota agreed with Harris and sent a telegram to Roosevelt, asking that the president denounce Dill's proposal. Schall called the proposal for radio to set up its own news-gathering agencies an "attempt to destroy our press services and in their stead create a government-sponsored press agency."[47] Again, these actions masked concerns over advertising and fear of the Roosevelt administration.

In 1935, the ANPA Committee on Radio hid its concerns over radio's siphoning of advertising revenue from newspapers and reported publicly that the focal point of the press-radio relationship was the property right of the newspapers to the news they or the press associations had gathered. Protection of those rights was paramount, and the Press-Radio Bureau was to coordinate and preserve these rights in news broadcasting. The committee also noted that the main issue between broadcasters and newspapers was the commercial sponsorship of news. The ANPA argued such sponsorship could permit advertisers to censor or edit news and that such "news" would degenerate into propaganda for the advertiser, representing only the advertiser's views and opinions.[48]

When radio challenged the Press-Radio Bureau, the confrontation rested on anti-monopoly practices, not free press grounds. Transradio Press Service, a large consortium of stations that served more stations than the Press-Radio Bureau in early 1935, filed a million-dollar suit against the ANPA, AP, UP, INS, CBS, NBC, E. H. Harris of the ANPA radio committee, and ten other individuals for violation of restraint on trade provisions in the Sherman and Clayton Anti-Trust Acts and the Communications Act. Transradio alleged that these companies and individuals had destroyed its ability to sell its news services. The ANPA denied the allegations and said it was defending the property rights of the newspapers to news stories they published. The suit ultimately died, and Transradio received no compensation.[49]

Meanwhile, other press and radio organizations took up the call for changes in or abandonment of the Press-Radio Bureau. Newspapers that owned stations, as well as the United Press and International News Service, began to oppose strict adherence to the bureau's directives, and in May 1935, the UP and INS offered radio stations news services. Newspapers began to increase their ownership of stations, and from the bureau's beginnings in 1934 to its end in 1938, newspaper ownership grew from 100 stations to 211. The UP and INS found ready customers in these stations. In addition, stations and networks expanded or began their own news-gathering operations as war loomed in Europe and the Far East. By

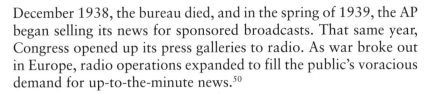

December 1938, the bureau died, and in the spring of 1939, the AP began selling its news for sponsored broadcasts. That same year, Congress opened up its press galleries to radio. As war broke out in Europe, radio operations expanded to fill the public's voracious demand for up-to-the-minute news.[50]

Conclusion

The rivalry of print and radio over radio's dissemination of information intertwined both public interest and free speech issues. In efforts to control radio's access to information, newspapers charged radio with irresponsible news-gathering that was contrary to the public interest. Newspapers also accused radio of not being a "free institution" as stations had to operate under government licenses issued by what they perceived as a biased board. To recognize radio news would be to accept officially sanctioned news, they argued. In the Press-Radio War that ensued in the 1930s, newspapers said their plan gave stations and their listeners carefully crafted, accurate accounts of the day's events. It also acted to protect newspapers from what they considered unauthorized use or piracy of their news. The arrangement did not last long.

As radio matured during the early 1930s, concerns evolved over which medium was the proper protector of freedom of expression. Newspaper publishers argued they were, while the upstart radio operators insisted they, too, could advance First Amendment freedoms in bringing the public news and information. Arguments focused largely on property rights in news dissemination and the licensing of stations by a government agency as an inhibition to dissemination of uncensored news. Underlying these arguments, however, were publishers' concerns over the exodus of advertising dollars from print to broadcast, not the advancement of freedom of expression. In facing declining revenues, some publishers were willing to constrict radio's freedom of expression through controls on its ability to disseminate news. These restrictions did not work, and as the later 1930s brought increasing desires on the part of the American public for news from unsettled regions of the world, especially Europe, restrictions on radio as a news-gathering institution died.

11 ➯ "ROGUE" STATIONS AND CONTROVERSIAL ISSUES OF PUBLIC IMPORTANCE: PROTECTING NONCONFORMIST SPEECH

While newspapers sought to protect what they perceived as their lawful prerogative to disseminate news and information from interlopers encroaching upon their territory, radio owners sought to control dissemination of material they deemed too radical or un-American. This desire for control found unparalleled support in the Federal Radio Commission. The FRC's power to compare station requests for the same wavelength was nowhere more evident than in its decisions regarding applications for frequencies operated by groups espousing unpopular minority viewpoints, especially WEVD, operated by the Socialist party in honor of Eugene V. Debs, and WCFL, operated by the Chicago Federation of Labor. From their inception through the early 1930s, both stations suffered with low-power assignments, had limited operational hours, and had to fend off commercial operations coveting their frequencies.[1]

Often, these stations were the only outlets commonly open for dissemination of disdained views on subjects such as socialism, economic reform, and birth control. Attempts at silencing them and others were not without consequences, however. Through the ACLU's efforts, bills were introduced in Congress to amend Section 18 of the Radio Act, which afforded political candidates protections, to guarantee additional nondiscrimination for supporters of political candidates and to maintain unbiased coverage of controversial issues of public importance. This chapter focuses on both the stations' efforts as outlets for dissenting opinions and attempts to pass legislation protecting coverage of differing views. With these attempts, definitions of "freedom of the air" and "public interest" on radio took on further attributes emphasizing non-mainstream ideas and opinions and enhancing First Amendment rights.

WEVD Versus the FRC

WEVD began operation after the FRC approved the purchase of WSOM in the summer of 1927. The station's inaugural broadcast was October 20, 1927, the first anniversary of the death of Eugene V. Debs, renowned Socialist and reformer. Station announcements emphasized WEVD's devotion to freedom of speech, stating its policy of no censorship over programming, except to prevent obscene, indecent, or profane broadcasts. WEVD would open its doors to groups and individuals with whom station managers did not agree, such as the American Legion. Views on religion as divergent as those held by the American Association for the Advancement of Atheism and mainstream religious groups would be heard. As a small operation, the station faced nearly insurmountable odds in achieving its goals. It transmitted with only 500 watts and had to share its wavelength at one time with eleven other stations. As a nonconformist station, WEVD was nearly forced off the air several times by the FRC.[2]

As with all stations, the FRC asked WEVD to justify its existence in its general orders in 1928 and 1929. The station's license was renewed, but by July 1930 WEVD was again required to show cause why its license should be continued, and hearings were scheduled for October 14 before FRC examiner Elmer Pratt. Pratt reviewed WEVD's operation from April 17 to October 8, 1930, and found that the station deviated from its assigned frequency, failed to disclose phonograph record usage, announced its call letters improperly, employed an engineer whose license had expired, and operated an unlicensed transmitter. Station management explained their technical difficulties and successfully refuted allegations that the transmitter was unlicensed and that they employed unlicensed personnel. They claimed poverty as the main reason for their shortcomings and added that violations were due to imperfections in equipment or unintentional negligence. Equipment and personnel were expensive, but as soon as WEVD learned of its technical problems, they were corrected. According to prominent Socialist and perennial presidential candidate Norman Thomas, the real investigation of WEVD focused on the station's exercise of "freedom of the air," as WEVD offered unique service to labor and other minorities ignored by mainstream stations.[3]

Even with these explanations, Pratt ordered the station to close October 31, 1930, but over Pratt's objections, the FRC gave WEVD a ninety-day extension. When the extension ended, the threat of license revocation reemerged, and Pratt conducted another investigation. Again, he found the station's operation wanting. WEVD appealed to the FRC and approached others for financial and moral support in maintaining the station. To its benefactors, WEVD presented the FRC's efforts as attempts to throttle and hamstring the station's presentation of more liberal, progressive opinions. Press releases noted loss of the station would be an irreparable blow to an open-minded free speech forum.[4]

WEVD also formed a national committee to fight nonrenewal,[5] and the committee hired Louis Caldwell, former FRC general counsel, to represent the station. Caldwell filed exceptions to each of Pratt's charges and showed how the commission reversed Pratt's license renewal decisions in at least ten other situations for violations similar to WEVD's.[6] In addition, other stations, especially large network-owned-and-operated stations, were not cited for violations similar to WEVD's. During the January 1931 hearing, Caldwell observed that Pratt's unfavorable recommendations reflected a predisposed negative attitude toward WEVD.[7]

Caldwell asserted that Pratt had applied unduly rigid interpretations to the station identification requirement to broadcast call letters every fifteen minutes. FRC regulations allowed "natural breaks" to be used for announcements, not rigid fifteen-minute intervals, and many of WEVD's citations were for instances when interruption would have needlessly annoyed the public, such as during musical and poetry recitals. Key network stations regularly allowed more than fifteen minutes to elapse without station identification. If the commission held one station strictly to the standard, all should be so held or the commission needed to discern why such discrimination was made.[8]

Further, WEVD's departure from its assigned frequency, Caldwell stated, resulted only from broken crystals in transmitters. When functioning properly, the station did not deviate. Likewise, station use of phonograph records was announced, but not in a fashion suiting Pratt. At times, WEVD announced both sides of a record at one time instead of individually. During initial hearings before Pratt, the station had to produce a certified copy of a memo showing that FRC rules allowed both sides of a record to be announced together. In other instances, material had been broadcast "live," not recorded as Pratt had concluded.[9]

Caldwell also explained charges of alleged use of unlicensed equipment and employment of unlicensed personnel. Testing improvements in equipment as authorized by the FRC and employment of a licensed first-class amateur operator were legal under FRC rules at the time of the alleged offenses. Only after May 1931, when the FRC adopted rules making amateur licenses illegal in broadcast station operations, were such activities prohibited. Caldwell reminded the commission that "time and time again you have renewed station licenses in the face of admissions, or of conclusive evidence, of violations of the same character as those charged against my client."[10]

He then noted Pratt's favorable summary of the variety of speakers aired and subjects covered during WEVD's broadcasts. Pratt wrote that these programs bolstered station claims of advancing "the cause of free speech and free discussion of matters of public interest and importance—in other words, to serve as an open forum free from censorship or discrimination."[11] Usually over two dozen educational, informative programs aired each week, more than any other part-time station, but even with this commendatory finding, Pratt concluded that no need existed for WEVD as other stations could provide the same service. As for financial backing, Caldwell outlined the contributions, actual and pledged, to the station and the number of reputable organizations underwriting WEVD's endeavors. He asserted that the station was not on the fiscal rocks.[12]

Caldwell concluded that two reasons existed for license renewal. First, "WEVD is giving practical application to the time-honored principle which forms part of the groundwork of our civilization—freedom of speech, and of the press" in allowing airtime to speakers on all sides of matters of public interest. Caldwell contended that this policy influenced other stations and the press in setting higher standards for themselves in accepting or rejecting viewpoints, for "they know that when they reject a speaker or a writer who desires to address the public, that speaker or writer may go to WEVD to get an audience." Second, WEVD was a monument to Eugene V. Debs, whose followers chose to honor him with construction of a radio station instead of a marble monument. Caldwell begged the commission "to think carefully before you lay destroying hands on this monument."[13]

The FRC scrutinized reports on WEVD closely and found that no violations had really occurred after mid-1930. The commission also noted that programs carried in late 1930 through 1931 were diversified and of interest to the public. During the last quarter of 1930, WEVD carried over 125 different organizations and aired between four thousand and five thousand speeches on a wide range of topics. As for technical violations, the commission concluded that most resulted from carelessness of station employees, who had been dismissed or restricted in operational influence. Current employees were "competent and adequate to insure the proper future operation of the station." Planned equipment updates also would aid in compliance with commission engineering standards.[14]

Because these changes had been made, the commission voted three to two to renew WEVD's license, with chairman Charles Saltzman and commissioner W. D. L. Starbuck dissenting. Saltzman believed WEVD had committed numerous violations and was so poorly managed with scant financial resources that renewal was unwarranted. Starbuck concurred and added that simply being a minority did not entitle one to rights. "A minority is not a thing apart and entitled to preferential treatment as a right," he noted. Minorities could not claim privileges if they abused them, which Starbuck believed WEVD did.[15]

On January 13, 1931, the FRC granted renewal, but in an unprecedented move, the commission reversed itself on the initial order within three days and voted to reconsider its previous decision. WEVD suspected pressure from a commercial broadcaster, because the FRC had also set a hearing for an application from commercial station WFOX, operated by Paramount Broadcasting Corporation of Brooklyn, for a change in frequency and operation to those used by WEVD.[16] WFOX shared time with three other stations and operated about twenty-seven hours per week. The station's owners wanted to expand their broadcast day because, they said, WFOX was unable to meet demands of commercial advertisers and charitable and civic organizations wanting time. To do so, the station's management said they needed WEVD's assigned hours.[17] G. August Gerber, managing director of WEVD, chided the commissioners for their decision to reconsider WEVD's renewal, which he claimed endangered all station licenses and neglected to follow the FRC's own rules. He also likened the action to Star Chamber proceedings.[18] Hearings were held in April 1931 to determine if the public interest would be served by forfeiture of WEVD's facilities in granting WFOX's application.[19]

After these hearings, FRC examiner Elmer Pratt ruled in favor of WFOX. He noted that WFOX operated on a commercially successful basis, had well-trained, efficient personnel, maintained excellent studio and transmitter facilities, had rendered good program and community service, and had sufficient talent available to increase live program offerings. He added that Brooklyn needed the public service programs provided by WFOX, especially to help Brooklyn's unemployed. Reviving charges that WEVD frequently used phonograph records, had less efficient studio and transmitting equipment, and was careless and negligent in its station operations, Pratt recommended WFOX's modification be granted.[20]

Naturally, WEVD challenged the report and again retained Louis Caldwell. In filing the station's exemptions, Caldwell stated that Pratt had erred in ruling WFOX was superior to WEVD. He listed Pratt's misinterpretation of station staffing, misunderstanding of equipment and facilities, misconceptions of financial issues, and flawed description of WFOX's programming. Regarding the latter, Caldwell showed that a number of programs WFOX listed as "charitable public service" were really commercial and paid for by the organizations involved. He noted that WEVD's signal was superior to WFOX's since installation of new equipment in October 1930. WFOX had also been guilty of using unlicensed equipment and playing phonograph records as well as carrying charitable and civic organizations' programming on a regular basis only if those programs were paid for. Caldwell asked for oral argument before the FRC on these exemptions.[21]

Instead of granting the oral argument, the commission scheduled further hearings a few months later. As the review continued, editorials appeared favoring WEVD and applying pressure for the station's continuance. For instance, a *Christian Century* editorial told its readers to watch the FRC's decision closely: "If it [WEVD] is taken off the air, and its license turned over to a station of the type recommended by the examiner, that can be taken as evidence that the radio commission is against the future development of non-commercial, minority group broadcasting."[22]

NBC officials also supported WEVD's continuation. In early January, NBC president Merlin Aylesworth told the ACLU's Morris Ernst in private that he was interested in WEVD's welfare, and NBC vice president John Elwood agreed to attend a private conference on WEVD's continuance.[23] Aylesworth and Elwood supported WEVD as an outlet for viewpoints that might raise the ire of advertisers and audience members alike, and neither man wanted such vexatious views carried on NBC's networks. Supporting WEVD behind the scenes tacitly protected the networks from pressure to carry more radical or unconventional programming. In addition, WEVD offered little commercial competition with the network.

The meeting with WEVD officials was finally held at Hotel Belvedere, the site of WEVD's studios, on May 11, 1931. Its purpose was to devise a plan for the station's ownership and operation by "responsible agencies" of the labor, liberal, and Socialist movements of New York.[24] The committee's report concluded that four major areas of operation had to be considered for station reorganization. First, the station had to be moved to a better locale and needed adequate equipment installed so listeners within a radius of one hundred miles could hear the broadcasts. Second, funds needed for operation, about $50,000, would be raised through sale of stock in the station. Third, a corporation and membership association needed to be formed to plan policies and programs for support of the station's work. Last of all, WEVD was to be maintained as "a radical university of the air" with daily educational programs, including a newspaper of the air and educational courses sponsored by different groups. In addition, a programming committee would carefully supervise advertising material in its attempt to offer programs having unique educational value. WEVD improved its equipment and staff, and the FRC gave it the summer to improve its programs, with additional hearings to be held September 9.[25]

While these hearings emphasized WEVD's reorganization and modifications made to overcome criticism of its operation, the FRC again voted in the same three-to-two split that WEVD retain its license. The majority noted the public service WEVD performed and its diversified programming. With equipment improvements and elimination of other problems, three commissioners believed WEVD would continue to serve the public interest. Saltzman and Starbuck again dissented. Both believed WFOX's license should be modified as requested and WEVD closed for repeated violations of FRC mandates. To them, WFOX would provide superior programming and operate far more efficiently than WEVD. Starbuck quoted his earlier dissent to WEVD's license renewal where WEVD successfully argued its case about silencing a minority viewpoint: "A minority is not a thing apart and entitled to preferential treatment as a right. A minority has a proper place and being but its existence cannot justifiably be made an excuse to abuse the privileges granted to it by the government under which it exists."[26] With this renewal, WEVD's existence finally seemed assured. Ironically, by 1935 the station had become more mainstream as an NBC network affiliate and a member of the National Association of Broadcasters.

WCFL Versus the FRC

WCFL also encountered problems with FRC rulings. Operated by the Chicago Federation of Labor, WCFL considered itself the voice of labor throughout the country. The station shared time on 970 kilocycles with KJR in Seattle, and the time-split did not allow WCFL to broadcast at night. In early 1929, it applied for a full clear channel, 50 kilowatts of power, and the right to rebroadcast its signal nationwide over small stations. Hearings were held on the request for higher power, a better frequency, and full-time status; the commission granted a construction permit for 50 kilowatts but denied the station the right to rebroadcast.[27]

The channel WCFL requested was 720 kc, then assigned to WGN, owned by the *Chicago Tribune*. The radio examiner for the Chicago area, Ellis Yost, suggested that WGN be assigned a temporary license. Naturally, WGN and the *Tribune* complained that any change would negatively affect WGN's listeners. WGN's counsel argued that WCFL had not operated in the public interest, especially because it used phonograph records and ran excessive advertising and other matters that should not be permitted into the home. The *Tribune* also protested Yost's failure to define WCFL as operating solely as the mouthpiece of labor and therefore as operating for private interests and not in the public interest.[28] When the

FRC took no action, WCFL applied for a clear channel in 1930, but by then it appeared that the FRC wanted to eliminate the station for carrying inferior programs and propaganda, failing to name sponsors of ads, and competing for the assignment with stations having prior claims to the frequency.[29]

Throughout these hearings, several powerful U.S. senators backed WCFL and promised further assistance in establishing a station reflecting labor interests,[30] so when WCFL again requested a clear channel in March 1931, it argued vociferously for legislation assigning one clear channel frequency to "recognized labor organizations which in the opinion of the Commission are most representative of the labor interests in the United States." Such a resolution passed the Senate unanimously. WCFL's Edward Nockels criticized what he termed "the radio trust" and continued his condemnation of efforts to silence the voice of labor. Of particular concern was FRC General Order No. 40, which prohibited station changes in frequencies and other rights to use the airwaves without FRC approval. Nockels believed this order established and perpetuated vested property rights in airwave assignments. He praised the Glenn Amendment, introduced in February by Republican senator Otis Glenn of Illinois, that would give organized labor a clear channel.[31]

Nockels decried an American Bar Association pronouncement against the amendment and stated that the report's author, ABA radio committee chairman Louis Caldwell, was advocating the position of his undisclosed client, WGN, which held a clear channel. The report had concluded: "There is not room in the broadcast band for every school of thought, religious, political, social and economic, each to have its separate broadcasting station, its mouthpiece in the ether. If franchises are extended to some, it gives them an unfair advantage over others, and results in a corresponding cutting down of general public service stations. It favors the interests and desires of a portion of the listening public at the expense of the rest."[32] Nockels called denial of a clear channel to labor on these grounds "a public display of grossest prejudice, and 100 percent un-American." He condemned the action as an attempt to serve someone other than the ABA,[33] strongly hinting that WGN might be behind the report.

Senator H. D. Hatfield of West Virginia introduced another bill granting labor a clear channel with unlimited operational time at maximum power, and hearings were held in Washington on March 15, 1932. WCFL representative Edward Nockels again charged the FRC with prejudice in favor of a "radio trust" in frequency allocation that ignored labor's needs,[34] and FRC actions seemed to bear out his allegations. When WCFL made its first request for increased power and time and a clear channel, the FRC had licensed a station to the Insull public utility interests, which had acquired a semi-moribund station. The Insull station was immediately assigned a clear channel, and by 1931 it was affiliated with NBC.[35]

At the hearings, the formidable NAB opposed clear channel use by labor and told a Senate subcommittee in March 1932 that Hatfield's bill authorizing the FRC to grant a clear channel to labor was not in the interest of broadcasting. NAB president Harry Shaw stated that under the proposed measure, the FRC could not police the station as labor would virtually own the frequency. "The bill would grant a vested right to labor forever," he noted. In defending itself before the committee, the commission noted, "There are numerous groups of the general public which might similarly demand the exclusive use of a frequency for their benefit." The FRC warned, "[C]lassification could be carried on until more groups than frequencies would be found. Since there is only a limited number of available frequencies for broadcasting, this Commission is of the opinion that there is no place for a station catering to any group, but all stations should cater to the general public and serve public interest as against group or class interest." Even granting WCFL maximum power of 50,000 watts on a clear channel would enable it to reach only a small percentage of laborers. FRC spokespersons indicated that the station would be able to serve listeners only within a two-hundred-mile radius on a consistent basis.[36] The station did not receive the channel or the increase in power, and its problems continued through passage of the Communications Act of 1934.[37]

Alluding to the WEVD and WCFL decisions in a 1932 review of communications law, the ABA assailed the FRC's procedural inconsistency. Its report stated that "formal regulations are strictly enforced in some cases and completely ignored in others." As for hearings, the report noted that out of over two hundred cases during the last year, the commission sat in only five hearings and allowed oral arguments in only eight, although many more stations requested that privilege. The report also complained that station owners had to come long distances at their great inconvenience and expense.[38] While the ABA complained of this capriciousness, the FRC did little to correct it.

Instead, stations presenting nonconformist views were targeted for closer review than stations carrying more mainstream programming. During the early 1930s, stations such as WEVD and WCFL had to monitor themselves carefully, or they would lose the ability to broadcast and the diversity of ownership and opinion would diminish. In addition, much like KTNT, KFKB, and KGEF, these stations were easier targets than larger commercial operations. But, unlike KTNT, KFKB, and KGEF, WEVD and WCFL had sizable backing by recognized industry and political constituencies. Consequently, they were able to mount successful campaigns to keep their licenses. Their experiences, though, led the ACLU and others to undertake an important—but ultimately unsuccessful—crusade in the early 1930s for inclusion of amendments to the Radio Act to balance coverage of controversial issues and to provide outlets for speakers espousing unorthodox views.

Expanding Political Discussion

In all, by mid-1930 two legislative measures of major importance and a half dozen or so minor bills affecting radio failed to be enacted, while two others passed both houses and became law. The measures passed by the 71st Congress included those indefinitely extending the life of the Federal Radio Commission and amending provisions of the radio law relating to court procedure. The first bill became law on December 18, 1929, and Hoover signed the second into law on July 1, 1930.[39] While these laws did not revise the communications law overall, they set the stage for passage of the Communications Act of 1934.

As those revisions were made, licensing and station censorship of programming and speakers formed a significant part of the discussions. Leading discussions promoting diversity of both ownership and viewpoint presentation were the ACLU and its offspring, the National Council on Freedom from Censorship. Formed the spring of 1931, the National Council on Freedom from Censorship focused on all forms of media censorship, including broadcasting. Two of its goals were preventing station censorship of speakers and programs and curbing FRC censorship through control of licenses. Council members believed both goals could be achieved through changes in the law limiting interpretation of "public interest, convenience, or necessity" (PICON) to technical matters and allowing speakers on controversial issues of public importance access to radio. As revisions to the Radio Act were proposed, Roger Baldwin of the ACLU's board of directors wrote Senator Clarence Dill about adding an amendment to prevent censorship and suggesting the ACLU's Morris Ernst as an aide in drafting legislation. Ernst and Dill conferred in early 1932, and Ernst began drafting language for an amendment to Section 18.[40]

In late February 1932, Gordon Moss, secretary of the ACLU, forwarded a review draft of what would become the controversial issues–PICON definition amendment to Bethuel Webster, former FRC general counsel. This amendment stated, first, that interpretations of PICON would be limited to technical and mechanical factors involved in obtaining efficient radio broadcasting, except for violations of profanity and defamation. When profanity and libel charges were made, radio would be held accountable in the same way print was.[41] Second, because the council's study revealed that nearly all charges of censorship arose from station refusal to broadcast all sides of public questions, the council's draft put controversial issues on the same basis for treatment as candidates for public office. It also extended equal opportunities to candidates' supporters. The amendment gave radio the same immunities and responsibilities as print in matters of public issues, and the draft was included in the Senate Commerce Committee report on the radio bill.[42]

The bill's specific language added that broadcast stations affording use of broadcast facilities to "any person who is an exponent or advocate of one side of a controversial social or public issue" had to offer equal opportunity "to opposing exponents or advocates of such issues."[43] The council believed stations had a right to abstain completely from covering public questions, but when they did air such debates, all sides deserved to be heard. Powerful members of Congress, including Senators Dill and Robert Wagner, supported the measure, and it was adopted by the Senate committee.[44] Other legislators, fearing that the phrase "social or public issue" was too vague and ill-defined, modified it to state equal opportunities be afforded public questions up for a vote. To expand issues covered by the amendment, the National Council on Freedom from Censorship wanted further changes to include questions to be voted upon by any legislative body.[45]

Council members rationalized that, if equal opportunities were limited to candidates, campaign issues, and a few questions the public would vote upon directly, extensive one-sided propaganda on other important questions was possible. Scarcity of spectrum that limited numbers of radio stations sustained this argument. "This franchise," the National Council on Freedom from Censorship argued, "should not be used to achieve the selfish political ends of station owners or their friends." The council recognized that some limitations were needed or issue advocates would besiege stations, so their proposal limited issues to subjects of legislation. Until bills on the topic were introduced, a station could editorialize as one-sidedly as it wished. "The instant such a subject has been introduced, however, it becomes a controversial public question of importance, and deserves the right to impartial discussion if it is to be discussed at all," the council concluded.[46]

The council reasoned that radio coverage of issues differed from newspaper analysis. A newspaper could have an official political bias because "it is essentially a *news*paper, and *must* deal largely with public questions. It depends on wide, intelligent, and impartial coverage of *news facts* to sustain the circulation on which its profitable advertising rates are based. This economic factor, and the presence of an unlimited potential field of competition, is sufficient to insure the public against too one-sided information concerning public questions" (emphasis in original).[47]

Radio, on the other hand, received a government franchise and was not required legally or economically to disseminate information of a public character. Radio could be maintained solely by entertainment programming or other material not covered in the amendment, and its effective competition was limited to other licensed stations crowding onto eighty-nine wavelengths. "With no economic or competitive pressure driving stations to the discussion of public questions, and with no legal obligation to treat such matters impartially, *there is absolutely nothing to prevent a radio station from using its government franchise to further the selfish political ends of itself or its friends*" (emphasis in original). Radio either had to stay out of public questions or had to give equal opportunity to all sides of controversial issues. The council concluded broadcasters "cannot be permitted to freely use the tremendous power of a limited government commodity as an instrument of one-sided propaganda on important public questions."[48]

Council members worried that new provisions would tempt stations to avoid all discussion of controversial issues or evade the intent of the law by charging impossibly high rates that minority issue groups could not pay.[49] These issues, though, were not as important to broadcasters and Congress as clarifying license revocation procedures, restricting foreign ownership of stations, and narrowing procedural policies of hearing examiners reporting to the FRC.[50]

Throughout December 1932 and early 1933, the ACLU and the National Council on Freedom from Censorship fought a continuing battle for inclusion of an amendment allowing supporters of candidates and exponents of any side of a public question on the air, but by then Senator Dill had had second thoughts on the measure. Dill stated confidentially to council members that neither the Senate committee nor radio operators wanted to throw the medium open to controversial issues for fear of what might happen, noting that radio stations would confine themselves entirely to entertainment, if the proposal were adopted. Consequently, he could not back the amendment.[51] At the height of the Depression, fears that radio might cause societal disruption underlay Dill's apprehensions. He and other senators were all too familiar with demagogues who reached vast audiences with their messages, and extending radio's use to coverage of controversial issues was perceived as too volatile in times of social unrest.

To say the ACLU and the National Council on Freedom from Censorship were disappointed in Dill's reaction is an understatement. Bethuel Webster wrote Dill to protest. He argued that because broadcasters used public grants of the airwaves, amendments guaranteeing nondiscrimination in coverage of controversial issues were reasonable. Nor did he believe an enacted proposal would stifle or discourage broadcasting's coverage of controversial issues. Webster noted he had counseled stations to allow all sides on the air, and "it is the experience of such stations that that policy gives them a freedom and independence and prestige that they would not otherwise possess." When pressured from special interest groups, Webster stated the stations could insist upon impartiality.[52] Throughout the month of December 1932, committees for both groups corresponded with Dill in attempts to change his mind,[53] but when he did not, the ACLU turned to Representative Ewin Davis and Senator James Couzens for help in getting the amendment passed.[54]

Davis had long sought ways to promote diversity of opinion, while Couzens had been defeated in the 1932 election and was eager to leave his mark on communication legislation before leaving office in March 1933. Both men promoted the expanded equal opportunities provision, and when a new report came out on communication law revisions on January 10, 1933, the Senate had revised the equal opportunity law to include "presentation of views on any side of a public question to be voted upon at an election" and added the phrasing "or to be decided by a governmental agency."[55] ACLU members were thrilled and became more enthusiastic as the House broadened Section 18 to ensure equitable presentation of views on public questions and to mandate equality of treatment among candidates for public office, including protection for their supporters.[56] The House struck governmental agencies from its measure and added a new sentence: "Furthermore, it shall be considered in the public interest for a licensee, so far as possible, to permit equal opportunity for the presentation of both sides of public questions."[57]

On February 26, 1933, after the conference ironed out wording differences, the House voted unanimously to accept the conference report on H.R. 7716, and Senate passage came within a week. With passage of a bill including equal opportunity extensions to presentation of public questions, supporters rejoiced, but their celebration was short-lived. Because President Hoover believed many bills passed in the waning days of his administration increased government expenditures, he pocket vetoed many new laws passed by the lame-duck Congress, including the Radio Act of 1932. The opportunity to expand free speech protections of Section 18 was now gone, even though, when the new Congress reconvened, it wasted no time in reintroducing bills expanding provisions on equitable treatment of speakers on all sides of public questions in the equal opportunities provisions. Promoters of communication legislation, including Dill and Davis, recognized that communication issues would be neglected in favor of legislation offering emergency relief from the Depression.[58] The moment for fundamental change in Section 18 or its successor had passed.

As the new administration took over, many wondered how Roosevelt would ultimately approach radio. He had already proposed creation of a Federal Communications and Power Commission to combine the FRC and Federal Power Commissions with the Interstate Commerce Commission's supervision of interstate communications.[59] Of more concern to broadcasters, however, was apprehension over presidential power under the Radio Act, which permitted presidential jurisdiction over radio in times of war or national emergency. In February 1933, Morris Ernst told ACLU members that he would not be surprised if Franklin Roosevelt exercised his presidential powers to assume control over radio in time of war or national emergency because "the country is in a state of fear, and we are very close to the strict censorship prompted by the last war."[60]

While Roosevelt did not take over radio, fears of administration intervention did lead to broadcaster censorship of speeches critical of administration policies. On March 8, a few days after FDR's inauguration, NBC station WGY in Schenectady, New York, barred Devere Allen of the *World Tomorrow*, a radical publication. His speech's offending passages stated that nations had more men under arms than in 1913, and in spite of worldwide poverty, global armaments cost nearly $5 billion each year. Growing harmony among nations did not exist; instead, "aggravated tensions, augmented fears, and the development of new enginery [*sic*] of destruction" flourished in postwar years. Allen decried economic war that led to the masses seeking guidance elsewhere for relief from the Depression, concluding: "[I]f there are those who still hold hopefully to the ordinary, time-tried methods of capitalist business and finance, let me remind them that we have had a significant depression in this country, since the Civil War, on the average of once every seven years. What is the promise of a system which, at best, can only bring us out the crisis and keep us out just long enough to catch a deep breath before we go down again?"[61]

NBC earmarked these sections and asked Allen to drop them. He refused, and NBC banned his speech as undermining "faith and confidence" in ongoing economic recovery efforts. When Allen tried to get newspapers in WGY's broadcast area to print the speech, they refused, and one declared that WGY should be treated as if it were "a fellow-journal, and that therefore to criticize it or play up its censorship would be a violation of journalistic ethics." The *World Tomorrow*'s editors concluded that in the Depression, Americans had learned a great deal about capitalism's ineptitude and misrule and surmised that as the reason airwaves were increasingly closed to those "who, for unselfish reasons of loyalty to the masses, want them to know the truth that alone can set them free."[62]

A few weeks after the Allen episode, FRC commissioner Harold LaFount wrote both the ACLU and the National Council on Freedom from Censorship for information about past FRC censorship. Both organizations reiterated WEVD's difficulties and Reverend Robert Shuler's inability to get license renewal, and both deplored "censorship" policies "which permit the channels of expression over radio to be loaded with advertisement as distinguished from controversy, propaganda, or education. . . . Private ownership of these channels of communication itself gives rights to individual censorship in each station."[63] As remedy for these problems and to promote balance, the organizations championed FRC rules affecting access, government ownership of stations, and laws designed to present all sides of controversial issues.[64]

While the ACLU wanted the controversial issues amendment reinstated in any new communications bill, some of its officers began to doubt passage of any measure that would promote or encourage discussion in the face of FRC inaction. Stations fearing loss of their licenses prohibited speakers who criticized government policies. Some even prohibited critiques of foreign government actions. Complaints about such censorship fell on deaf ears, according to the ACLU, because the FRC lacked an interest in advocating free speech. The few stations voicing critical or radical views were constantly in danger of going out of business, while station managers at larger stations engaged in censorship "with an eye to protecting the status quo."[65] Complaints to the FRC and these larger stations were met with apathy and indifference, and the ACLU believed the overall picture was bleak for freedom of the air. At a minimum, the ACLU wanted an amendment mandating access to broadcast facilities for all sides of controversial issues and changes in libel laws as related to radio so stations could not be held liable in discussions decreed by law.[66] It got neither, as Congress investigated radio and drafted new communication laws.

In October 1933, Roger Baldwin wrote a colleague that the ACLU would cooperate with any efforts to review and eliminate all forms of radio censorship in any new federal legislation. He then advised his colleague to seek a sponsor other than Dill for any amendment as "Senator Dill . . . although he knows the subject well, is a weak sister when it comes to decisive action."[67] Baldwin noted Dill was "not so friendly to our suggestion [on inclusion of political issues] but [Ewin] Davis, chair of House committee, may be."

Baldwin had reservations about the amendment's ability to pass because of broadcaster opposition. He wondered if the ACLU should abandon attempts to pass the original Bethuel Webster version of the amendment, which included all controversial issues of public importance, in favor of a narrower focus on issues up for public vote only.[68]

Broadcasters tied their opposition to any change to possible liability under *Sorenson v. Wood*, which held broadcasters liable for slander or libel spoken over their stations. In testifying before the Senate Committee on Interstate Commerce, NAB executive and CBS vice president Henry Bellows argued that broadcasters did not want their liability for slander increased to a point where they would have to ban from the air all candidates for public office, all their supporters, and all discussions of public questions to be voted on at an election. Bellows complained that a revised equal opportunities provision had a worse effect on free speech than did the original Section 18 of the Radio Act.[69] That revision, now Section 315(a), read:

> If any licensee shall permit any person who is a legally qualified candidate for any public office to use a broadcasting station, he shall afford equal opportunities to all other such candidates for that office in the use of such station; and if any licensee shall permit any person to use a broadcasting station in support of opposition to any candidate for public office, or in the presentation of views on a public question to be voted upon at an election, he shall afford equal opportunity to an equal number of other persons to use such station in support of an opposing candidate for such public office, or to reply to a person who has used such broadcasting station in support of or in opposition to a candidate, or for the presentation of opposite view on such public questions. Furthermore, it shall be considered in the public interest for a licensee, so far as possible, to permit equal opportunity for the presentation of both sides of public questions.[70]

Bellows declared that enacting this provision as stated, plus the *Sorenson v. Wood* decision, would drive political discussion off the air. Because the Supreme Court had declined to hear appeals of *Sorenson v. Wood*, broadcasters were in an untenable situation. Under current equal opportunity provisions they could not censor, yet they were held responsible for what was aired. Broadcasters believed they could not protect themselves from charges of libel and slander unless they could censor political speeches, and laws prohibited such censorship.[71] Their only recourse was to ban all political exchange. Congressional representatives and senators realized the veiled warning in Bellows's statement: Broadcasters would deny politicians access of any kind if changes were made in the 1927 Radio Act's equal opportunity provisions.

While legislators mulled over these proposed changes, an interdepartmental committee under Secretary of Commerce Daniel Roper recommended in late January 1934 that one central governmental agency regulate all communication systems, including telegraph, telephone, and radio. The "Roper Report" also reviewed nationalization of radio, as had been done in Canada, and concluded ownership should remain in private hands in the United States. When the administration's communications control bills were finally introduced, broadcasters assailed the proposal as going far beyond the ideas Roosevelt espoused in his message calling for one agency to deal with communications issues. While both the Rayburn bill (H.R. 8301) and the Dill bill (S. 2910) transferred FRC powers to a communications commission, the Dill bill contained provisions for a zone system, a one-year license term, and extension of equal opportunity to public questions up for a vote in an election.[72]

Both broadcasters and telephone executives criticized the bill. Henry Bellows asserted that it removed all existing legal safeguards from radio broadcasting, made the new commission a criminal court, and decided technical points that should be left up to the new commission. Heavy fines were especially condemned. Bellows claimed that under the bill, licenses might be revoked without hearing and that broadcast fines of $1,000 per day after infringement could result in bills as high as $180,000. Bellows also claimed that the even more stringent penalties for slander would make it impossible to permit political speeches on radio. AT&T president Walter Gifford attacked the bill as going beyond Roosevelt's proposal and for providing for government management of the communication industries. He claimed regulations would severely damage the existing Bell System by giving the commission virtually complete authority over most, if not all, business transactions.[73]

The bill had its supporters, including the ACLU and powerful newspapers. In February 1934, the *New York Times* endorsed unification of communication regulation under one governmental agency.[74] Bethuel Webster suggested Roosevelt appoint a special commission, independent of Congress, to prepare a careful, comprehensive investigation of broadcasting to ensure consistent, reliable service. He believed the Radio Act did not assure maximum beneficial use of available facilities and crystallized the status quo of 1926 of private enterprise for private gain. Prevailing economic forces and government regulatory policy vested control of the most desirable facilities in a few private agencies, especially NBC and CBS. Webster believed the commission unworkable, "given to internal friction, timidity and ineptitude." Selection of one commissioner from each of five zones as well as the Davis Amendment handicapped sound policy making. Because broadcasting was essentially different from all other forms of electrical communication, "in some respects like the newspapers, in others like the theatre or movies," it warranted further study. If no study were undertaken, attempts to deal with broadcast communications would be "disappointing."[75] But, Congress conducted no further research, as it had too many other pressing matters at hand in dealing with the Depression in early 1934.

To complement Senate provisions imposing a limited obligation on broadcasters to permit the use of their stations to people wishing to speak out on public questions, Representative Louis McFadden of Pennsylvania introduced H.R. 7986 to provide that no radio station should discriminate against legally qualified candidates for public office or against speakers sponsored by religious, charitable, or educational organizations.[76] He argued that many people who did not read newspapers listened to the radio and formed their opinions from that source. Consequently, the power of radio was significant, especially in its use for propaganda, advertising, and political campaigns. McFadden believed that the party in power could control the sentiment of the citizenry in ways it could not be controlled by any other media, including the press. He also warned against the censorship power of the networks, which he claimed controlled 80 percent of the stations in the country through their collective programs. He warned that without special protections, the networks' monopoly power would expand and censorship of organizations that the networks disagreed with might have problems securing time. Therefore, he sought a resolution to protect freedom of speech via the airwaves. It stated that no radio broadcasting station should discriminate in the use of that station in favor of or against political candidates, religious organizations, charities, educational groups, or any other associations.[77]

The measure had virtually no chance of passing, as most congressional representatives and senators believed the new commission could investigate radio and overcome any censorship concerns. They also dreaded their own exclusion from the airwaves if broadcasters removed all political discussion from radio for fear of libel suits. These fears underlay their overall lack of support for modifications, and when the bills were reported out of committee, the offending provisions had been struck.[78]

Conclusion

Proposed changes in the equal opportunity section were defeated because commercial broadcasters and key legislators did not support modifications. Fears that Roosevelt might take over the airwaves under the president's emergency powers led broadcasters to be cautious, so they continued censorship of speeches critical of administration policies. *Sorenson v. Wood's* outcome made broadcasters fear their liability in cases of slander revolving around changes in the equal opportunities doctrine to allow issues as well as candidates' supporters equal opportunity to the airwaves. If changes were made, broadcasters threatened to ban all candidates for public office, all their supporters, and all discussions of public questions to be voted on at an election. Because congressional representatives and senators did not want to lose access to their constituents via the airwaves, they did not liberalize Section 18. Thus, only equal opportunity for candidates, and not discussion of controversial issues of public importance nor extension of equal opportunity to candidates' supporters, remained in the law after passage of the Communications Act of 1934.

Even though passage of these modifications was unsuccessful, the proposals did delineate the meanings of "freedom of expression" and "public interest" for radio. In the climate of fear fostered by the Depression, freedom of expression emphasized mainstream speech, and challenging the reigning powers was not allowed because it was not in the public interest to advocate societal change. The public's welfare depended too much upon social stability, which needed to be maintained at all cost.

12 ⋙ CONGRESS ACTS—AGAIN

While amendments to Section 18 caused anxiety for commercial broadcasters, more distressing for them was a concurrent call for setting aside a fixed percentage of spectrum for noncommercial broadcasters. These amendments had powerful congressional proponents, who fought for permanent reallocation of the airwaves with anywhere from 10 to 25 percent of the distribution going to nonprofit broadcasters. To commercial broadcasters, covering controversial issues of public importance and offering equal opportunities to candidates' supporters were relatively insignificant compared to losing one's license permanently through spectrum reallocation. The simultaneous introduction of reallocation measures with bills for extension of equal opportunity forced commercial broadcasters to champion their coverage of public affairs and their presentation of educational and cultural material as a part of their public service responsibility. As the Communications Act was debated in 1933 and 1934, commercial broadcasters successfully fended off reallocation plans.

By 1934, setting aside a fixed percentage of broadcasting facilities for nonprofit radio broadcasters had become a priority in communication bills in Congress. An amendment to the Senate bill proposed up to one-fourth of the radio facilities within any communication commission's jurisdiction be allocated to educational, religious, agricultural, labor, and similar nonprofit associations.[1] Senators Robert Wagner of New York and H. D. Hatfield of West Virginia supported this amendment, largely to counter the Great Lakes Statement and under pressure from noncommercial broadcasters. In the Great Lakes Statement, the commission noted its preference for "general public-service" stations over "special purpose" stations.[2] Usually the more "general" a station was, the more likely it was a commercial operation, while nonprofit stations were more likely to be categorized as a "special purpose" concern. The NAB endorsed the position of the Great Lakes Statement and maintained that all radio stations should serve the public as a whole. Its officers testified against the set-aside amendment,[3] while nonprofit broadcasters argued vociferously in its favor as Congress considered bills that resulted in the Communications Act of 1934.

The Communications Act of 1934 ultimately brought together radio regulation and telecommunications common carrier law. Merging oversight of these media was nothing new; it had been advanced as early as 1929. Under President Roosevelt in 1933, an interdepartmental committee studied the regulation of all communications. When Roosevelt received the resulting "Roper Report," his message to Congress stressed only the need for unified control over the entire field of communications and urged adoption of an act to consolidate all aspects of communication law.[4]

During these challenging years, hard-pressed noncommercial stations and broadcast reformers raised free speech issues coupled with public interest concerns, such as setting aside frequencies for noncommercial purposes, to little avail. As Robert McChesney chronicles in his book *Telecommunications, Mass Media, and Democracy*, such allocation requests ranged from 10 to 25 percent of existing frequencies. Calls for allocations, feared by commercial broadcasters, ultimately died when the newly formed Federal Communications Commission told Congress in 1935 that "the present system was functioning successfully and that there was no need for legislation to set aside channels for the exclusive use of nonprofit and educational broadcasters."[5] Only later, in 1941, did the FCC reverse course with set-asides as FM emerged as a viable radio service. This chapter chronicles the fight noncommercial broadcasters mounted for set-asides and their unsuccessful use of free speech and public interest issues in their battle.

Readin', 'Ritin', 'Rithmetic, and Radio

From radio's inception, educators dreamed the "R" of radio would be added to the traditional "readin', 'ritin', and 'rithmetic,"[6] but declining numbers of educational stations show how quickly those dreams ended. In May 1927, just after the Radio Act went into effect, 94 educational stations (out of 681) were licensed, but by January 1934, that number had decreased to 49 out of 583.[7] One study by the National Association of Educational Broadcasters (NAEB) showed that the proportion of college- and university-owned stations dropped from 19.5 percent in 1926 to only 6.3 percent in 1934.[8] According to contemporary documents, this trend grew out of two overarching factors: the public interest (PICON) standard, as it "required a station attempt by its bill of fare to be all things to all men, women and children," and economic determinants, as "slimly financed stations [had] to spend money defending their licenses before the Commission or by court appeal when challenged by competing commercial stations."[9] In other words, educational stations were too narrowly focused in programming to suit regulators and too poorly underwritten by financial backers or institutions to compete on a level playing field in the marketplace. They faced a daunting uphill battle for equity with commercial broadcasters.

Financial and other problems for noncommercial broadcasters had come to a head in August 1928 with FRC General Order No. 40, which established channels for broadcast station operation. The following September, General Order No. 42 established transmitter power limits. These orders modified most broadcast assignments, with only network-owned and -operated stations or stations affiliated with a network remaining unchanged.[10] Nonprofit stations often had to share hours of operation with stations the FRC deemed more worthy of getting the lion's share of airtime. Eventually, many smaller stations closed completely or sold out to larger commercial enterprises. Only stations such as WCFL and WEVD with large supportive constituencies survived to fight the battles necessary to win public acceptance.

As radio's educational and noncommercial roles slipped, the Bureau of Education reacted. On May 21, 1929, Secretary of the Interior Ray Lyman Wilber called a conference of the Bureau of Education (housed in the Interior Department) and the Federal

Radio Commission to review both radio's educational efforts and what role the federal government should play in such endeavors.[11] FRC commissioner Ira Robinson told the conference that a key question was whether commercial companies or the Bureau of Education should lead in finding the best uses for radio as an educational agent. Of course, commercial companies thought they should be in charge of any program. NBC vice president John Elwood noted that NBC's twenty-eight affiliates aired numerous educational programs heard by three to five million students each day. Everett Case, secretary to the NBC Advisory Council, asserted that radio chains were eager to work with educators and noted that limits existed to what networks could do nationally. FRC vice chairman Eugene Sykes warned that working out educational programs "must be gone at slowly" as people did not want too much educational matter, not more than two or three hours in the day and a half hour or so at night. As with so many commissions, this one concluded with few recommendations except to ask President Hoover to appoint a fact-finding commission to ascertain what radio could do for education and what the federal government's role in any such program should be.[12] Hoover turned this request over to Commissioner of Education William J. Cooper, who appointed a fact-finding board called the Advisory Committee on Education by Radio (ACER). ACER members included the presidents of NBC and CBS as well as other commercial broadcasters and some educators but no other noncommercial broadcasters.[13]

One ACER committee member, Armstrong Perry of the Payne Fund, conducted a separate fact-finding tour of the United States, which convinced him of two intertwined problems: first, commercial broadcasters had little interest in promoting educators' efforts via radio, and second, the FRC favored commercial enterprises at the expense of noncommercial operations, especially college and university stations. These observations persuaded Perry to back development of educational stations run by educators over commercial enterprises giving grants of time for educational programs.[14]

An ACER subcommittee concurred, and its December 30 report reverberated with many of Perry's sentiments. While recognizing the need for separate facilities, however, the report shied away from any radical proposals and called for commercial broadcasters and educators to work together toward a solution. In separate dissents, both CBS and NBC challenged the report's criticism of commercial broadcasters and their disregard for educators and lack of willingness to carry educational broadcasts. Perry issued his own report, concluding noncommercial educational channels had to be reserved. The networks challenged Perry's findings and asserted that "broadcasting companies are willing to give ample time for educational programs and would exercise no censorship whatsoever" over programming. When the full committee met to write its final report, it considered Perry's recommendations yet made no mention of educational channel reservations in its full report of February 18, 1930. Instead, the full committee recommended a permanent radio branch be created in the Office of Education to coordinate efforts between broadcasters and educators and to conduct research on education by radio.[15] Commercial broadcasters were elated, while educators saw such commercial control of radio as a threat.[16]

At the National Education Association (NEA) meeting in July 1930, FRC commissioner Ira Robinson asked the NEA to help strike down any commercial interest monopoly as a great danger to the American republic. "The doctrine of free speech must be preserved," he declared. "The use of the air for all and not merely for a few must be protected. The average man has the natural right to speak over the air as well as to listen to others."[17] Robinson noted that "the sanctity of the home and the school, the very foundations of our government, should be preserved and nurtured by the use of radio," then asked, "Should education by radio be left to the direction of commercial interests?" He challenged commercial broadcasters' views that educational programming had to be sugar-coated and questioned the right of radio operators to censor in selecting speakers and topics for presentation while rejecting opposing views. "Shall one group or any individual say what shall be said at such long range to millions of listeners? If so, there is a clear violation of the guarantee of free speech."[18]

The NEA recommended legislation to set aside a reasonable share of broadcast channels for the use of radio for education and government. That resolution spoke of allotting "a reasonable share of the radio broadcasting channels" based, not upon free speech concerns, but upon policies the federal government used when it allotted one or two sections of townships for educational purposes during westward expansion.[19] The NEA recommended no specific set-aside in its resolution and left that decision to the Conference on Radio and Education, which would meet in Chicago three weeks later.

This gathering brought together FRC representatives, commercial broadcasters, educators, and other educational groups. The meeting was to deal with "the fear that before education knows what it wants to do, commercial stations will have practically monopolized the channels open for radio broadcasting."[20] The conference adopted two recommendations: first, that Congress enact legislation to assign a minimum of 15 percent of all existing or future channels to educational institutions and governmental educational agencies permanently and exclusively, and second, that leading educational organizations form a committee to protect and promote educational broadcasting. Formed under the chairmanship of NEA president Joy Elmer Morgan, the organization took the name National Committee on Education by Radio (NCER).[21]

The commissioner of education endorsed the recommendations of the Conference on Radio and Education and appealed to Congress to set aside 15 percent of the available facilities for noncommercial educational uses. Senator Simeon Fess of Ohio introduced the bill on January 8, 1931. This 15 percent figure was slightly more than the percentage of noncommercial stations on the air in 1927. Under the bill, only educational agencies and federal or state government institutions would be allowed to use the set-aside frequencies.[22] The bill faced formidable opposition. Fess gave little indication of wanting to push it, a majority of the FRC opposed it, and commercial broadcasters saw no need for it.[23]

Commercial broadcasters repeatedly declared their willingness to give educators all the free time they could use, "when and if the educators come prepared with educational programs which do not bore too great a portion of their audiences." Critics accused commercial broadcasters of using the airwaves in their own private interest and in the private interest of their commercial advertisers and noted that even if educators could purchase time, they would not be able to buy costly evening time periods. They charged that commercial stations would also insist programs interest the majority of their listeners, lest competing stations win them away, and stated broadcasters would censor educational broadcasts adversely affecting their advertising clients.[24]

Commercial broadcasters found an ally in another educational organization, the National Advisory Council on Radio in Education (NACRE) formed in 1930 by the American Association for Adult Education. NACRE's philosophy was one of cooperation with commercial broadcasters, and its leaders saw little reason for separate allocations for noncommercial and educational stations advocated by the NCER.[25] NACRE was financed by John D. Rockefeller Jr. and the Carnegie Corporation, while the Payne Fund supported the NCER. According to McChesney, tensions between the two groups "reflected the conflict between the Carnegie Corporation and the Payne Fund over which organization, and which approach, would prove dominant in determining the course of education by radio."[26] Their conflict ultimately led to the demise of any allocation plan.

NACRE accepted the existing organizational structure of broadcasting, while the NCER charged NACRE with being a smoke screen for commercial operations. NACRE had taken no stand on the question of public versus private ownership and believed that commercial broadcasters should play a major role in developing educational programming. While NACRE's membership was largely educational, representatives of NBC and CBS were also members.[27]

Educational institutions used FRC data to document the loss of free speech and program diversity.[28] In early 1931, the FRC sent 605 stations a survey to analyze programs presented the week of January 11, and 522 returned the questionnaire. Of the stations, educational institutions operated only 42, and religious institutions controlled about another 10 percent. According to station answers, about 10 percent of commercial stations' airtime was devoted to educational programs, while educational stations devoted about 28 percent. The survey showed overall on-air hours of commercial stations outnumbered those of educational stations thirty-three to one.[29]

In response to the study, the NCER charged commercial broadcasters with subordinating education to show business and protested what it saw as a trend toward commercial monopoly of broadcast channels.[30] At the same time, FRC commissioner Harold LaFount responded that educators had little grounds for complaint. Educational stations, licensed to be on the air 3,669.2 hours per week, used only one-third of the available time. Of time actually used, only 283.85 hours were devoted to education. LaFount concluded that educational radio was healthy and educators ought to be happy.[31]

To educators, though, the commission blatantly favored business interests. Educators knew they had been assigned less desirable frequencies, were forced to share time with commercial interests, and were compelled to upgrade equipment so suddenly that no time was allowed for academic budgeting intricacies. They also believed commercialism and fear of offending advertisers affected educational programming accepted by commercial broadcasters, and their supposition found strong backers. At NACRE's 1931 annual meeting, FRC chairman C. McK. Saltzman warned that commercialism on the air was becoming "nauseating" even though he believed the private system was superior to the government-owned system in Great Britain. He predicted that stations permitting excessive advertising would one day be judged on whether they operated in the public interest.[32]

At the same meeting, CBS vice president and NAB executive Henry Bellows blamed the public, not broadcasters, for the state of affairs. No advertiser trying to reach the public would knowingly offend a large segment of the population. In addition, he contended educators did not take advantage of unsold time available on commercial stations, and much educational programming done was "depressingly dull." He added that allocating 15 percent of the spectrum to educational stations would be highly detrimental to broadcasting. FRC chief examiner Ellis Yost agreed. He said his experience showed that commercial broadcasters were most willing to extend their facilities to educational institutions and offered more time than educational entities could use.[33]

By 1931, arguments favoring educational radio set-asides revolved around protecting the public's rights to the airwaves and safeguarding educational and civic uses of radio from encroachment by commercial interests.[34] "It is doubtful whether the cause of good citizenship is served by having lodged deeply in the subconscious of thousands of boys and girls that they have received their instruction 'by courtesy of the Standard Oil company,' or whatever the sponsoring corporation may be," Paul Hutchinson wrote in April 1931 in his *Christian Century* series on radio. He also recognized that educators had done little with the frequencies they had. Of stations owned by schools, fifty-three reported that they averaged eight hours *weekly* on the air, and of this time, only two and a half hours were considered educational, with the balance of programming largely consisting of phonograph records. A NACRE survey of 280 commercial stations reported they broadcast an average of fifty-seven hours per week of which seven hours and twenty-five minutes, or 13 percent, were educational. During 1930, NBC said it devoted about one-fourth of its daytime hours and one-twelfth of its nighttime hours to what it called educational programs. NBC also emphasized its eagerness to give time to educators, but strings came attached to these offers: "Educational" programs had to have some "official" sponsorship or sanction. Programs also had to avoid being "boring," as defined by the commercial broadcasters.[35]

By mid-1931, arguments about educational radio were heating up. On one side were those who believed that educational programming was on the increase, and on the other, those who did not. When Commissioner Harold LaFount addressed the Second Annual Institute for Education by Radio in Columbus, Ohio, he noted that since stations had to show how their operations were in the public interest, convenience, or necessity, commercial stations carrying educational material had increased dramatically. FRC standards of "well-rounded programming" included educational shows in addition to religion, entertainment, discussion of public questions, and coverage of important public events, news, weather, and market reports. LaFount defended the FRC's record regarding the number of educational radio stations and attacked Armstrong Perry's article "Freedom of Speech Almost Lost."[36]

Perry's article had claimed that "educational stations, attacked constantly by commercial broadcasters on one hand and unprotected by the Federal Radio Commission on the other, are reduced to a mere handful with inadequate power and time to make their work effective." LaFount responded that the commission never canceled any license of an educational institution. "The reduction in the number of educational stations since 1927 has occurred by virtue of the voluntary assignment or surrender by educational stations of their licenses," he said. Stations gave up their frequencies because they did not have adequate programming or they were unable to maintain them financially. As a whole, the forty-nine educational stations used only one-third of the time allotted to them, and of this time, only 23 percent was devoted to education. For the rest of the time, facilities presented entertainment, religious activities, agriculture, sports, and commercial advertising. Commercial stations, on the other hand, he said, devoted an average of 10 percent of their time to covering educational issues. Because this time seemed to be on the increase, LaFount believed "the public will be much better served than it can possibly be by confining education exclusively to a percentage of the whole number of existing stations."[37]

Commercial broadcasters' attitudes could be paraphrased as "We have built up great audiences, and we have learned how to hold them," according to James Rorty in a *Harper's Monthly* article. He stated that commercial broadcasters believed they were "interested in education too—real education, the kind people want. We'll *give* educators all the time on the air they can use, provided they will agree not to bore too great a proportion of *our* audiences too much." Rorty concluded that "when it breaks in Congress, the war will be a holy war. The educators are bitter, determined, and not without allies, the newspaper business being what it is today. The commercial broadcasters are bitter, virtuous, and inspired by a flaming conviction: 'The Show Business for Business Men.' They will also come provided with a capacious war chest, so that they may win, this time. If they do, they will merely have to fight again, on this or some other front."[38]

Congress indeed was the battleground, and to deflect the spotlight they found themselves in, the Senate adopted a resolution on January 12, 1932, directing the FRC to survey and then report to Congress on the commercial uses of broadcasting. The resolution also called for information on the possibilities of government ownership of stations and included an amendment by Senator Clarence Dill for information on the use of commercial facilities by educational institutions.[39] While this resolution was not adopted, it laid the groundwork for the later Federal Communications Commission investigation under the Communications Act of 1934 of radio's educational undertakings.

Challenges to radio's claims as an aid to education continued, and reformers were not without their critics. In former FRC general counsel Bethuel Webster's opinion, NCER efforts "to obtain facilities for educational purposes have been marked by ineptitude and lack of sufficient basic information and planning." Webster also had a jaded opinion of setting aside 15 percent of broadcast facilities for educational use. "The records of the commission showed again and again that stations conducted as adjuncts of educational enterprises were used mainly for dull professorial speeches and uninteresting amateur talent," he wrote to Roger Baldwin of the ACLU, adding that many of these stations did not meet usual engineering standards. The NCER's work had been worthwhile in promoting better educational broadcasts, he felt, yet it failed to offer a comprehensive plan for broadcasting in general and for educational broadcasting in particular. Webster confessed he was always suspicious of lobbyists, especially educational lobbyists. "Frequently their ranks are recruited from unsuccessful or publicity seeking teachers . . . and there is an element of racketeering in their attitudes and methods," he noted, adding that if he were in charge, he would want the best engineering and legal advice and would not present "half-baked schemes."[40]

Meanwhile, the networks began heavily promoting their non-commercial programming. CBS issued a handsome booklet reviewing its programming efforts for 1933, reporting it averaged sixteen hours per day on the air and that 70 percent of the broadcasting was noncommercial. The booklet contained a long list of programs in the fields of education for children and adults, civic welfare, religion, national and foreign events, news, serious and light music, drama, and sports. Much of the educational programming appeared on Sunday or during daytime hours, which went begging for advertisers. CBS had sold virtually all its evening schedule for six evenings a week, 8:00 to 10:30 P.M. EST.[41]

NBC's Advisory Council focused on educational broadcasting and free speech during its April 1934 meeting. Educational radio programming was far more available than generally believed, NBC president Merlin Aylesworth claimed. Robert M. Hutchins, president of the University of Chicago and chair of the Advisory Council's educational committee, noted that NBC offered more serious-minded educational programs and called for the equivalent of an *Amos 'n' Andy* show in educational programming. To him, educators placed too much attention on the selection of outstanding speakers and too little on interesting approaches. At the same meeting, conductor Walter Damrosch noted that many high schools had begun bands or orchestras in response to morning broadcasts of concerts. Morgan O'Brien, chairman of the council's committee on religious activities, stated that during 1933, religious broadcasts educated listeners, created a better understanding among the various faiths, increased religious tolerance, and supplied religious services to shut-ins, invalids, and lighthouse keepers and others living in remote places.[42]

During the year, Hutchins had also warned publicly that radio had to be more effective in education or it would find itself more drastically regulated. A colleague at the University of Chicago, Grace Abbott, advocated establishing government radio channels for educational purposes, while NACRE's president Robert Millikan warned that changes should not be too radical. "The man who is shuddering today at the loss of freedom of speech and of the press the world over, the man who believes that human progress dies when that freedom of expression is gone, will feel that all advantages that government control of radio might bring are bought at too high a price because of the danger to the freedom of speech and action of the individual."[43] A more liberal interpretation of "public interest, convenience and necessity" would "provide a good theoretical case for public control of broadcasting," according to William Orton of Smith College. To him, congressional action should achieve several objectives, including central control of all popular broadcasting, redistribution of facilities, and taxation of programs and broadcasters based on nature of programming (for example, cultural versus commercial) and transmitter power of the station.[44]

Thus, this battle between commercial and educational radio continued during 1933 and 1934 as new laws were discussed for broadcasting. The conflict focused on whether to set aside frequencies for noncommercial stations; the role of radio in private, commercial, for-profit stations versus publicly owned radio; government ownership of stations; and commercial development of quality educational programs. Radio was seen not so much as a medium of free expression as a medium of commerce, much like motion pictures. Educators had valid concerns over diversity of radio programs and the medium's commercialization but lacked the cohesiveness to realize reform.

Noncommercial Spectrum Set-Asides?

Typifying educational and noncommercial operations was New York City station WLWL, operated by the Missionary Society of St. Paul the Apostle, or the Paulist Fathers. It was the only Catholic station east of the Mississippi. The Department of Commerce licensed WLWL in 1925 to operate at 5,000 watts with unlimited time, but by 1934 the time had been reduced to weekday evenings from 6:00 to 8:00 P.M. and two and a half hours on Sundays, split between an afternoon program and evening church services. The station had struggled for five years in a losing battle to gain its share of time on the air. The FRC assigned WLWL to share time with a commercial station in Atlantic City with 110 ½ hours per week going to the commercial station and only 14 ½ hours to WLWL. Reverend

John Harney, superior of the order, wanted adoption of a set-aside to prevent commercial control over radio and proposed assigning one-fourth of all facilities to "educational, religious, agricultural, labor, cooperative and similar non-profit-making associations." This distribution, supported by powerful Senators Robert Wagner and H. D. Hatfield, would alleviate the discrimination he felt had been leveled at his station and other noncommercial ventures.[45]

In House testimony on the amendment, Harney emphasized that "human welfare agencies" operated less than 2.5 percent of all broadcast facilities in the United States. He reiterated the need to allocate 25 percent of radio facilities to these groups, and when asked why such allocations were needed, especially if commercial stations were carrying cultural or educational programs, Harney replied, "I do not want to hand my manuscript over to them and then have them say, 'We do not like it. You tone this down. Cut this out.'" He added that he believed in freedom of the air and said, "If these commercial stations were simply told, 'You must give 25 percent of your time,' that [still] makes them masters of what shall be put on the air." He also refuted what the NAB's legislative committee had told the House Interstate Commerce Committee the day before.[46]

The NAB had contended that nonprofit groups were wrong to think that special allocation of broadcasting facilities to particular groups or denominations was necessary to protect their right of free speech. NAB officials thought the exact opposite would be true. In its supplementary statement on the Harney proposal, the NAB noted that "such a system of special allocation would, in fact, deprive millions of people of the right either to utter or to hear free speech. In the field of religion alone, it is obvious that an assignment to religious organizations of 25 or even 50 percent of the total facilities would by no means take care of everyone." It continued:

> Suppose that religious organizations are assigned 10 "cleared" channels. There are 3 or 4 times that many religious denominations or groups of national scope, many of which would inevitably be shut out in the race for broadcasting facilities of their own. Would the Methodist, the Christian Scientists, the Jew be invited to make free use of the facilities controlled by another denomination as today they are all invited to use the facilities of the general service broadcasting stations? There would be freedom of speech only for those groups lucky, rich, or influential enough to secure all the available allocations; for the rest there would be no freedom at all.[47]

The statement emphasized that "freedom of speech can be maintained in radio only by insisting that every station shall serve every listener within its normal range, whether Democrat or Republican, conservative or radical, rich or poor, Catholic or Jew, city dweller or farmer. It can most quickly be destroyed by assigning facilities to a favored few among the groups which seek to appeal to a special and limited audience."[48]

The NAB also claimed that reallocating one-fourth of the present facilities was "utterly destructive to the rights of the radio-listening public, to the broadcasting industry, and to the work of the Communication Commission itself." The statement concluded that "radio must always stand firmly for the right of free speech. It [the NAB] insists, however, that neither public service nor freedom of speech can be assisted by making service to a particular class, group or creed, the test of fitness for a broadcasting license instead of service to the people as a whole."[49] Harney countered that all the amendment "really asks is that Congress make due provision for the radio welfare of those organizations that are seeking human betterment rather than selfish pecuniary profit."[50]

Senators Wallace White and Clarence Dill opposed the amendment and argued that making such allocations fairly would be difficult. They also noted that many organizations would not have the financial means to operate a station sans commercials and would ultimately become commercial broadcasters to make ends meet. To them, commercial stations already devoted a lot of time to religious and educational programs.[51] During discussions, Dill asked if the plan was really a scheme by some who called themselves educational, religious, or nonprofit but who in reality were planning to enter the commercial field and sell a tremendous amount of their time for commercial purposes. Dill argued that in effect it was a proposal to transfer control of 25 percent of radio facilities to organizations or individuals who said they were going to broadcast for nonprofit groups but who in reality would sell commercial time. Consequently, he believed the amendment was fatally flawed. No method had been presented to ensure radio's use for educational, religious, fraternal, and nonprofit purposes. Senator James Couzens agreed and added that once an organization got a license, it was not required to carry any nonprofit programming and could sell all of its time for commercial purposes. He concluded that the new commission should study the situation. Senators Wagner and

Hatfield disagreed and argued that the FRC had been studying the situation since the passage of the Radio Act. The time was ready for congressional action.[52]

In final comments on the amendment, Senator White reminded the other senators that when the 1927 law was enacted, land grant colleges were especially vocal in urging that they get preferential treatment in the new law. Then, as now, it would be difficult to allocate a finite number of stations to a seemingly infinite number of nonprofit organizations. While White deplored commercialization of American radio, he did not believe any set-aside amendment should be adopted. The Senate killed the amendment, forty-two to twenty-three, with thirty-one senators not voting, but approved its version of a new communications act on May 15, 1934.[53]

Discussion on a similar amendment in the House raised the same issues: How was the allocation to be accomplished, and by whom? Who would decide among the various religious sects? What made a station "nonprofit" or "educational"? Speaker of the House Sam Rayburn argued any new allocation plan would result in revocation of all broadcast licenses, thus upsetting a successful national communication system. He thought it would be better for the proposed Federal Communications Commission to investigate and report back to Congress; then Congress could take any necessary action to correct flaws in the system.[54]

On June 7, House and Senate committees agreed to a compromise bill that included Section 307(a), which ordered the FCC to study radio's use for educational, religious, and nonprofit purposes as well as review apportionment of a fixed percentage of broadcasting facilities for nonprofit programs and to report back by February 1, 1935.[55] Chief changes included increasing the commission to seven members from the five proposed by the Senate and elimination of the Senate provision that would have modified and extended the political broadcast provisions,[56] discussed in chapter 11. With its passage, President Roosevelt told the Radio Manufacturers' Association that radio broadcasting "should be maintained on an equality of freedom similar to that which has been and is the keystone of the American press," and he signed the bill into law on June 20.[57]

In many ways, Roosevelt got what he wanted in the new Communications Act. His administration essentially wanted nothing more than to have all communications, including common carrier regulation then administered by the Interstate Commerce Committee, housed under one administrative agency, the newly formed Federal Communications Commission. The Wagner-Hatfield Amendment, which would have drastically changed the face of radio, did not have his support for several key reasons. First, he needed the support of commercial broadcasters to counter the negative publicity his administration's policies received in the print media. Second, as radio grew in popularity, he saw it as one of the few continuing financial success stories in the Depression. Third, radio offered the public "free" entertainment, plus growing news and information programs, during the Depression years. Radio sets were among the last modern conveniences given up by financial stressed individuals, and doing anything to upset radio's success might generate unnecessary public antagonism. For the time being, it was better to leave well enough alone and let the newly formed FCC grapple with the feasibility of any proposed changes in set-asides for nonprofit channels.[58]

FCC Hearings on Use of Radio for Education

With a mandate to report to Congress on spectrum set-asides by February 1, 1935, the FCC scheduled hearings to begin October 1.[59] Nearly six hundred radio stations would be affected if redistribution were successful, according to CBS executive Henry Bellows's testimony on behalf of the NAB. Bellows believed the only way to handle the question was through cooperation between educators and broadcasters, and he added: "We are going to bring out overwhelming evidence to show that there has been no covert censorship or control of educational programs by broadcasters as some educators allege. All broadcasters have insisted is that programs be reasonably interesting."[60]

Before hearings began, the ACLU noted that one of their frequent spokespersons, Bethuel Webster, opposed allocation of frequencies for educational and nonprofit organizations. In a memo for the ACLU's radio committee, Clifton Read stated that Webster believed that programs broadcast by these organizations "would be extremely dull" and doubted if they could command "consistent listener interest." Webster suggested that instead of backing a percentage proposal, the ACLU should back regulations requiring all stations and networks to devote a reasonable amount of time on a regular basis to broadcasts on controversial subjects.[61]

Reaction to Webster's suggestion split the committee so sharply that members met over a luncheon to iron out their differences before FCC hearings began. Levering Tyson, director of NACRE, agreed with Webster, while Morris Ernst wanted emphasis placed on programs by nonprofit organizations with not only a 25 percent set-aside for nonprofit stations but also one-quarter of time on commercial stations earmarked for noncommercial programming. Henry Eckstein was less adamant and believed simply that whatever was decided, all noncommercial interests should stick together to present a united front to commercial interests. Roger Baldwin wanted surrender of a specified amount of "good time" on commercial stations for public discussion and educational features not under station control. He did not want to strike any compromise with broadcasters opposed to the set-aside.[62] The main purpose of the proposals as he saw it was to break up the monopoly to get noncommercial material on the air, "because only thus do we escape advertisers' pressure and open up [broadcasting to] controversial discussion."[63] When they were unable to agree among themselves, the committee adopted Webster's approach and asked him to represent the ACLU before the FCC.[64]

Hearings before three members of the FCC Broadcast Division—Hampson Gary, Thad Brown, and Eugene Sykes—began October 1. As they commenced, the *New Republic* castigated the attitudes supporting commercial radio, especially those of Commissioner LaFount, who had said: "[C]ommercialism is the heart of broadcasting in the United States. What has education contributed to radio? Not one thing. What has commercialism contributed? Everything—the life blood of the industry." The magazine noted that educational material in Britain was double that of the U.S. and had an overall superior quality. Noting the quality of news reports on British radio, the publication lamented the dearth of coverage brought about by newspapers confining broadcasters to two brief summaries a day under the Biltmore Agreement. While others, notably Jerome Davis of Yale, promoted taxation on advertising to pay educational radio's bills, the *New Republic* suggested setting up a few government-owned stations to furnish advertising-free programming. "They [commercial broadcasters] could hardly complain, moreover," the magazine concluded, "since they have repeatedly argued that no one but themselves understands what the American public wants, or is competent to furnish it."[65]

Most educators appearing before the commission pleaded for an increase in better time slots for their programs and for programs free from advertising and designed to promote the public welfare. Nine national educational organizations joined in Joy Elmer Morgan's appeal for better programming and frequency allocations to noncommercial stations. Networks were assailed for tying up large groups of stations, and Dr. Harry Eubank of the University of Wisconsin said noncommercial stations were essential to safeguard the rights of the public. The proportion of stations owned by colleges and universities dropped from 19.5 percent in 1926 to 6.3 percent in 1934, according to NAEB director Joseph Wright. While all speakers conceded commercial stations' attempts to aid educational groups, they stressed the uncertainty and possible censorship of future programs. They also underscored the lack of desirable hours and complained that educational stations were impaired by low power, crowded channels, and limited time.[66]

CBS chief William Paley opposed proposals for set-asides and those forcing broadcasting companies to grant free radio time for educational and religious programming. He challenged the assumption that commercial radio was not providing adequate educational programs, noting that two-thirds of CBS programming for the first three-quarters of 1934 had consisted of sustaining programs. Of these, more than one-fourth had been devoted to religious, scientific, and educational material. Such a policy could be developed by others, he noted, and added that a call for government development of educational programs was an unnecessary duplication of a system that already worked well. He stated:

> Columbia has carefully refrained from imposing on its audience any small personal concepts of what that audience ought to receive. Rather it has sought so far as possible to act as editors and directors of a great news and educational and entertaining service. Columbia's broadcasting facilities and periods have been alike extended to business men, to religious institutions and labor groups, to government representatives and to the political opposition, to women's clubs and organizations devoted to community welfare, to any and all responsible groups which had a message of real interest for a representative public.[67]

Paley emphasized that because radio was a sound business enterprise, it could make continuous contributions toward U.S. cultural development, but it needed commercials for financing as taxpayers were unwilling to pay for service through taxes or other assessments as other nations did. Radio's program schedule had to serve a universal audience and "never [be] systematically restricted to subject matter of interest only to certain groups." An analysis of CBS programming showed numerous educational, cultural, and informative programs with about 32 percent appearing in evening hours. Some of these programs were commercially sponsored. To destroy what commercial radio had built would damage radio's educational efforts, he concluded.[68]

Dr. Floyd Reeves, personnel director of the Tennessee Valley Authority and formerly of the University of Chicago, had long been interested in possible benefits of radio for rural Americans and told the commissioners that government ownership, operation, and control of a national radio system should be developed to compete with the commercial networks. His remarks surprised the commissioners, who asked him what radio channels he would use and how much the system would cost. He replied that while details had not been worked out, he had a five-point plan that included (1) government set-up, ownership, and operation of a national system of radio stations; (2) allocation of these frequencies with as little disruption of current commercial operation as possible; (3) government financing of the stations' mechanical operation; (4) control of programming placed under a presidentially appointed committee of foremost educators and nonprofit, cultural agencies; and (5) making these facilities available for educational programming to nonprofit groups, including government departments. Reeves stated that because programs were "supplied almost entirely through commercial profit," they were not satisfactory for "meeting the needs of the educational and cultural agencies of America." He said radio should be freed from the influence of advertising and that freedom of speech should be ensured by elimination of commercial as well as political pressure. Reeves suggested that fees on receivers pay for radio's expenses.[69]

In his widely reported testimony on behalf of the ACLU, Bethuel Webster deplored broadcasters' determination of what listeners would hear through unlimited powers of censorship. "It is a remarkable paradox that while Congress and this commission are expressly forbidden to abridge freedom of speech, the law has placed in the hands of network and station owners practically unlimited power of censorship," he said. Speaking for the ACLU, he emphasized controversial issue discussion over the airwaves. "We believe that every station in the country should be required to set aside definite, desirable periods on a non-profit basis for free discussion of educational, political and social matters," he said. If promotion of public discussion over all stations could be arranged without disturbing the status quo, Webster said the ACLU would abandon support of spectrum reallocation. He noted that greater freedom of discussion over the air existed in the U.S. than elsewhere and that groups requesting allocations be set aside "have made remarkably unimpressive showings."[70]

Instead of recommending radical revision of broadcasting's structure, Webster advocated that regulations be formed in which regular use of all stations for uncensored discussion be assured. Local factors in communities served in addition to the character and size of the station would be the criteria for the manner in which the time would be used and allocated. Networks and their affiliates would call meetings of national organizations engaged in promotion of public discussion so those groups could allocate time periods during parts of the broadcasting day set aside for public discussion. Stations and networks would be responsible only for technical aspects and could not censor the programs, except as to legal liability for defamation.[71] Henry Bellows thought broadcasters would be more receptive to Webster's proposal if they were freed from libel or slander suits on proposed public time. Then only speakers and their sponsors would be responsible for defamation.[72]

Webster also called for a publicly operated major radio network to join existing radio networks. He urged the number of current stations be reduced by at least half and advocated reallocation of existing commercial network stations to give them a maximum of clear channels in a scientific distribution plan. The new network would be given a five- or six-year trial and would be composed of one to four full-time regional or local stations in each state.[73]

Webster's views ran counter to the majority of NACRE's members, who disapproved of government ownership and operation of a network. In speeches debating government control, E. H. Harris, chair of the ANPA Committee on Radio, favored private ownership and control and warned government dominion would lead to censorship of radio. Bruce Bliven, editor of the *New Republic*, supported Webster and favored government control. He charged that many radio programs consisted of "moronic drivel and oral garbage" and countered that censorship already existed—he had been victim to it. To that, Dr. Morris Fishbein, editor of the *Journal of the American Medical Association*, stated, "[T]he government has not demonstrated ability to function as well as private interests. Under government radio control the word education will be used for propaganda." NEA president Joy Elmer Morgan asked the FCC to set aside more and better time for educational broadcasts, free from advertising, to promote the public welfare.[74]

Commercial broadcasters presented a united front against these educational broadcasters. The central theme of their testimony was that commercial broadcasters already made adequate provision for religious and cultural programs. Changes in the allocation scheme would be harmful to both the industry and the American public. Citing sworn statements submitted by nearly three hundred radio stations, Henry Bellows asserted that commercial stations worked closely with nonprofit groups to provide programs gratis for them and other government and local groups. Bellows testified that commercial broadcasters in cooperation with educational institutions devoted more time to educational programs than stations operated by educational institutions. He denied specific allegations that educational programs were rejected when time could be sold, that only "useless daytime hours" were available for educators, and that commercial broadcasters failed to realize the benefits of educational broadcasts. He claimed that colleges and universities often wanted time for non-educational features such as broadcast of football games and rallies and musical clubs and added that some stations picked up costs of campus studios, including line hookups. He complained that educators often turned down free time because they were not interested in the time or could not bear their share of program production costs. Despite complaints about "dry" educational programs from listeners, some commercial stations persisted in carrying programs. In all, commercial broadcasters *were* meeting educators' needs.[75]

NBC vice president Frank Russell told the FCC that in the year ending September 1, NBC had carried 871 speeches, totaling 250 hours, by government officials. He warned against changes, as did several radio engineers. Engineer John Hogan said setting aside educational wavelengths would "rob" rural areas of service, while C. M. Jansky stated such action would mean that "a large portion of the United States would receive no reliable night time service whatever."[76] Conductor Paul Whiteman and the stars of *Amos 'n'*

Andy appeared for NBC, while Dr. Thomas Reed of the University of Michigan said that "perfect freedom of speech" was available under existing plans.[77]

Commercial broadcasters argued that too much time had been allotted for educational purposes and that educators had been unable to use their time wisely. NBC's Merlin Aylesworth told the FCC that "people do not want education, they want entertainment. Education on radio can be made entertaining and if it is not, the radio audience will turn to other programs." He added that many educators lacked "showmanship" in their program productions and that "it would be too bad to destroy the great force of radio education because of monotony and poor showmanship."[78] The *New York Times* editorialized that NBC should carry educational programming. "There is no telling when some boy Abraham Lincoln of the twentieth century, hungry for knowledge, will stumble upon one of the N.B.C.'s monotonous lectures with results transcending the aggregate social effect of twenty star comedians at $5,000 a week."[79] In mid-November, the five-week hearings came to a close, and the FCC's report was expected in January or early February 1935.[80]

In January 1935, the FCC issued its report, concluding that no fixed percentages of radio broadcasting facilities be allocated for nonprofit radio. The FCC added that it would "assist in the determination of the rightful place of broadcasting in education. . . . Every sound, sensible, and practical plan for the betterment of the broadcast structure will be speedily affected."[81] The report emphasized commercial broadcasters' contributions to educational and sustaining programming. The commission underscored the NAB's report, which argued that a little over 11 percent of commercial stations' programming was educational, "using the term 'educational' in its broadest sense to embrace all programs having a cultural or informative value." The report added that "representatives of some of the most important institutions of learning were definite in their statements that they had ample opportunity for the development of their radio activities under present arrangements, and they were definite in their opposition to any rearrangement which would place the burden of maintaining broadcast stations upon educational institutions."[82] No general increase in number of stations could result from reallocation of frequencies, and the services of too many other stations would be affected. Action might also result in some areas of the country not being able to receive radio signals.

To their misfortune, the nonprofit organizations had not presented a united front, nor had they come up with definitive proposals for actual use of reallocated stations. Some stated their organizations were not financially able to build and maintain their own broadcast operations even if facilities were allocated. The FCC saw "no evidence of a real demand on the part of the great body of nonprofit organizations or on the part of the general public for the proposed allocation of definite percentages of broadcast facilities to particular types or kinds of non-profit activities." Nonprofit organizations could be served by existing facilities through cooperative efforts of commercial broadcasters and the respective organizations under the FCC's direction.[83]

In short, the FCC saw no need to fix the percentage of radio time for religious, educational, and labor programming. The commission said it had ample authority to provide equitable distribution of broadcasting programs, that it would protect existing stations, and that it had the power to revoke or suspend for thirty days the licenses of stations. The FCC found that "there are insufficient facilities available in the present development of the art to provide for specialized broadcast service consistent with a fair and equitable distribution of facilities and services throughout the country."[84] Spectrum scarcity then became the rationale for denying allocation for noncommercial stations.

Conclusion

Spectrum scarcity was only one reason for refusing allotments for noncommercial stations. The FCC agreed with the NAB argument that special treatment for noncommercial broadcasters would be detrimental to listeners' receipt of information and entertainment. Freedom of the air and the public interest were enhanced by service to all the public at all times, not select segments of the public at specific times. By presenting a united front against educational and other nonprofit broadcasters, commercial broadcasters successfully argued that they made adequate provision for religious and cultural programs and thereby enhanced freedom of the air and the public interest. Changes in spectrum allocation would harm both the industry and the American public. The January 1935 FCC report emphasized commercial broadcasters' contributions to educational and sustaining programming to the ultimate detriment of educational and other noncommercial endeavors on radio.

13 ⇒ THE PAST IS PROLOGUE

In its debate over a new communications law, Congress revisited major free speech considerations of censorship, speakers' rights, broadcasters' rights, and listeners' rights to receive information. By 1930, with one exception, anxiety over ownership monopoly had moved largely from the realm of free speech to concerns over restraint of trade. That one exception was diversity of ownership in terms of commercial and noncommercial stations. Inclusion of political broadcast rules, anti-censorship rules, and prohibitions on broadcast profanity and indecency reinforced much of the FRC's work. By the time the Communications Act of 1934 became law, the parameters for freedom of the air and the public interest and their relationship to electronic media were firmly established in the American psyche.

Freedom of the Air

Affecting free speech's emergence on radio were religious values and morality; definitions of what constituted diversity in the interwar years; notions of speaker responsibility; coverage of government officials, their actions, and public issues; and the nation's economic conditions, including radio's commercialization and the Depression. Freedom of the air became a symbolic construction to form and maintain the power structure of both government and corporations involved in radio in the 1920s and 1930s. During its formative years, courts, regulators, and broadcasters saw radio much more as a medium for commerce than expression. To them, radio was a for-profit, show business, entertainment medium that both paralleled motion pictures and differed from newspapers and other public opinion outlets. As a result, radio was not viewed as an information business with legal analogues to newspapers; rather, it was a commercial enterprise that could be legitimately regulated in much the same way motion pictures were regulated in the 1920s and 1930s. Thus, "freedom of the air" came with limitations for expression in a new, potentially powerful medium. By accepting the standards that evolved, broadcasters tacitly accepted what would eventually become a second-class status in First Amendment rights when compared to print media.

As radio evolved in the 1920s, government agencies and the broadcast industry influenced concepts of freedom of the air and public interest as they worked together to get service to the American public. Their interaction is best exhibited through the four radio conferences, when the Department of Commerce and chief industry leaders RCA and AT&T worked behind the scenes to set the resulting agenda—and potential outcomes—for these meetings. Concepts of freedom of the air emerged during the conferences and focused on who could speak and when. Attendees at the conferences did not construe freedom of the air or free speech via radio as promoting diversity of ideas per se, but rather interpretations rested on the appropriateness of speakers and under what conditions they could use the medium. Those meriting the right to speak over radio had to use the medium responsibly to protect the welfare of the American public. Broadcast programs, consequently, were conservative, discreet, and restrained.

The Public Interest

During the 1920s, public interest concepts linked clear signal reception with responsible programming. Coupled to the standard was the medium's use of the supposedly scarce resource of the ether. This scarcity, though, was constructed and resulted from regulators' and broadcasters' attempts to clear up the airwaves during the radio conferences and hearings on the Radio Act. Discussion then of the public interest standard centered on technical issues and outcomes, with promises of program diversity brought to listeners by a reliable, largely corporately controlled radio industry. While this initial understanding of public interest held throughout the mid-1930s and still holds in part today, the meaning of public interest began changing as broadcasters and the Federal Radio Commission wrestled with decisions on programming in the latter part of the 1920s. What was appropriate broadcast service, and whom should broadcasting serve, and how? With FRC pronouncements that programming could be controlled if it did not serve the general public, the definition of public interest began shifting so that, by the early 1930s, understanding of public interest from technical and economic standpoints was augmented with notions of program diversity and program quality.

Freedom of the Air and the Public Interest

Actual program censorship in radio from its inception to passage of the Communications Act came in two forms: indirect government censorship and overt broadcaster censorship. Often broadcasters had to discern what was acceptable to audiences as well as to government officials to protect their licenses under conservative interpretations of free expression that existed in the 1920s and early 1930s. While exchange of ideas was important, especially for democratic governance, responsibility came with the exercise of speech on radio where fears of radio's instantaneous nature and potentially disruptive power surfaced. In the general social structure of the 1920s and 1930s, most public discussion was legally protected as a part of self-governance, but even it could be curbed if speech threatened the public's general welfare. At the same time, the private domain could be limited as it centered upon commerce, private actions of individuals or corporations, and other expression not dealing with self-governance. For the most part, broadcasting was considered part of this private domain.

Offensive and inappropriate programming subsequently became the focus of celebrated incidents involving freedom of the air and the public interest. Among issues considered unsuitable for broadcast by both government and broadcasting officials were pacifism, socialism, atheism, sex, birth control, and discussion of eliminating Prohibition. As the Depression deepened, speakers found their evaluation of economic conditions censored. Not only were outright bans on materials effective but so too were policies assessing charges for airtime that kept dissidents and others expressing supposedly un-American views off the air. Broadcasters considered these practices "editing" in the name of protecting the public's welfare and promoting social accord.

Speakers afforded special privileges from radio's very beginnings, however, were political candidates. Broadcasting began changing American politics forever in the 1920s, but at best, the political speech that was offered protection came primarily to the major political parties. Use of the medium was often tied to the ability to pay for airtime, and the major parties had the coffers to pay for this time that others holding minority viewpoints did not.

Radio also affected the manner in which political speeches were delivered. Shorter, more folksy speeches with less dramatic oratory became the order of the day, while networks carried political programs such as conventions and campaigns as a public service for network goodwill and name recognition. Broadcasters formed industry policies providing equal opportunity for candidates several years before they were actually written into law as Section 18 of the Radio Act. Broadcaster-devised provisions focused on presenting candidates equitably through impartially assessing charges for airtime. By levying the same rates for time, broadcasters could control who used the airwaves without complaint of discrimination, as usually only major party candidates could afford to purchase time. While radio operators had reservations about equal opportunity being written into law, they ultimately welcomed provisions as a way to control unpopular viewpoints and to repress unpopular speech. Free broadcast time for all candidates did not enter discussions revolving around political candidates' access to the medium. Hence, the equal opportunity provision adopted first in 1927 did not enhance listeners' ability to receive a diversity of political viewpoints.

In reworking the Radio Act in 1932 and early 1933, Congress attempted to expand Section 18's provisions to stipulate that coverage of controversial issues be accorded the same treatment as candidates for public office. Bills also sought to extend equal opportunities to candidates' supporters. While the amendments passed both houses of Congress in early 1933, President Hoover pocket vetoed the bill along with numerous other legislative measures as an unnecessary expansion of government expenditures. In doing so, the moment passed for key, fundamental changes in the definition of equal opportunity, which would have enhanced the First Amendment through dispersal of diverse viewpoints and partisan opinion and programming.

One major fear of networks and stations concerned their liability if candidates engaged in profanity, indecency, slander, or libel over the air. By 1930, new laws and court cases had extended regulations in these unprotected speech areas to radio. In reaction to *Sorenson v. Wood* and because of fear of FRC license refusal, stations laid down rules for both candidates and spokespersons for candidates that resulted in censorship. While the FRC stated that the Radio Act's anti-censorship clause in Section 29 meant that no one would be deprived of free speech over the airwaves, the commission emphasized that this proviso protected expression of views, not what it called "impolite or annoying" language, or defamation, especially when the public's welfare was concerned.

Balancing Section 29's prohibition against censorship with application of the "public interest, convenience or necessity" standard, the FRC decided freedom from censorship was a qualified right, subject to commission policies, with their fundamental consideration the public welfare or the public interest. Further, the commission stated that its actions were consistent with the First Amendment because the First Amendment did not protect "obnoxious and indecent language." Thus, political speech on radio had its limits, too. These limits and the general climate of fear of license denial led to broadcasters' censorship of speakers.

Another perspective on free speech, public interest, and broadcasting developed in the 1920s that would pass constitutional muster in the 1970s in cases seeking to protect children from indecent material: programs had to be maintained "free of malice and unwholesomeness" to protect children and the home environment. Broadcasters saw their actions in deciding programming as safeguarding the home and providing what they determined as beneficial and ethical programming. Consequently, broadcasters developed industry policies that were conservative and restrained in deciding programming needs. As broadcasters and regulators attempted to determine "what the public wanted" in programming, a rather circuitous decision-making process evolved.

Overall, stations had to provide well-rounded programming designed for the tastes, needs, and desires of all substantial groups of listeners. Stations could not operate exclusively in the private interest of individuals or groups as not enough spectrum existed

for every school of thought, whether it was religious, political, social, or economic. To regulators, "propaganda" stations had lesser
claims to the broadcast airwaves than did other "general public
service" stations.

Two stations, WEVD and WCFL, had more difficulty than other
stations proving their worthiness to the FRC because they were seen
as "special interest stations." While some attacks on programming
were initiated against these stations in the late 1920s, the FRC often assailed their technical or financial operations rather than their
programming because these functions were easier to assault in the
name of public interest than the latter, which could be deemed as a
violation of free speech. Even though these stations ultimate met
every challenge leveled by the commissioners, they were reminded
constantly that holding minority viewpoints did not entitle them to
preferential treatment. In fact, quite the contrary was true. Their
minority views often made them targets for government attempts
at incursion into their affairs.

In its directives, the FRC stated that holding a radio station license imposed an inescapable obligation on the licensee to serve the
public interest and to promote the public welfare. Promoting personal or community strife and turmoil by means of radio communications were not in the public interest, nor were a station's unjust attacks or attempts to destroy legitimate organizations or
individuals to further personal interests and business. While unspo-
ken, the concept of a "clear and present danger" to the health and
well-being of the American public was evident in getting errant
broadcasters such as John Brinkley and Norman Baker off the air,
while Robert Shuler's loss of license for use of radio for personal
controversy, slanderous attacks on individuals, and exploitation of
his personal views gave broadcasters further illustration of what
freedom of the air meant for radio.

In addition, because the home was the main site for radio reception, broadcasts appraised as vulgar, immoral, or indecent by
contemporary standards were forbidden. To ward off crusades
against potentially indecent radio programming, station and network censors modified songs and skits. For the most part, they
worked hard to keep "blue material," including profane and indecent language, off the air, whether such material appeared in song
or skit. Later, as public acceptance of material changed, broadcasters modified what they allowed on the air.

By 1930, radio was a rising competitor of newspapers for dissemination of news and—more importantly from the publishers' standpoint—advertising dollars. As radio evolved, concerns emerged over which medium could properly advance and protect freedom of expression and accuracy in news reporting. Newspaper publishers argued they were, while the upstart radio operators insisted they, too, could advance freedom of the press in news broadcasting. Arguments focused largely on property rights in news dissemination and the licensing of stations by a government agency as an inhibition to dissemination of uncensored information. Underlying these arguments, however, were publishers' concerns over the exodus of advertising dollars from print to broadcast during the Depression when every advertising dollar was especially coveted.

Educational and noncommercial broadcasters fomented another challenge to commercial radio. By 1931, arguments favoring educational radio revolved around two intertwined concerns: protecting the public's rights to ownership of the ether by keeping radio from falling solely into private hands, and safeguarding educational and civic uses of radio from encroachment by commercial interests. Commercial broadcasters controlling valuable airtime became more and more reluctant to give educators choice time periods. Educators often found their long-term educational programs disrupted or discouraged through such tactics as stations or networks choosing what professors could lecture and when. For commercial stations, educational material was presented during hours unsalable for advertising and rarely during times when audiences the educators desired were home.

In incorporating all of the provisions of the Radio Act into the new communications law in 1934, Congress revisited major free speech considerations of censorship, speakers' rights, broadcasters' rights, and listeners' rights to receive information. Inclusion of political broadcast rules, anti-censorship rules, and prohibitions on broadcast obscenity, indecency, and profanity reinforced much of the FRC's work, assuaged industry concerns over their use of radio, and solidified the common threads weaving together the meaning of freedom of the air and the public interest. Issues of broadcaster and government censorship over programming, speakers' rights of access to the medium, listeners' rights to receive information via the airwaves, and broadcasters' rights to use the airwaves in any manner they desired were generally voiced in conservative

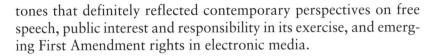

tones that definitely reflected contemporary perspectives on free speech, public interest and responsibility in its exercise, and emerging First Amendment rights in electronic media.

Emerging Media and the First Amendment

In the 1920s and 1930s, the First Amendment was interpreted in an narrower context than it is today. Speech negatively affecting the public welfare or the home environment could be substantially curtailed under contemporary interpretations of the First Amendment as applied to radio without as much debate as occurs today with application of First Amendment rights in newer technology. Viewpoints on what constitutes freedom of the air, a free press, and permissible speech have changed since the mid-1930s as the media have evolved from print, radio, and motion pictures to include television, cable, and computer-based information technologies. Attitudes of owners who are responsible for information provided on their channels are now resurfacing in discussions of new electronic media and telecommunication services.

Today's First Amendment rights in media are far greater than those evident in the 1920s and 1930s. To varying degrees, the free speech–free press clauses protect motion pictures, broadcast, cable, and other electronic distribution services in addition to magazines, newspapers, and some commercial material. Subject matter covered in these media is also more diverse than material covered in the 1920s and 1930s, as can be seen on any current television program, radio talk show, or on-line chat room. But if one reviews the conservative nature of radio's interaction with expression issues in the interwar years, one realizes that today's electronic and telecommunications media may bear the same anxieties and considerations as they move toward the goal of free interchange among viewers/subscribers and services. Controlling information dispersal via today's new media services is far more difficult than with radio; fewer than seven hundred stations were on the air in 1934, while millions of subscribers can post and retrieve information by way of on-line electronic services. If these new media need control, as is argued by some, the question of who is to control them, and how, will again be central to discussion of freedom of expression.

How government and communication industries see the dissemination of messages over newer technologies such as computer lines, satellite links, and telephone/common carrier equipment will determine the role they will play in any future regulation of all media, including broadcasting. If they see a multiplicity of voices existing on innumerable available broadband channels, scarcity will not be an underpinning of regulation, and broadcasting may be freed from laws first set in the 1920s.

As this book goes to press, it seems unlikely that a few industry giants may control access to cyberspace and other newer technologies. But if industry-imposed limits on expression and access evolve, government may have to mandate access for political and other viewpoints. In addition, further protections than what is currently found in telecommunications law may be needed for privacy and to shield children and unwitting cyberviewers from indecent material. Such rules will seek to balance free expression concerns with other compelling societal interests, such as protection of individual privacy and children from indecency that may come across a computer screen. Speaker/publisher rights will have to be reconciled with desires to protect individuals and businesses from defamation and to safeguard copyrighted material. On-line sexually explicit material may face the same controls as similar material found in other media outlets. The challenge will be to foster an environment where First Amendment and freedom of expression rights are preserved for both those who post and those who access material in cyberspace.

The lessons learned from radio's formative days show an approach to freedom of the air and the public interest that curtailed and balanced expression with what were perceived as societal needs. Post–World War I perspectives on freedom of expression influenced radio's development as much as current First Amendment perspectives will affect contemporary communication regulation. Today's balancing of perceived social needs with expression will form new ways of viewing not only old media such as print, broadcast, and common carrier but also evolving cyberspace media. In the 1920s and 1930s, radio regulations grew through agreements and accommodations of all involved in the policy-making process as a civic consensus for radio developed. The customs, practices, and policies of this culture set standards of acceptable speech in broadcasting for years to come, and a continuing discussion will lead to ever-changing boundaries for freedom of expression in emerging telecommunications and electronic media today.

NOTES
INDEX

⇒ NOTES

The following abbreviations are used frequently in the notes. Papers cited from these collections are used with permission of the collections.

ACLU   American Civil Liberties Union Archives, Seeley G. Mudd Manuscript Library, Princeton University Library. Used by permission of the Princeton University Library and the American Civil Liberties Union.

ANPA   American Newspaper Publishers Association Collection, Newspaper Association of America, Vienna, Virginia. Reprinted with permission of the Newspaper Association of America.

AT&T   American Telephone and Telegraph Collection, AT&T Archives, Warren, New Jersey

BPL   Broadcast Pioneers Library collection, Library of American Broadcasting, Hornbake Library, University of Maryland, College Park

HHPL   Herbert Hoover Presidential Library, West Branch, Iowa

LC   Library of Congress, Manuscript Division, Washington, D.C.

MCHC   Mass Communication History Center, State Historical Society of Wisconsin, Madison

NA   National Archives, Washington, D.C.

NAB   National Association of Broadcasters, Washington, D.C.

ODY   Owen D. Young Collection, Owen D. Young Library, St. Lawrence University, Canton, New York

Payne Fund   Payne Fund, Inc., Records, Ms 4315, Western Reserve Historical Society, Cleveland, Ohio

RG   Record Group of the manuscript and document collection in the National Archives, Washington, D.C.

Sarnoff   David Sarnoff Papers, David Sarnoff Corporation, Princeton, New Jersey

1. Spirit, Whither Goest Thou?

1. Information for these introductory paragraphs comes from material in the HHPL and from materials in the NA, RG 173, Predecessor Agencies to the Federal Communications Commission. The Kaltenborn incident will be developed in detail in chapter 3.

2. Margaret A. Blanchard, "Filling in the Void: Speech and Press in State Courts Prior to *Gitlow*," in *The First Amendment Reconsidered*, ed. Bill Chamberlin and Charlene Brown (New York: Longman Inc., 1982), 20.

3. Three eminent nineteenth-century legal scholars developed a freedom-responsibility nexus used later by others in free speech decisions. Columbia law professor and chancellor of the state of New York James Kent, Supreme Court Justice Joseph Story, and Thomas Cooley, a professor of law and American history at the University of Michigan and a Michigan state supreme court justice, provided the basic principles used later either to support or to rebut claims in speech and press decisions. Scholars at the turn of the century and through the war years built on the traditions established by Kent, Story, and Cooley. For further expansion of these concepts, see Margaret A. Blanchard, "Filling in the Void"; Robert R. Schneider and Stephen B. Presser, "James Kent," in *The Guide to American Law*, vol. 9 (St. Paul: West Publishing Company, 1984), 12–16; James Kent, *Commentaries on American Law*, 5th ed., 2 vols. (New York: printed for the author by James Van Norden and Co., 1844), 2:17; Joseph Story, *Commentaries on the Constitution of the United States*, 2nd ed., 2 vols. (Boston: Little and Brown, 1851), 2:597–98; Thomas M. Cooley, *A Treatise on the Constitutional Limitations Which Rest Upon the Legislative Power of the States of the American Union*, 2nd ed. (Boston: Little, Brown and Co., 1871), 454–55; David Rabban, "The First Amendment in Its Forgotten Years," *Yale Law Journal* 90 (1981): 514, 566; David Rabban, "Free Speech in Progressive Social Thought," *Texas Law Review* 74 (1996): 951–1038; Robert R. Schneider and Stephen B. Presser, "Roscoe Pound," *The Guide to American Law*, vol. 8 (St. Paul: West Publishing Company, 1984), 241–44; Roscoe Pound, "Interests of Personality," part 2, *Harvard Law Review* 28 (1915): 445; Charles Merriam, "Freund, Ernst," in *Dictionary of American Biography*, vol. 11, supplement 1, ed. Harris Starr (New York: Charles Scribner's Sons, 1944), 323–24; Ernst Freund, *The Police Power: Public Policy and Constitutional Rights* (Chicago: Callaghan and Co., 1904), 509–21; Theodore Schoeder, "The Meaning of Unabridged 'Freedom of Speech,'" *Free Speech for*

Radicals (1922; reprint, New York: Benjamin Franklin, 1969), 37; Theodore Schoeder, "Concerning the Meaning of 'Freedom of the Press,'" *"Obscene" Literature and Constitutional Law* (New York: private printing, 1911), 151; Theodore Schoeder, "'Due Process of Law' in Relation to Statutory Uncertainty and Constructive Offenses, Part II," *"Obscene" Literature and Constitutional Law,* 362–63; and Henry Schofield, "Freedom of the Press in the United States," *American Sociological Society: Papers and Proceedings* 9 (1914): 67, 79, 81, 105. Pound advocated a balancing test. Freund viewed most speech as protected under the freedom of speech and religion clauses of the First Amendment. Schoeder advocated the position that all speech, including advocacy of criminal conduct, was protected unless actual harm resulted, while Schofield did not want to protect falsehoods.

4. See, for example, Robert McChesney, *Telecommunications, Mass Media, and Democracy: The Battle for the Control of U.S. Broadcasting, 1928–1935* (New York: Oxford University Press, 1994); Philip Rosen, *The Modern Stentors* (Westport, Conn.: Greenwood Press, 1980); and Erik Barnouw, *A Tower in Babel* (New York: Oxford University Press, 1966).

5. Willard D. Rowland Jr., "The Meaning of 'The Public Interest' in Communications Policy, Part I: Its Origins in State and Federal Regulation," *Communication Law and Policy* 2 (1997): 309–28, and "The Meaning of 'The Public Interest' in Communications Policy, Part II: Its Implementation in Early Broadcast Law and Regulation," *Communication Law and Policy* 2 (1997): 363–96.

6. See Paul Murphy, *The Meaning of Freedom of Speech: First Amendment Freedoms from Wilson to FDR* (Westport, Conn.: Greenwood Publishing Co., 1972); Frederick Allen, *Only Yesterday: An Informal History of the 1920s* (New York: Harper-Row, 1931); Roderick Nash, *The Nervous Generation: American Thought, 1917–1930* (Chicago: Rand-McNally and Co., 1970); John Braeman, Robert Bremmer, and David Brody, eds., *Change and Continuity in Twentieth Century America: The 1920s* (Columbus: Ohio State University Press, 1964); Otis Graham, *The Great Campaigns: Reform and War 1900–1928* (Englewood Cliffs, N.J.: Prentice-Hall, 1971); Mark Sullivan, *Our Times,* vol. 6 (New York: Scribner's Sons, 1946); Elizabeth Stevenson, *Babbitts and Bohemians: The American 1920s* (New York: Macmillan Co., 1967); Isabel Leighton, *The Aspirin Age 1919–1941* (New York: Simon and Schuster, 1949); Joan Hoff Wilson, *The Twenties: The Critical Issues* (Boston: Little, Brown, and Co., 1972); Frederick Paxton, *Postwar Years: Normalcy 1918–1923* (Berkeley: University of California Press, 1948); Don Kirschener, *City and Country: Rural Responses to Urbanization in the 1920s* (Westport, Conn.: Greenwood Publishing Co., 1970); Kenneth Jackson, *The Ku Klux Klan in the City 1915–1930* (New York: Oxford University Press, 1967); David M. Chalmers, *Hooded Americanism: The First Century of the Ku Klux*

Klan 1865–1965 (New York: Doubleday, 1965); William Preston Jr., *Aliens and Dissenters: Federal Suppression of Radicalism 1903–1933* (Cambridge, Mass.: Harvard University Press, 1963); Robert Murray, *Red Scare: A Study in National Hysteria 1919–1920* (Minneapolis: University of Minnesota Press, 1955); and Irving Bernstein, *The Lean Years: A History of the American Worker 1920–1933* (Boston: Houghton Mifflin Co., 1960).

7. Murphy, *The Meaning of Freedom of Speech*, 8.

8. Ibid., 25.

9. Ibid., 25–37.

10. Ellis Hawley, *The Great War and the Search for a Modern Order: A History of the American People and Their Institutions* (New York: St. Martin's Press, 1979), 68, 81–94, 103; William Leuchtenberg, *The Perils of Prosperity, 1914–32* (Chicago: University of Chicago Press, 1958), 178–79; Preston William Slosson, *The Great Crusade and After, 1914–1928* (New York: The Macmillan Company, 1937), 186–88, 228; John D. Hicks, *Republican Ascendancy, 1921–1933* (New York: Harper and Row, Publishers, 1960), 50; J. H. Wilson, *The Twenties*, 39; and Ellis Hawley, "Herbert Hoover, the Commerce Secretariat, and the Vision of an Associated State, 1921–28," *Journal of American History* 61 (June 1974): 116–40.

11. Hawley, *The Great War*, 101–4.

12. Louise Benjamin, "Working It Out Together: Radio Policy From Hoover to the Radio Act of 1927," *Journal of Broadcasting and Electronic Media* 42.2 (spring 1998): 69–84.

2. Corporations and Censorship to 1926

1. Rosen, *The Modern Stentors*, 3–34.

2. Benjamin, "Working It Out Together," 69–84.

3. Westinghouse Engineering Department to Goldsmith, 8 July 1924, NAB, 351K; and Clark to Curtis, 2 June 1936, George H. Clark Collection, Archives Center, Natural Museum of American History (hereafter NMAH), Smithsonian Institution, CL14, General History, 439A.

4. "The History of Broadcasting in the United States by H. P. Davis," Apr. 5, 1928, H. P. Davis Collection, 64:21, box 4, Archives Service Center, University of Pittsburgh.

5. *Tenth Annual Report of the Secretary of Commerce*, (Washington, D.C.: U.S. Government Printing Office, 1922), 13–14, 35, 217–18.

6. For the full story of this struggle, see Rosen, *The Modern Stentors*, 3–33.

7. "Statements on Radio Telephone Conference," Feb. 18, 1922, Notes on Agenda for Radio Telephony Conference, Feb., Mar., Apr. 1922, NA, RG 173, Records of the FCC, Accession 54-A258, box 20; "Policy

As to Radio," *Washington Star,* Feb. 12, 1922, NA, RG 111, box 840, file 337, folder 1.

8. "Report of the Department of Commerce Conference on Radio Telephony," 1922, HHPL, Commerce Papers, box 496, Radio Conference—National First.

9. "Notes for Introduction to Subject," Feb. 23, 1922, Notes on Agenda for Radio Telephony Conference, Feb., Mar., Apr. 1922, NA.

10. Squire to Hoover, Feb. 24, 1922, NA, RG 111, box 840, file 337, folder 1.

11. "Statement by the Secretary of Commerce at the Opening of the Radio Conference on February 27, 1922," HHPL, Commerce Papers, Radio Correspondence, Press Releases, Misc.

12. "Minutes of Open Meetings of Department of Commerce Conference on Radio Telephony," Washington, D.C., Feb. 27 and 28, 1922, HHPL, Commerce Papers, box 496, Radio Conference—National First, Minutes, 39.

13. Ibid., 95–96.

14. Ibid., 123–24.

15. "Radio Telephone Conference of Department of Commerce," memorandum, Mar. 7, 1922, AT&T, box 2005, file: Radio Conference—First National—Department of Commerce, 1922.

16. "Report of the Department of Commerce Conference on Radio Telephony," 1922, HHPL.

17. Ibid.

18. *An Act to Amend an Act Entitled, "An Act to Regulate Radio Communication," Approved August 13, 1912, and for Other Purposes,* 67th Cong., 2nd sess., S. 3694; Notes on Executive Sessions of Radio Telephony Conference, Apr. 17–20, 1922, NA, RG 173, Records of the FCC, Accession 54-A258, box 20.

19. Notes on Executive Sessions of Radio Telephony Conference, April 17–20, 1922, NA; *To Amend an Act to Regulate Radio Communication, Approved August 13, 1912, and for Other Purposes,* 67th Cong., 2nd sess., H.R. 11964, and *An Act to Amend an Act Entitled, "An Act to Regulate Radio Communication," Approved August 13, 1912, and for Other Purposes,* 67th Cong., 2nd sess., S. 3694.

20. Barnouw, *A Tower in Babel,* 121; Rosen, *The Modern Stentors,* 56; "The Urgent Need for Radio Legislation," *Radio Broadcast,* Jan. 1923, HHPL, Public Statements, Bible #276; *To Amend an Act to Regulate Radio Communication, Approved August 13, 1912, and for Other Purposes,* 67th Cong., 2nd sess., H.R. 11964; and *To Amend the Radio Act of 1912,* 67th Cong., 4th sess., H.R. 13773.

21. *Hoover v. Intercity Radio Co., Inc.,* 286 F 1003 (D.C. Cir.), Feb. 5, 1923.

22. Clarence Dill, *Radio Law Practice and Procedure* (Washington, D.C.: National Law Book Co., 1938), 68–69; Rosen, *The Modern Stentors*, 53–54; Hoover to Solicitor General, Department of Justice, Feb. 17, 1923, NA, RG 40, Department of Commerce, file 80524; and Intercity Radio File, NA, RG 173, FCC, General Records, Radio Division, file 1102.

23. "The Urgent Need for Radio Legislation," *Radio Broadcast,* Jan. 1923, HHPL.

24. Ibid.

25. Press release, Department of Commerce, Mar. 6, 1923, HHPL, Commerce Papers, Radio: Conferences, National—Second.

26. Interdepartmental Radio Conference, Mar. 20, 1923, and press release for use Monday morning, Mar. 19, 1923, HHPL, Commerce Papers, Radio: Conferences, National—Second.

27. Memorandum to Mr. Carson, Nov. 27, 1922, HHPL, Commerce Papers, Radio: Interdepartmental Problems.

28. S. M. Kintner, "Factors That Have Made Radio Broadcasting Possible," broadcasted from KDKA, WJZ, KYW, WBZ, Dec. 20, 1922, and William H. Easton, "What the Radio Audience Tells Us," broadcasted from KDKA, WJZ, KYW, WBZ, Dec. 16, 1922, MCHC, Batsel Papers, 1 folder.

29. "H. P. Davis, Vice President of the Westinghouse Electric and Manufacturing Company, Speaks from KDKA on the Problems of Radio Broadcasting," Dec. 1922, MCHC, Batsel Papers, 1 folder.

30. L. W. Chubb, "Broadcasting Conditions," broadcasted from KDKA, WJZ, KYW, WBZ, Dec. 30, 1922, MCHC, Batsel Papers, 1 folder; C. W. Horn, "Radio Broadcasting Conditions," broadcasted from KDKA, WJZ, KYW, WBZ, Jan. 3, 1923; M. C. Batsel, "Selectivity," broadcasted from KDKA, WJZ, KYW, WBZ, Jan. 10, 1923; and P. Thomas, "The Speech Microphone, the Brain of the Broadcasting Set," broadcasted from KDKA, WJZ, KYW, WBZ, Jan. 29, 1923, MCHC, Batsel Papers, 1 folder.

31. Memorandum, "Wave Length for Broadcasting," Mar. 12, 1923, AT&T, box 61, National Radio Conference—Second, 1923.

32. Memorandum for Mr. Edgar S. Bloom regarding Hoover Radio Conference [on] March 20, 1923, Mar. 15, 1923, AT&T, box 61, National Radio Conference—Second, 1923.

33. "Radio Broadcasting," Mar. 19, 1923, AT&T, box 61, National Radio Conference—Second, 1923; A. H. Griswold to Edgar S. Bloom, memorandum, Mar. 29, 1923, AT&T, box 61, National Radio Conference—Second, 1923; "Report of the Second National Radio Conference," NA, RG 173, Records of the FCC, Accession 54-A258, box 20.

34. "Minutes of Open Meetings of Department of Commerce Conference on Radio Telephony," Washington, D.C., Feb. 27 and 28 and Mar. 21, 1922, NA, RG 173, Records of the FCC, Accession 54-A258, box

20. (This last date is mislabeled on the original. It should read "Mar. 21, 1923.")

35. Ibid.

36. *New York Times,* Mar. 25, 1923; "Recommendations of the National Radio Committee," Mar. 24, 1923, HHPL, Commerce Papers, Radio: Conferences, National—Second; D. B. Carson to Secretary of Commerce, memorandum, Mar. 28, 1923, HHPL, Commerce Papers, Radio: Conferences, National—Second; "Radio Service Bulletin," No. 72, Apr. 2, 1923, HHPL, Commerce Papers, Radio: Conferences, National—Second; and "Report of the Second National Radio Conference," Mar. 1923, NA.

37. Barnouw, *A Tower in Babel,* 121.

38. Ibid., 121–22; Rosen, *The Modern Stentors,* 56–59; "Recommendations of the National Radio Committee," Mar. 24, 1923, HHPL; D. B. Carson to Secretary of Commerce, memorandum, Mar. 28, 1923, HHPL; "Radio Service Bulletin," No. 72, HHPL; and "Report of the Second National Radio Conference," Mar. 1923, NA.

39. D. B. Carson memorandum, "Amendments to Regulations," Apr. 4, 1923, NA, RG 173, Records of the FCC, Accession 54-A258, box 20.

40. "Report of the Second National Radio Conference," Mar. 1923, NA.

41. Barnouw, *A Tower in Babel,* 122.

42. Ibid.; "Report of the Second National Radio Conference," Mar. 1923, NA.

43. Barnouw, *A Tower in Babel,* 122–23.

44. William Harkness to Edgar Bloom, memorandum, Jan. 16, 1924, AT&T, box 50, Broadcasting—Station WEAF Increase in Power—1924.

45. William Peck Banning, *Commercial Broadcasting Pioneer: The WEAF Experiment 1922–1926* (Cambridge, Mass.: Harvard University Press, 1946), 134–36; Barnouw, *A Tower in Babel,* 117; and G. E. Folk to George Schubel, Sept. 27, 1923, AT&T, box 50, Patent Infringement Suit, Station WHN, 1924.

46. Statement made before the Radio Trade Association, New York, Mar. 13, 1924, AT&T, box 61, Radio Broadcasting Infringement Problems, 1924; Elam Miller to Mr. W. E. Harkness, memorandum, Apr. 9, 1924, AT&T, box 62, Radio Broadcasting, Licensing Non-Licensed Stations, 1924.

47. P. W. Armstrong to Mr. Elam Miller, memorandum, Nov. 7, 1924, AT&T, box 62, Radio Broadcasting, Licensing Non-Licensed Stations, 1924; Barnouw, *A Tower in Babel,* 118; and Banning, *Commercial Broadcasting Pioneer,* 139.

48. G. E. Folk to Duell, Warfield, and Duell, Mar. 17, 1924, and "The Situation of the American Telephone and Telegraph Company with Radio Broadcasting—H.B. Thayer—1924," AT&T, box 50, Patent Infringe-

ment Suit, Station WHN, 1924; Banning, *Commercial Broadcasting Pioneer*, 209; and Barnouw, *A Tower in Babel*, 118–19.

49. J. A. Holman to the staff of WEAF, memorandum, Mar. 12, 1924, AT&T, box 50, Patent Infringement Suit, Station WHN, 1924; Barnouw, *A Tower in Babel*, 176; and Banning, *Commercial Broadcasting Pioneer*, 213.

50. "From—Information Department, American Tel. and Tel. Co.," Mar. 6, 1924 (press release), AT&T, box 50, Patent Infringement Suit, Station WHN, 1924.

51. Memorandum for Mr. S. L. Ross, Director of Programs, Mar. 11, 1924, with "Foreword" and "Speech," AT&T, box 61, Radio Broadcasting Infringement Problems, 1924.

52. Ibid.

53. House, *Report of Federal Trade Commission on the Radio Industry*, 67th Cong., 4th sess., H.R. 548.

54. Ibid., 69.

55. Barnouw, *A Tower in Babel*, 201.

56. E. E. Plummer to Herbert Hoover, telegram, Mar. 7, 1924, HHPL, Commerce Papers, Plumby, E.-Plymouth Coal.

57. Herbert Hoover to E. E. Plummer, telegram, Mar. 10, 1924, HHPL, Commerce Papers, Radio, Radio World's Fair. Also in HHPL, Commerce Papers, Plumby, E.-Plymouth Coal.

58. "Hoover Takes Stand on Question," *Radio Digest*, Mar. 22, 1924.

59. Statement by Secretary Hoover for release to Monday afternoon papers, Mar. 10, 1924, HHPL, Commerce Papers, Radio Correspondence, Press Releases, Misc. and Bible #363.

60. Statement by Secretary Hoover at hearings before the Committee on the Merchant Marine and Fisheries on H.R. 7357, "To Regulate Radio Communication, and for Other Purposes," Mar. 11, 1924, HHPL, Commerce Papers, Radio Correspondence, Press Releases, Misc.

61. "The Government's Duty Is to Keep the Ether Open and Free to All," *New York World*, Mar. 16, 1924.

62. Radio Talk by Secretary Hoover, Washington, D.C., Mar. 26, 1924, HHPL, Commerce Papers, Radio Correspondence, Press Releases, Misc.

63. Ibid.

64. Statement made before the Radio Trade Association, New York, Mar. 13, 1924, AT&T.

65. P. W. Armstrong to Mr. Elam Miller, memorandum, Nov. 7, 1924, AT&T; Barnouw, *A Tower in Babel*, 176.

66. Elam Miller to Mr. W. E. Harkness, memorandum, July 16, 1924, AT&T, box 62, Radio Broadcasting, Licensing Non-Licensed Stations, 1924.

67. W. E. Harkness to E. S. Bloom, memorandum, July 17, 1924, AT&T, box 62, Radio Broadcasting, Licensing Non-Licensed Stations, 1924.

68. R. W. Armstrong to W. E. Harkness, memorandum, Aug. 5, 1924, AT&T, box 62, Radio Broadcasting, Licensing Non-Licensed Stations, 1924.

69. Payton Spence to Mr. Elam Miller, memorandum, Subject: Suggested Policy for Licensing Infringing Broadcast Stations, With Appendix A, Nov. 4, 1925, AT&T, box 62, Radio Broadcasting, Licensing Non-licensed Stations, 1925.

70. Barnouw, *A Tower in Babel,* 119.

71. Elam Miller to Mr. J. C. Lynch, memorandum, Subject: Licensing Infringing Broadcasting Stations, Oct. 18, 1926, AT&T, box 62, Radio Broadcasting, Licensing Non-Licensed Stations, 1926–29.

72. Confidential memorandum and subjects for consideration at the next radio conference, July 25, 1924; memorandum for Mr. Elam Miller, July 25, 1924; memorandum for file, Aug. 1, 1924; and memorandum for Miller, Aug. 23, 1924, AT&T, box 61, National Radio Conference, Third, 1924.

73. Memorandum for file, Sept. 10, (1924), AT&T, box 61, National Radio Conference, Third, 1924; Sarnoff to H. P. James, Mar. 19, 1924; and memorandum from Guy Tripp: A Plan of Super-Broadcasting to the Nation, 1924, Sarnoff Library, David Sarnoff Papers, *Sourcebook for Early Reports,* vol. 1, 1914–1924; "Draft of April 15, 1925, III. Joint Proposals," ODY, box 96, AT&T Wireless.

74. Memorandum for Mr. Elam Miller, Aug. 30, 1924, and memorandum for file, Sept. 29, 1924, AT&T, box 61, National Radio Conference, Third, 1924.

75. J. G. Harbord to Owen Young, Oct. 20, 1924, ODY, box 141, General Harbord.

76. Opening address by Herbert Hoover, Secretary of Commerce, in Recommendations for Regulation of Radio, Oct. 6–10, 1924, HHPL, Commerce Papers, Radio: Conference, National—Third, Correspondence; "Secretary Hoover Address Third National Radio Conference," release for use Tuesday morning, Oct. 7, 1924, HHPL, Commerce Papers, Radio: Conference, National—Third, Reports. Seventeen stations carried it: WCAP, Washington, D.C.; WGR, Buffalo; KSD, St. Louis; WOAW, Omaha; WCCO, Minneapolis; KLZ, Denver; WEAF, New York City; WMAF, South Dartmouth, Massachusetts; WDAF, Kansas City; KGO, Oakland, California; WOO, Philadelphia; WOC, Davenport, Iowa; WJAR, Providence, Rhode Island; WLW, Cincinnati; KDKA, Pittsburgh; WMAQ, Chicago; and WTAM, Cleveland.

77. Coolidge address, "Third Radio Conference, Called by and under the Auspices of the United States Department of Commerce," Oct. 6–10, 1924, HHPL, Commerce Papers, Radio: Conference, National—Third (Proceedings).

78. Report of Proceedings of Sub-Committee No. 3 Dealing with Gen-

eral Problems of Radio Broadcasting, Oct. 6–10, 1924, HHPL, Commerce Papers, box 496, Radio: Conferences, National—Third (Proceedings); "Digest of Progress Reports, Third National Conference," Oct. 9, 1924, NA, RG 173, Records of the FCC, Accession 54-A258, box 20.

79. "Digest of Progress Reports, Third National Conference," Oct. 9, 1924, NA.

80. "Third Radio Conference Called by and under the Auspices of the United States Department of Commerce, Report of Proceedings," Oct. 6–10, 1924, NA, RG 173, Records of the FCC, Accession 54-A258; Report of Proceedings of Sub-Committee No. 3 Dealing with General Problems of Radio Broadcasting, Oct. 6–10, 1924, HHPL.

81. "Third Radio Conference Called by and under the Auspices of the United States Department of Commerce, Report of Proceedings," Oct. 6–10, 1924, NA.

82. Report of Proceedings of Sub-Committee No. 3 Dealing with General Problems of Radio Broadcasting, Oct. 6–10, 1924, HHPL.

83. Ibid.

84. Memorandum for file, Sept. 10, 1924, AT&T; and Sarnoff to James, Mar. 19, 1924, with memorandum by Guy Tripp, Sarnoff Library. Also, see following items in ODY, box 96, AT&T Wireless: David Sarnoff to E. P. Edwards, Jan. 13, 1922, with Memorandum of the Three-Company Executive Broadcasting Committee, Jan. 12, 1922; Edwards to Sarnoff, Jan. 16, 1922; A. H. Griswold to E. S. Bloom, memorandum, Subject: American Telephone and Telegraph—General Electric Company License Agreement, Aug. 14, 1922; Sarnoff to Young, Aug. 16, 1922; and "Draft of April 15, 1925, III. Joint Proposals."

85. Report of Proceedings of Sub-Committee No. 3 Dealing with General Problems of Radio Broadcasting, Oct. 6–10, 1924, HHPL.

86. Ibid.

87. Ibid.

88. Ibid.

89. Recommendations for Regulation of Radio, Oct. 6–10, 1924, HHPL.

90. See Hawley, *The Great War*, 87–90, 107–13.

91. Memorandum for file, Subject: Conference Luncheon with Dr. Goldsmith with Regard to the Forthcoming National Radio Conference, Oct. 9, 1925, AT&T, box 61, National Radio Conference, Fourth, 1926.

92. Memorandum, Subject: General Policy of the Bell System Representatives to Be Followed at the Fourth National Radio Conference, Oct. 31, 1925, AT&T, box 61, National Radio Conference, Fourth, 1926.

93. Ibid.

94. See the lists of delegates to the third and fourth conferences, NA, RG 173, Records of the FCC, Accession 54-258A, box 20.

95. Questions for Consideration by General Conference, Fourth Na-

tional Radio Conference, Department of Commerce, Nov. 9, 1925, and "Hoover Calls Radio Conference," press release for use not earlier than Oct. 7, 1925, HHPL, Commerce Papers, Radio: Conferences, National—Fourth.

96. "Proceedings and Recommendations for Regulation of Radio," Fourth National Radio Conference, Nov. 9–11, 1925, NA, RG 173, Records of the FCC, Accession 54-A258, box 20. This report is also in HHPL, Commerce Papers, Radio: Conference, National—Fourth.

97. Report of Sub-Committee No. 2 (Fourth Radio Conference), NA, RG 173, Records of the FCC, Accession 54-A258, box 20.

98. Ibid.

99. "Fourth National Radio Conference, Resolutions Adopted by Committee No. 4 on Operating Regulations, November 10, 1925," NA, RG 173, Records of the FCC, Accession 54-A258, box 20.

100. "Committee No. 8—Legislation," NA, RG 173, Records of the FCC, Accession 54-A258, box 20.

101. "Proceedings and Recommendations for Regulation of Radio," Fourth National Radio Conference, Nov. 9–11, 1925, NA.

102. Secretary of Commerce Hoover, "Radio Problems and Conference Recommendations," an address broadcast from Washington, D.C., Nov. 12, 1925, HHPL, Commerce Papers, Radio: Conferences, National—Fourth.

103. "Radio Affairs—Letter to T. Stevenson," Nov. 19, 1925, HHPL, Public Statements, Bible #524A.

3. To Speak, or Not to Speak, That Is the Question: Political Speech to 1926

1. *Schenck v. United States,* 249 U.S. 47, 52 (1919). Also, see *Frohwerk v. United States,* 249 U.S. 204, 206 (1919).

2. Rabban, "The First Amendment in Its Forgotten Years," 514, 562–67, and "Free Speech in Progressive Social Thought," 951–1038. According to Rabban, during this century's first three decades, four scholars were particularly important in their analyses of free speech issues: Henry Schofield, professor of law at Northwestern; Ernst Freund, University of Chicago law professor; Roscoe Pound, Harvard University law professor; and Theodore Schoeder, guiding force behind the Free Speech League, a precursor to the American Civil Liberties Union. Also see Schneider and Presser, "Roscoe Pound," 241–44; Pound, "Interests of Personality," 445; Merriam, "Freund, Ernst," 323–24; Freund, *The Police Power,* 509–21; Schoeder, "The Meaning of Unabridged 'Freedom of Speech,'" 37, "Concerning the Meaning of 'Freedom of the Press,'" 151, and "'Due Process of Law,'" 362–63; and Schofield, "Freedom of the Press in the United States," 67, 79, 81, 105.

3. Untitled editorial, *The Nation,* Apr. 16, 1924, 413; David Ostroff,

"Equal Time: Origins of Section 18 of the Radio Act of 1927," *Journal of Broadcasting* 24 (1980): 367, 370.

4. Speech delivered by W. E. Harkness, "Radio Broadcasting in Metropolitan Area," Feb. 1923, MCHC, E. P. H. James Papers, box 1, folder 2: NBC Background File, Speeches Re Inception of Commercial Broadcasting, 1922–23; Harkness to E. S. Bloom, memorandum, Feb. 2, 1924, AT&T, box 42, Radio Broadcasting, Bell System Activity, 1922–23, 1925–26.

5. H. M. Crist, Managing Editor, *Brooklyn Eagle,* to H. B. Thayer, President, AT&T, Sept. 22, 1924, AT&T, box 57, Radio Broadcasting, Complaint by the *Brooklyn Eagle,* 1924; H. V. Kaltenborn, "Reminiscences," 104, MCHC, Kaltenborn Papers; Barnouw, *A Tower in Babel,* 138–40; and Banning, *Commercial Broadcasting Pioneer,* 156.

6. William Harkness, "Reminiscences," 35, Columbia University Oral History Collection, New York, cited in Barnouw, *A Tower in Babel,* 140–41.

7. Crist to Thayer, Sept. 22, 1924, AT&T.

8. Thayer to Crist, Sept. 24, 1924, and Crist to Thayer, Sept. 25, 1924, AT&T, box 57, Radio Broadcasting, Complaint by the *Brooklyn Eagle,* 1924; and Crist to Gordon Moss, Apr. 29, 1931, ACLU Papers.

9. *Brooklyn Eagle,* June 12, 1924, cited in Giraud Chester, "The Radio Commentaries of H. V. Kaltenborn: A Case Study in Persuasion" (Ph.D. diss., University of Wisconsin, 1947), 88.

10. Barnouw, *A Tower in Babel,* 141–42; Gleason Archer, *History of Radio to 1926* (New York: American Historical Society, 1938), 396.

11. *Congressional Record,* 67th Cong., 4th sess., 1924, 64, pt. 3: 2781–82.

12. House Committee on the Merchant Marine and Fisheries, *To Regulate Radio Communication, and for Other Purposes: Hearings on H.R. 7357,* 68th Cong., 1st Sess., Mar. 11, 1924, 36 (hereafter cited as "Hearings on H.R. 7357").

13. Ibid.

14. E. B. Mallory speech before the Second Annual Radio Conference under the Auspices of the Music Master Corp. of Philadelphia, Mar. 6, 1924, p. 38, HHPL, box 489.

15. W. A. McAdoo to Owen Young, Jan. 5, 1924; J. G. Harbord to H. V. Morrison, Jan. 18, 1924; Morrison to McAdoo, Jan. 24, 1924, ODY, box 10, file 1-93, McAdoo.

16. Henry E. Marschalk speech before the Second Annual Radio Conference under the Auspices of the Music Master Corp. of Philadelphia, Mar. 6, 1924, p. 22, HHPL, box 489.

17. Hearings on H.R. 7357, 83.

18. Minutes of the First Annual Convention of the National Association of Broadcasters, BPL, file: VF-NAB-History.

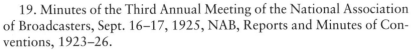

19. Minutes of the Third Annual Meeting of the National Association of Broadcasters, Sept. 16–17, 1925, NAB, Reports and Minutes of Conventions, 1923–26.

20. William G. Shepard, "Blotting Out the Blah," *Colliers,* Aug. 23, 1924, 11.

21. "The Use of Bell System Facilities in the Broadcasting of the Political Campaign of 1924," AT&T, box 42, Radio Broadcasting, Bell System Activity, 1922–23, 1925–26, 2 (hereafter cited as "Use of Bell Facilities, 1924").

22. Ibid., 2–3.

23. Ibid., 6–7, and Harkness to Sarnoff, May 28, 1924, George H. Clark Collection, Archives Center, NMAH, CWC 134-1164A.

24. "Use of Bell Facilities, 1924," 7–10.

25. Ibid., 16–18.

26. Wilson to Hale, Feb. 27, 1924; Wilson to Abbot, Feb. 29, 1924; Abbott to Wilson, Mar. 3, 1924; Peirce to Cooper, Mar. 4, 1924; Clark to Wilson, Mar. 7, 1924; Wilson to Clark, Mar. 8, 1924; Wilson to DuBois, Mar. 13, 1924; AT&T memorandum, "Long Distance Telephony as an Adjunct to Radio Broadcasting"; and pamphlet, "Why Chicago Did Not Rebroadcast President Coolidge Message," AT&T, box 46, Radio Broadcasting, Long Distance Facilities Required, 1924.

27. Mr. Quinn to Mr. Pierson, confidential memorandum, no date, ODY, box 90, RCA; and "Republican National Committee Receives Offer," *New York Times,* Jan. 6, 1924, 3.

28. "Use of Bell Facilities, 1924," 11–15.

29. Gleason Archer, "Conventions, Campaigns and Kilocycles in 1924: The First Political Broadcasts," *Journal of Broadcasting* 4 (1960): 110.

30. WJZ logs, Tuesday, June 10, to Thursday, June 12, 1924, MCHC, NBC Papers, General Files, Historical Files, 1923–27, 1930, box 98, folder: WJZ Logs, May–June 1924.

31. "J. P. Sousa Will Direct Band," *New York Times,* Apr. 25, 1924, 19; "Plans for Broadcasting," *New York Times,* June 8, 1924, sec. 8, p. 19; "Opening Session Broadcast by 15 Stations," *New York Times,* June 11, 1924, 4; "Coolidge and Dawes Nominated," *New York Times,* June 13, 1924, 1; "3,000,000 Listened In," *New York Times,* June 17, 1924, 24; "Will Rogers' Commentary," *New York Times,* June 13, 1924, 7. Also see convention coverage on page 1 of *New York Times* of June 11 and 12, 1924; Art Ronnie, "First Convention on Radio," *Journal of Broadcasting* 8 (1963): 245; and Lewis Weeks, "The Radio Election of 1924," *Journal of Broadcasting* 8 (1960): 233.

32. "Statement by Robert LaFollette, Jr.," *New York Times,* June 11, 1924, 5; "Formal Announcement of Candidacy," *New York Times,* June 16, 1924, 1; Archer, "Conventions, Campaigns and Kilocycles," 112–13; and Weeks, "Radio Election of 1924," 236.

33. "Use of Bell Facilities, 1924," 22.

34. Untitled editorial, *The Nation*, July 23, 1924, 85.

35. Hawley, *The Great War*, 78–79; Hicks, *Republican Ascendancy*, 89–101; and Donald McCoy, *Coming of Age* (Middlesex, England: Penguin Books, Ltd., 1973), 98–102.

36. "Use of Bell Facilities, 1924," 1, table 1; Weeks, "Radio Election of 1924," 235.

37. "Use of Bell Facilities, 1924," 21–22.

38. Ibid., 21; Barnouw, *A Tower in Babel*, 149–50; Archer, "Conventions, Campaigns and Kilocycles," 111–12; Weeks, "Radio Election of 1924," 235–36; and Ronnie, "First Convention on Radio," 246.

39. Leuchtenburg, *The Perils of Prosperity*, 132–33.

40. Archer, "Conventions, Campaigns and Kilocycles," 112.

41. "The Spellbinder and Radio," *Saturday Evening Post*, Aug. 23, 1924, 20.

42. Leuchtenburg, *The Perils of Prosperity*, 134; Hawley, *The Great War*, 78–79.

43. Leuchtenburg, *The Perils of Prosperity*, 134–35.

44. "Use of Bell Facilities, 1924," 10.

45. Archer, "Conventions, Campaigns and Kilocycles," 115. Elam Miller to W. E. Harkness, memorandum, July 17, 1924; "Suggested Stations for National Broadcasting," report, July 21 1924; and R. W. Armstrong to Elam Miller, memorandum, July 3, 1924, MCHC, James Papers, box 1, file: NBC Background File, 1924–25 Memoranda. "Activities of the American Telegraph and Telephone Company," AT&T, box 1062, Radio Broadcasting, Activities of AT&T Co., 1921–26.

46. Elam Miller to W. E. Harkness, memorandum, July 17, 1924, MCHC.

47. "Use of Bell Facilities, 1924," 1–8, table 1. The interconnected stations were combinations of WEAF, New York City; WCAP, Washington, D.C.; WNAC, Boston; WMAF, South Dartmouth, Massachusetts; WDBH, Worcester, Massachusetts; WJAR, Providence, Rhode Island; WSB, Atlanta; WGY, Schenectady, New York; WGR, Buffalo; KDKA, Pittsburgh; WTAM, Cleveland; WSAI and WLW, Cincinnati; WGN, WMAQ, and WEBH, Chicago; KSD, St. Louis; and WDAF, Kansas City.

48. "Statement from Mr. Owen D. Young for *The Wireless Age*," ODY, box 105, Wireless Press.

49. "Radio Monopoly and Mr. LaFollette," press release, Oct. 16, 1924, HHPL, Bible #405.

50. Ibid.

51. Weeks, "Radio Election of 1924," 238–39.

52. Report of Proceedings of Sub-Committee No. 3 Dealing with General Problems of Radio Broadcasting, Oct. 6–10, 1924, HHPL, 44–45.

53. Martin Rice to MacLafferty, June 6, 1924, ODY, box 127, Broadcasting.

54. "Operating a Broadcast Station," talk given by W. E. Harkness to A.I.E.E., Nov. 12, 1924, AT&T, box 59, Operating a Broadcasting Station.

55. "Socialist Party Plans Radio in Place of Soap-box Orators," *New York Times,* May 4, 1926, 1.

56. "Debs' Death," *New York Times,* Oct. 22, 1926, 11.

57. "Socialists to Erect Debs Radio Station," *New York Times,* Dec. 22, 1926, 16.

58. *Hoover v. Intercity Radio Co., Inc.; United States v. Zenith Radio Corporation,* 12 F2d 614 (N.D. Ill, 1926); 35 Ops. Atty. Gen. 126 (July 8, 1926).

59. House Committee on the Merchant Marine and Fisheries, *To Regulate Radio Communication: Hearings on H.R. 5589,* 69th Cong., 1st sess., Jan. 6, 7, 14, and 15, 1926, 56–58.

60. Ibid., 83–87.

61. *Congressional Record,* 69th Cong., 1st sess., 1926, 67, pt. 5: 5491.

62. *Congressional Record,* 67, pt. 11: 12501; "Coolidge Rebuff in Dill Radio Bill," *New York World,* May 7, 1926, ACLU Papers, 1926, vol. 300.

63. Isabelle Kendig to Lucille Milner, May 5, 1926, ACLU Papers, 1926, vol. 310.

64. *Congressional Record,* 67, pt. 5: 5483, 5560–61.

65. Minutes of the Fourth Annual Meeting of the National Association of Broadcasters, Sept. 14, 1926, 10, NAB, Reports and Minutes of Conventions, 1923–26.

66. Ibid., 10–11.

67. Ibid., 11.

68. ODY:S to James Hotchkiss, Oct. 23, 1926, ODY, box 128, Broadcasting.

69. M. H. Aylesworth to Herbert Merrill, Dec. 20, 1926, MCHC, NBC Papers, Central Files, Correspondence, box 5, file: Socialist Party, 1926–28.

70. J. G. Harbord to Editor, *New York World,* Oct. 27, 1926, ODY, box 128, Broadcasting.

71. ODY:LM to James Hotchkiss, Oct. 23, 1926, ODY, box 128, Broadcasting.

72. Herbert Merrill to Kolin Hagar, Nov. 3, 1926, and M. H. Aylesworth to Merrill, Dec. 20, 1926, MCHC, NBC Papers, Central Files, Correspondence, box 5, file: Socialist Party, 1926–28.

73. Herbert Merrill to Director of Radio-Broadcasting Sta. W.J.Z., Dec. 9, 1926, MCHC, NBC Papers, Central Files, Correspondence, box 5, file: Socialist Party, 1926–28.

74. M. H. Aylesworth to Herbert Merrill, Dec. 20, 1926, MCHC.

75. Bertha Brainard to M. H. Aylesworth, Jan. 11, 1927, MCHC, NBC Papers, Central Files, Correspondence, box 5, file: Socialist Party, 1926–28.

76. Memorandum for Mr. Edgar S. Bloom, Apr. 20, 1926, MCHC, NBC Papers, Central Files, Correspondence, box 5, file: Norman Thomas, 1926.

77. Norman Thomas to G. F. McClelland, Apr. 21, 1926; Thomas to McClelland, Apr. 22, 1926; and newspaper article, "Norman Thomas Defies Riot Act; Put in N.J. Jail," *New York Morning World,* Apr. 15, 1926, MCHC, NBC Papers, Central Files, Correspondence, box 5, file: Norman Thomas, 1926.

78. Norman Thomas, "Is There Radio Censorship?" *Popular Radio,* Aug. 1926, 335, and "How to Win the Radio from Reaction, an Address Which Was to Have Been Delivered over WMCA, New York City," May 22, 1926, ACLU Papers, 1926, vol. 304.

79. Ibid.

80. "A Page with the Editor," *Popular Radio,* Aug. 1926, 306; and "Cancel Radio Talk by Norman Thomas," *New York Times,* May 17, 1926, ACLU Papers, 1926, vol. 315.

81. "Editor of *Radio News* Answers Dr. Thomas," June 8, 1926, *New York Times,* ACLU Papers, 1926, vol. 301. Other newspaper articles covering this situation from unnamed newspapers are in the ACLU Collection, 1926, vol. 315.

82. Thomas, "How to Win the Radio from Reaction," May 22, 1926, ACLU Papers.

83. Thomas, "Is There a Radio Censorship?," 335.

84. Heywood Brown, "It Seems to Me," *New York Morning World,* Apr. 22, 1926; "WEAF Bars Thomas from Radio Speech" *New York Herald Tribune,* Apr. 20, 1926; "Norman Thomas Barred by WEAF," *New York Evening World,* Apr. 20, 1926; "Last Night on the Radio," *New York Herald Tribune,* Apr. 21, 1926; "Hackensack Bars Speech by Thomas," *New York Times,* Apr. 21, 1926; "WEAF Answers Thomas," *New York Sun,* Apr. 21, 1926; "WEAF Denies Ban on Thomas Talk," *New York American,* Apr. 21, 1926; "Perhaps That's It," editorial, *Brooklyn Times,* Apr. 22, 1926; "Public Vigilance and Radio," *New York Evening World,* editorial, Apr. 22, 1926; F.P.A. column, *New York Morning World,* Apr. 22, 1926; and "Conning Tower in New York," *New York Morning World,* Apr. 22, 1926, MCHC, NBC Papers, Central Files, Correspondence, box 5, file: Norman Thomas, 1926.

85. M. Cuthbert to G. F. McClelland, memorandum, Apr. 21, 1926, MCHC, NBC Papers, Central Files, Correspondence, box 5, file: Norman Thomas, 1926.

4. Free Speech and the Formation of NBC

1. House, *Report of the Federal Trade Commission on the Radio Industry*, H.R. 548, 67th Cong., 4th sess. Also, see Christopher Sterling and Mike Kittross, *Stay Tuned: A Concise History of American Broadcasting*, 2nd ed. (Belmont, Calif.: Wadsworth Publishing, 1990), 53–58.

2. House, *Report of the Federal Trade Commission on the Radio Industry*, H.R. 548, 69.

3. *New York Times*, Jan. 24, 1924.

4. Barnouw, *A Tower in Babel*, 160–62, 181–84.

5. Gleason Archer, *Big Business and Radio* (New York: American Historical Company, 1939), 126–30; "In the Arbitration Proceedings Between the Telephone Group and the Radio Corporation Group, Roland W. Boyden, Referee," no date, ODY, box 96, AT&T Wireless (hereafter cited as "Arbitration Proceedings," no date).

6. "Arbitration Proceedings," no date.

7. Archer, *Big Business*, 150–65.

8. Barnouw, *A Tower in Babel*, 182; "In the Arbitration Proceedings Between the Telephone Group and the Radio Corporation Group," report, Nov. 1924; Albert Davis to Owen D. Young, June 4, 1924; and Davis to Gerard Swope, Nov. 15, 1924, ODY, box 96, AT&T Wireless.

9. Harbord to Owen D. Young, radiogram, Nov. 15, 1924, ODY, box 96, AT&T Wireless; Barnouw, *A Tower in Babel*, 183; Archer, *Big Business*, 170.

10. Harbord to Owen D. Young, radiogram, Nov. 17, 1924, ODY, box 96, AT&T Wireless; Barnouw, *A Tower in Babel*, 183; Archer, *Big Business*, 170–72.

11. Gifford to Harbord, Jan. 17, 1925, and Harbord to Gifford, Jan. 15, 1925, AT&T, box 50, Arbitration Proceedings—1925; A. G. Davis to Young, Mar. 31, 1925, and "Notes on Mr. Gifford's Memorandum of March 27, 1925," Mar. 30 and 31, 1925, ODY, box 96, AT&T Wireless; Barnouw, *A Tower in Babel*, 183.

12. Barnouw, *A Tower in Babel*, 183–84; Archer, *Big Business*, 193–98.

13. Barnouw, *A Tower in Babel*, 184; Archer, *Big Business*, 196–206; "Draft of April 15, 1925, to make use in the United States and to make and sell for export," report; "Mr. Sarnoff's Fundamentals," report, Feb. 5, 1925; L. V. Morrison to Owen Young regarding "Memorandum from A. G. Davis," Mar. 7, 1925; Young to W. S. Gifford, Mar. 31, 1925; Gifford to Young, Mar. 31, 1925, with "Suggestions" memorandum, Mar. 31, 1925; and "Memorandum—Proposed Negotiations Between Radio and Telephone Group," Mar. 31, 1925, ODY, box 96, AT&T Wireless.

14. Minutes, RCA Board of Directors, Jan. 6, 1922, ODY, box 93, RCA Board of Directors; E. P. Edwards to A. G. Davis, Jan. 6, 1922; Davis to Edwards, Jan. 7, 1922; Davis to E. W. Rice, Jan. 16, 1922; and ODY to

E. M. Herr, Rice, David Sarnoff (RCA Committee on Broadcasting), July 19, 1922, ODY, box 96, AT&T Wireless.

15. Memorandum of H. P. Davis, Oct. 12, 1925, AIS, Davis Collection, 64:21, box 1.

16. "To the Board of Directors, Radio Corporation of America," from David Sarnoff, H. P. Davis, and Albert G. Davis, RCA Committee on Broadcasting, ODY, box 93, RCA Board of Directors.

17. Minutes of the Board of Directors Meeting, Jan. 22, 1926, ODY, box 93, RCA Board of Directors.

18. David Sarnoff to J. G. Harbord, July 15, 1926, ODY, box 128, Broadcasting.

19. Report submitted by Ames and Norr Inc., Public Relations Counsel, Radio Corporation of America, to Mr. Sarnoff, July 14, 1926, ODY, box 128, Broadcasting.

20. "WEAF Sold; Air Combine Is Forecast," *New York Tribune,* July 22, 1926, 1; "WEAF Sale Only Part of Huge Deal," and "Coming Monopoly of Broadcasting by WEAF Is Seen," *New York World,* July 23, 1926, in ODY, box 128, Broadcasting.

21. Minutes of the Board of Directors of the Radio Corporation of America, Aug. 10, 1926, ODY, box 93, RCA Board of Directors.

22. David Sarnoff, "Plan for the Support of National Broadcasting Through Formation of the Public Broadcasting Company," Aug. 12 (1925), Davis Collection, 64:21, box 1; Office of the President, RCA, to the Board of Directors, RCA, Sept. 13, 1926, and Minutes of the Board of Directors of the Radio Corporation of America, Sept. 17, 1926, ODY, box 93, RCA Board of Directors.

23. "Radio Still Up in the Air," *Literary Digest,* July 24, 1926, 2; Minutes of the Board of Directors of the Radio Corporation of America, Sept. 17, 1926, ODY. Also see "Broadcasting on a National Scale," *Literary Digest,* Oct. 2, 1926, 13, and "Radio Converts the Continent into an Auditorium," *Literary Digest,* Dec. 4, 1926, 26–27.

24. "Opening Remarks, Inaugural Program, National Broadcasting Company, Monday evening—November 15," delivered by Merlin Hall Aylesworth, President, ODY, box 128; Aylesworth to Owen Young, Oct. 2, 1926; Broadcasting and Advisory Council National Broadcasting Company, circa Nov. 1, 1926, memorandum; and Charles MacFarland to Stuart Parker, Apr. 25, 1927, ODY, box 154, Advisory Council. As to Rosenwald's status, also see J. G. Harbord to L. V. Morrison, Nov. 1, 1926, ODY, box 154, Advisory Council.

25. Owen D. Young to Elihu Root, Nov. 6, 1926, ODY, box 154, Advisory Council. The same or similar letters were sent to other proposed members.

26. Edwin Alderman to Owen Young, Nov. 12, 1926; and Morgan J. O'Brien to Young, Nov. 10, 1926, ODY, box 154, Advisory Council.

27. Owen Young to Charles E. Hughes, Nov. 18, 1926, ODY, box 154, Advisory Council. Similar letters were sent to other invited members.

28. NBC press release, Nov. 1, 1926, cited in Barnouw, *A Tower in Babel*, 188.

29. H. P. Davis to M. H. Aylesworth, Nov. 24, 1926, Davis Collection, 64:21, box 1; Aylesworth, President NBC, to Owen Young, Chairman of the Board, Dec. 28, 1926, ODY, box 128, Broadcasting.

30. Minutes of the Board of Directors of the National Broadcasting Company, Inc., Dec. 3, 1926, ODY, box 153, NBC—Board of Directors.

31. Memorandum of Minutes of the Advisory Council of the National Broadcasting Company, first meeting, Feb. 18, 1927, ODY, box 154, Advisory Council.

32. Ibid.

33. Ibid.

34. Memorandum of Minutes of the Advisory Council of the National Broadcasting Company, second meeting, and first draft of letter "To the Members of the Advisory Council of the National Broadcasting Company," n.d., ODY, box 154, Advisory Council.

35. Press release, "History Looks Backward as Radio Looks Forward," Nov. 14, 1941, MCHC, James Papers, box 4, file 4, Press Releases.

36. Hiram Jome, *Economics of the Radio Industry* (Chicago: A. W. Shaw Company, 1925), 175–76.

37. Untitled memorandum, Sept. 18, 1924, AT&T, box 61, National Radio Conference, Third, 1924.

38. House, *To Reduce and Equalize Taxation, to Provide Revenue, and for Other Purposes*, 68th Cong., 1st Sess., H.R. 6715.

39. *Congressional Record*, 68th Cong., 1st sess., 1924, 65, pt. 8: 7697; House, *To Reduce and Equalize Taxation, to Provide Revenue, and for Other Purposes*, H.R. 6715.

40. From J. L. Bernard, Information Bureau, Radio Corporation of America, New York City, N.Y., Apr. 7, 1924, press release, ODY, box 90, RCA.

41. J. G. Harbord to The Honorable Finance Committee of the United States Senate, Apr. 7, 1924, ODY, box 90, RCA.

42. *Congressional Record*, 65, pt. 8: 7698–99.

43. Ibid., 7700.

44. Zenith Corporation, *The Zenith Story: A History from 1919* (Chicago: Zenith Corporation, 1955), 8.

45. "Zenith Radio Case Decision and Necessity for Legislation Press Release," Apr. 20, 1926, HHPL, Commerce Papers, Radio Correspondence, Press Releases. Also, see Barnouw, *A Tower in Babel*, 180, and Rosen, *The Modern Stentors*, 93–95.

46. 12 F2d 614, 616–17 (N.D. Ill. 1926).

47. Statement by Secretary Hoover, Apr. 20, 1926, HHPL, Commerce Papers, Radio: Zenith Radio Corporation.

48. *Hoover v. Intercity Radio.*
49. 35 Ops. Atty. Gen. 126 (July 8, 1926).
50. "Bulletin—July 15, 1926," National Association of Broadcasters, NA, RG 173, box 168, file: FCC, 3601.
51. "To Every Station Owner," July 19, 1926, National Association of Broadcasters, and "Certificate of Promise," n.d., NA, RG 173, box 168, file: FCC, 3601.
52. "Bulletin—July 28, 1926," National Association of Broadcasters, NA, RG 173, box 168, file: FCC, 3601.

5. In the Public Interest: The Radio Act of 1927 and Actions of the Federal Radio Commission to 1933

1. From the 67th Cong., 1st Sess.: S. 31, *To Regulate the Operation of and to Foster the Development of Radio Communications in the United States;* S. 1627, *To Regulate the Operation of and to Encourage the Development of Radio Communication in the United States;* S. 1628, *To Regulate Radio Communication and to Foster Its Development;* H.R. 4132, *To Regulate the Operation of and to Encourage the Development of Radio Communication in the United States;* H.R. 5889, *To Regulate Radio Communication and to Foster Its Development;* and S. 2290, *To Amend Section 3 of an Act Entitled "An Act to Regulate Radio Communication," Approved Aug. 13, 1912.*

From the 67th Cong., 2nd Sess.: S. 3694, *To Amend an Act Entitled "An Act to Regulate Radio Communication," Approved Aug. 13, 1912, and for Other Purposes;* and H.R. 11964, *To Amend an Act to Regulate Radio Communication, Approved Aug. 13, 1912, and for Other Purposes.*

From the 68th Cong., 1st Sess.: S. 2796, *To Regulate Radio Communication, to Provide for the Collection of License and Radio Station Fees, and for Other Purposes;* S. 2524, *To Amend an Act to Regulate Radio Communication, Approved Aug. 13, 1912, and for Other Purposes;* and H.R. 7357, *To Regulate Radio Communication and for Other Purposes.*

From the 69th Cong., 1st Sess.: S. 1, *Reaffirming the Use of the Ether for Radio Communication or Otherwise to Be the Inalienable Possession of the People of the United States and Their Government, and for Other Purposes;* S. 1754, *Reaffirming the Use of the Ether for Radio Communication or Otherwise to Be the Inalienable Possession of the People of the United States and Their Government, Providing for the Regulation of Radio Communication and for Other Purposes;* S. 3968, *To Provide for the Regulation of Radio Communication, and for Other Purposes;* S. 4057, *For the Regulation of Radio Communications, and for Other Purposes;* S. 4156, *For the Regulation of Radio Communication, and for Other Purposes;* H.R. 5589, *For the Regulation of Radio Communications and for Other Purposes;* H.R. 9108, *For the Regulation of Radio*

Communications and for Other Purposes; and H. R. 9971, *For the Regulation of Radio Communications and for Other Purposes.* Also, see House Committee on Interstate and Foreign Commerce, *Regulation of Broadcast: Half a Century of Government Regulation of Broadcasting and the Need for Further Legislative Action, Study for the Committee on Interstate and Foreign Commerce on H. Res. 99, A Resolution Authorizing the Committee on Interstate and Foreign Commerce to Conduct Investigations and Studies with Respect to Certain Matters Within Its Jurisdiction,* 85th Cong., 2nd sess., 1958, 7–12.

2. *Congressional Record,* 67, pt. 11: 12335–59, and 68, pt. 1: 2556–90; and Donald Godfrey, "The 1927 Radio Act: People and Politics," *Journalism History* 4.3 (autumn 1977).

3. Godfrey, "The 1927 Radio Act," 75.

4. *Congressional Record,* 67, pt. 11: 12335–59.

5. Ibid., 5558.

6. House Committee, *Hearings on H.R. 5589,* 26.

7. Ibid., 56–57.

8. Senate Committee on Interstate Commerce, *Radio Control: Hearings on S. 1 and S. 1754,* 69th Cong., 1st sess., Jan. 8–9 and Feb. 26–Mar. 2, 1926, 228–29.

9. Ibid., 48–87, 121.

10. Ibid., 125–26.

11. Ibid., 128–34.

12. Clarence C. Dill, "Statement on Radio Bill," Apr. 22, 1926, HHPL, box 545.

13. "President Opposes Boards Not under Executive Control," *Washington Post,* Apr. 28, 1926, HHPL, Commerce Papers, President Coolidge.

14. *Congressional Record,* 67, pt. 11: 12375.

15. Ibid., 12501–5.

16. Ibid., 12503.

17. Ibid., 12335.

18. Ibid., 12335–59.

19. Ibid., 12353.

20. Ibid., 12356–58.

21. Ibid., 12502.

22. Ibid., 12618.

23. "Expect New Conference on Radio Control," *New York Times,* Oct. 19, 1926, 19.

24. Godfrey, "The 1927 Radio Act," 77; *Congressional Record,* 68, pt. 1: 3031.

25. Clarence Dill interview by Dan Godfrey, transcript, July 21, 1964, BPL. This interview may also be found in the Herbert Hoover Presidential Library.

26. *Congressional Record,* 69th Cong., 2nd sess., 1927, 68, pt. 3: 2556–58 and 2588–90.

27. Ibid., 2556.

28. Ibid., 2560–67.

29. Ibid.

30. Ibid., 2868–81, 3025–37, and 3117–24.

31. Ibid., 3025–27.

32. Ibid., 3027–29, 3034–35, and pt. 4: 4288, 4342, and 4938; and Public Law 632, 69th Cong., 2nd Sess., Feb. 23, 1927.

33. Orestes Caldwell, "Reminiscences," 9, Columbia University Oral History Collection, cited in Barnouw, *A Tower in Babel,* 214.

34. Press release, statement by Secretary of Commerce Herbert Hoover, released for use not earlier than Sunday, Mar. 6, 1927, and Hoover to Harvey Ingham, editor, *Des Moines Register,* Mar. 11, 1927, HHPL, Commerce Papers, Radio Correspondence, Press Releases; "Federal Radio Commission, March 15, 1927," HHPL, Commerce Papers, Radio: Federal Radio Commission—Clips, Press Releases; Orestes Caldwell, "The Administration of Radio Legislation in the United States," Dec. 1928, MCHC, Caldwell Papers, box 1, file: Writings and Talks by OHC.

35. Caldwell, "The Administration of Radio Legislation in the United States," MCHC.

36. Text of radio address by Judge Eugene O. Sykes, Vice Chairman, Federal Radio Commission, on Thursday, Mar. 17, at 7:45 P.M. Eastern Standard Time, NA, RG 173, box 309, FCC, file: Dep-4.

37. Minutes, fourth day, Conference held at Washington, D.C., before the Federal Radio Commission, Friday, Apr. 1, 1927, HHPL, Commerce Papers, Radio Conferences, Federal Radio Commission Minutes.

38. "President Aylesworth of the National Broadcasting Company Defines 'Freedom of the Air' in Address Before Civil Liberties Union," Apr. 29, (1927), ODY, box 128, Broadcasting.

39. Oliver H. P. Garrett, "Broadcasting as an Industry," *American Review of Reviews* (Nov. 1927): 523, in MCHC, NBC Papers, Central Files, Department Files, 1927–42, box 90, file: Press Relations, Mngr. G. W. Johnstone, 1927–29.

40. Alfred Goldsmith to Herbert Hoover, Dec. 5, 1927, and Goldsmith, "Analysis of Network Broadcasting" (speech), Nov. 28, 1927, HHPL, Commerce Papers, Radio Correspondence, Press Releases.

41. Henry A. Bellows, "Government and Radio," address at the dinner of the League of Women Voters, Washington, D.C., Apr. 27, 1927, NA, RG 173, box 310, FCC, file: Dep-4-e.

42. Federal Radio Commission, *Annual Report* (Washington, D.C.: U.S. Government Printing Office, 1927), 7–8.

43. Ibid., 8; General Order No. 12, May 26, 1927, LC, William Borah Papers, General Office Files, box 261, Radio/Radio Legislation, 1927–28.

44. Caldwell, "The Administration of Radio Legislation in the United States," Dec. 1928, MCHC.

45. J. H. Dellinger, Chief Engineer, FRC, "What the Government Is Doing to Advance Radio," talk broadcast from National Broadcast Company stations, Oct. 9, 1928, NA, RG 167, Personal Papers of J. Howard Dellinger, folder: Published Papers and Speeches (1910–62).

46. Proceedings, Fifth Annual Convention of the National Association of Broadcasters, Sept. 19–21, 1927, NA, RG 173, box 168, FCC, file 3601.

47. Untitled memorandum, marked "confidential," and bulletins of the National Radio Club of Washington, D.C., Jan. 9, 17, and 28, 1928, NA, RG 173, box 309, FCC, file: Dep-4.

48. The allocation had six purposes: (1) to arrange for maximum use of broadcast channels, (2) to divide stations among the five zones and, within these zones, among the states according to population, (3) to secure good radio reception to all parts of the country, especially in rural areas and towns more than 100 miles for any broadcast station, (4) to provide numerous local broadcast stations of limited power to serve local communities, (5) to continue operation of all licensed transmitters through time-sharing while at the same time (6) minimizing "modification of assignments of popular stations having great followings of listeners" (Caldwell, "The Administration of Radio Legislation in the United States," Dec. 1928, MCHC).

49. Caldwell, "The Administration of Radio Legislation in the United States," Dec. 1928, MCHC.

50. Federal Radio Commission, *Annual Report* (Washington, D.C.: U.S. Government Printing Office, 1928), 15–16.

51. Ibid., 17.

52. "Dill Again Assails Acts of Radio Board," *New York Times,* Sept. 22, 1929.

53. "Control of Radio," *Washington Post,* Aug. 12, 1929, in NA, RG 173, box 83, FCC, 1102.

54. "The Radio Law Is Challenged," *New York Times,* Sept. 28, 1930, sec. 9, p. 9.

55. Statement made by the commission on Aug. 23, 1928, relative to public interest, convenience, or necessity, Federal Radio Commission, *Annual Report,* 1928, 166.

56. In the Matter of the Application of the Great Lakes Broadcasting Co., FRC Docket No. 4900, Federal Radio Commission, *Annual Report* (Washington, D.C.: U.S. Government Printing Office, 1929), 32, modified later on other grounds (37 F2d 993 [D.C. Cir 1930]), certiorari dismissed 281 U.S. 706 (1930); "Station's Priority Is Superior Right," *New York Times,* Feb. 17, 1929, sec. 9, p. 18.

57. Opinion of the General Counsel, No. 29, in the Matter of the Con-

struction of Sections 9 and 29 of the Radio Act of 1927, Jan. 26, 1929, NA, RG 172, box 310, FCC, file: Dep-4-c.

58. "Report of the Forty-Seventh Annual Meeting of the American Newspaper Publishers Association," ANPA Bulletin 6114, May 4, 1933.

59. "Newspaper Loses Fight on Moving Station," ANPA Bulletin 6136, July 7, 1933.

60. "Report of the Forty-Seventh Annual Meeting," ANPA Bulletin 6114.

61. "Government Petitions Supreme Court to Review Ruling in WIBO-WPCC Case," *Glendale (CA) News,* Feb. 2, 1933, ACLU Papers.

62. "Radio's Toughest Fight Looms as Result of Supreme Court's Ruling in WIBO-WPCC-WJKS," *Variety,* May 16, 1933, ACLU Papers; "Supreme Court Upholds Quota System," ANPA Bulletin 6116, May 12, 1933.

6. "By Their Fruits Ye Shall Know Them": Brinkley, Baker, and Shuler

1. Mitchell Dawson, "Censorship on the Air," *American Mercury,* Mar. 1934, 259.

2. Ibid.; "Radio Commission Hands Down Decisions on Cited Stations," *NAB News,* Sept. 4, 1938.

3. "Seeks to Bar Radio to Quack Doctors," *New York Times,* Dec. 26, 1929.

4. "Radio Ethics Code Sought by Wynne," *New York Times,* Dec. 28, 1929.

5. "Radio Drive on Quacks, Announced by Wynne," *New York Times,* Dec. 31, 1929; "3 Groups Plan War on Radio Quacks," *New York Times,* Jan. 4, 1930, 12; "Sees Commercialism in Health Campaigns," *New York Times,* Mar. 7, 1930, 20; and "Radio and a Rogues' Gallery," editorial, *New York Times,* July 14, 1930, 18.

6. "Hold Radio Board Can't Stop Quacks," *New York Times,* Dec. 27, 1929.

7. James Rorty, "Order on the Air!" in *The John Day Pamphlets, No. 44* (New York: The John Day Company, 1934), 18.

8. Hearings, in Re Application of the KFKB Broadcasting Association, Inc., Milford, Kansas, Docket No. 835, NA, RG 173, FCC Docket Section 835, box 115 (hereafter cited as "Hearings, Docket 835").

9. Friends of Democracy, Inc., memorandum concerning Dr. John Richard Brinkley, Aug. 30, 1940, NA, RG 173, FCC General Correspondence, 1927–71, box 193, file 44-3, J. R. Brinkley (hereafter cited as "Friends of Democracy, Aug. 30, 1940").

10. Hearings, Docket 835, 502, and Friends of Democracy, Aug. 30, 1940.

11. Hearings, Docket 835, 514–18, 524–26.

12. *KFKB Broadcasting Association, Inc. v. Federal Radio Commission,* 47 F2d 670 (1931); "By Their Fruits Ye Shall Know Them," *Broadcasters' News Bulletin,* Feb. 7, 1931.

13. Friends of Democracy, Aug. 30, 1940.

14. See memos and correspondence in NA, RG 173, box 192, file 44-3, Dr. John Brinkley, Program Complaints, 1931–33; "Study Wave Length Theft," *Variety,* Dec. 26, 1931, ACLU Papers.

15. "Brinkley to Radio from XER in Mexico," *Omaha World Herald,* Oct. 18, 1931, NA, RG 173, box 192, file 44-3, Dr. John Brinkley, Program Complaints, 1931–33; Frank M. Kratokvil, Inspector in Charge, to FCC, Jan. 30, 1935, NA, RG 173, FCC General Correspondence, 1927–71, box 193, file 44-3, J. R. Brinkley.

16. "Broadcasting Conference Fails," ANPA Bulletin 6154, Aug. 16, 1933.

17. "Fortune Tellers Broadcast from Mexico," ANPA Bulletin 6098, Mar. 31, 1933.

18. Kratokvil to FCC, Jan. 30, 1935, NA.

19. Sterling and Kittross, *Stay Tuned,* 131, 195.

20. In Re Application of Norman Baker, Station KTNT, "Appearance by Applicant and Statement of Facts," received Oct. 7, 1930, NA, RG 173, FCC Docket Section 967, vol. 1.

21. In Re Application of Norman Baker, Station KTNT, Muscatine, Iowa, for Renewal of License, "Report of Ellis A. Yost, Chief Examiner," submitted Mar. 5, 1931, NA, RG 173, FCC Docket Section 967, vol. 1 (hereafter cited as "Yost report, Mar. 5, 1931").

22. Ibid.

23. Ibid.; "Brief of Iowa Medical Society, et al., Amicus Curiae," NA, RG 173, FCC Docket Section 967, vol. 1.

24. Yost report, Mar. 5, 1931; "Recommends Against KTNT," *Broadcasters' News Bulletin,* Mar. 7, 1931.

25. Gordon Moss to Norman Baker, Apr. 2, 1931; Baker to Moss, Apr. 7, 1931; and Moss to Baker, Apr. 17, 1931, ACLU Papers.

26. Hearing before the Federal Radio Commission, Washington, D.C., in Re: Norman Baker, Call Letters: KTNT, Docket No. 967, Wednesday, May 13, 1931, 20–23, NA, RG 173, FCC Docket Section 967, vol. 1.

27. Ibid., 28.

28. Ibid.

29. "Statement of Facts, Grounds for Decision and Order of the Commission," June 5, 1931, as corrected, NA, RG 173, FCC Docket Section 967, vol. 1.

30. Baker to ACLU, Apr. 12, 1934, ACLU Papers.

31. In Re Application of Trinity Methodist Church South (Station KGEF), Docket No. 1043, Statement of Facts, Grounds for Decision and Order of the Commission, Nov. 13, 1931, NA, RG 173, FCC Docket

Section 1043, box 166 (hereafter cited as "In Re Application, Docket 1043").

32. Rorty, "Order on the Air!" 17; Examiner's Report No. 241: In Re Application of Trinity Methodist Church South (Station KGEF), Docket No. 1043, Aug. 7, 1931, NA, RG 173, FCC Docket Section 1043, box 166 (hereafter cited as "Examiner's Report No. 241").

33. Edmund Wilson, "City of Our Lady, the Queen of Angels," *New Republic,* Dec. 9, 1931, cited in Rorty, "Order on the Air!" 17.

34. Examiner's Report No. 241. Also, see Reporter's Transcript of Testimony and Proceedings in Re Application for Renewal of Station License, vols. 1–14, Jan. 8–24, 1931, NA, RG 173, FCC Docket Section 1043, boxes 163–166 (hereafter cited as "Reporter's Transcript, Docket 1043").

35. Reporter's Transcript, Docket 1043, vol. 1, 77–81 and 95.

36. In Re Application, Docket 1043.

37. Reporter's Transcript, Docket 1043, vol. 1, 95, and vol. 2, 348–50.

38. Examiner's Report No. 241; In Re Application, Docket 1043.

39. Examiner's Report No. 241.

40. Ibid.

41. In Re Application, Docket 1043; "Shuler Offered Help by Union in Contempt Case," *Open Forum,* no date; "Union Behind Record in Fighting Contempt Charge," newspaper clipping, no date, ACLU Papers, vol. 385; and untitled précis, NA, RG 173, FCC Docket Section 1043, box 163, 10 (hereafter cited as "Untitled précis, Docket 1043").

42. Reporter's Transcript, Docket 1043, vol. 14, 2156–63; untitled précis, Docket 1043; "Flint Murder Motivated by Losses of Slayer," *Los Angeles Times,* July 15, 1930, 1; and "Shuler Tract in Evidence," *Los Angeles Times,* July 16, 1930, 2.

43. Untitled précis, Docket 1043, 55; "Throng at Meeting on Shulerism," *Los Angeles Times,* July 26, 1930, part 2, p. 1.

44. "Shuler Radio Quiz Promised," *Los Angeles Times,* July 22, 1930, part 2, p. 1.

45. Untitled précis, Docket 1043, 55–57.

46. Ibid., 58.

47. Ibid., 60.

48. Examiner's Report No. 241.

49. Ibid.; In Re Application, Docket 1043.

50. Exceptions to Report No. 241, NA, RG 173, FCC Docket Section 1043, box 166, 3.

51. Hearing before the Federal Radio Commission, In Re: Trinity Methodist Church, KGEF, Docket No. 1043, NA, RG 173, FCC Docket Section 1043, box 166, 29 (hereafter cited as "Hearing, KGEF, Docket 1043").

52. Exceptions to Report No. 241, NA, 4–5.

53. Ibid., 6.

54. Ibid., 9–12.

55. In Re Application, Docket 1043.

56. In Re Shuler, 292 Pacific Reporter 481 (1931).

57. Hearing, KGEF, Docket 1043, 4–30.

58. Ibid., 31–32.

59. Ibid., 32–54.

60. Ibid., 42, 58–60.

61. Ibid., 60–62.

62. Ibid., 69–74.

63. Statement of Facts, Grounds for Decision and Order of the Commission, Nov. 13, 1931, In Re: Trinity Methodist Church, KGEF, Docket No. 1043, NA, RG 173, FCC Docket Section 1043, box 166, 10–12; Rorty, "Order on the Air!" 17.

64. Gordon Moss to Robert Shuler, Nov. 14, 1931, ACLU Papers.

65. Bob Shuler to Gordon Moss, Nov. 18, 1931, ACLU Papers.

66. George Shoaf, "Federal Radio Commission Acts," *Open Forum,* Nov. 21, 1931.

67. 283 U.S. 697 (1931).

68. *Trinity Methodist Church, South v. FRC,* 62 F2d 850 (1932).

69. 288 U.S. 599 (1933).

70. Various newspaper articles regarding Shuler case, Jan. 1933, ACLU Papers.

71. "Liberals Join Fight on Schuler [*sic*] Air Ban," *Baltimore Evening Sun,* Jan. 24, 1933, ACLU Papers.

72. "Shuler Gets Help in Fight for Radio," *New York Times,* Jan. 24, 1933, ACLU Papers.

73. Brief in Support of Petition for Rehearing, *Trinity Methodist Church v. FRC,* Feb. 10, 1933, ACLU Papers; "Shuler Fights Radio Censor," *Los Angeles Times,* Feb. 11, 1933, ACLU Papers.

74. 288 U.S. 599 (1933).

75. "'Bob' Shuler Is Off the Air," *Christian Century,* Feb. 22, 1933, 245.

76. "Shuler: His Column," *Hawthorne Advertiser,* Feb. 27, 1933, ACLU Papers.

77. "Why Not Free Murder?" newspaper article (no paper listed), ACLU Papers.

78. RNB (Roger Baldwin) to Harris K. Randall (American Radio Audience League), Mar. 31, 1933, ACLU Papers.

7. To Reach the Voters: Political Speech, 1928–1934

1. "Large Radio Chain in June for National Conclaves," *New York Times,* Feb. 12, 1928, sec. 9, p. 14.

2. "Predicts Wide Use of Radio in Politics," *New York Times,* May 9, 1928, 18.

3. "Lays Curb on Radio to Fear of Hoover," *New York Times*, Mar. 31, 1928, 22.

4. "Brevity and Appeal to Reason Make Radio Talks Magnetic," *New York Times*, Mar. 25, 1928, sec. 10, p. 16.

5. "Fix Hotel Rates for Republicans," *New York Times*, Jan. 8, 1928, 9; "Party Conventions to Be Broadcast," *New York Times*, Feb. 4, 1928, 6.

6. "Broadcasting Conventions," editorial, *New York Times*, Feb. 7, 1928, 26.

7. "Large Radio Chain in June for National Conclaves," 14.

8. "Campaign Expected to Aid Broadcasters," *New York Times*, Mar. 11, 1928, sec. 9, p. 15.

9. "Would Check Radio by Standard Waves," *New York Times*, Apr. 10, 1928, 34; "Socialists Arrange to Carry Radio Speeches," *New York Times*, Apr. 11, 1928, 27.

10. "Record Radio Hook-Up as Republicans Meet," *New York Times*, Apr. 3, 1928, 35. NBC operated three networks at this time. The Red Network, comprised of the old WEAF/AT&T network, dominated, while the smaller Blue Network was comprised of the old WRC/Radio Group network. The Orange Network operated on the West Coast, and its stations affiliated with either the Red or Blue after permanent transcontinental links were established later in 1928.

11. Owen Comora, "From McNamee to Huntley-Brinkley: 40 Years of Political Convention Broadcasting," *Electronic Age* 23.3 (summer 1964); Quin Ryan, "Quin Ryan Recalls Early Conventions," *Chicago Tribune,* July 12, 1964, Radio section, p. 10, in BPL, box 82, Broadcasting in Political Campaigns.

12. "WMAQ Political Programs, 1922–1931," BPL, box 134, Judith Waller.

13. "Voice Personality Will Count in Race to the White House," newspaper clipping, MCHC, Martin Codel Papers, box 6, file: Misc. Loose Papers.

14. Ibid.

15. Ibid.

16. Ibid.

17. "Brevity and Appeal to Reason Make Radio Talks Magnetic," 16.

18. Graham McNamee, "The Elephant and the Donkey Take the Air," *American Magazine*, Nov. 1928, 15, 153.

19. "107 Radio Stations Linked for Hoover," newspaper clipping, MCHC, Martin Codel Papers, box 6, file: Misc. Loose Papers.

20. Frank R. Kent, "The Great Game of Politics," and anon., "Politics and Music Join in Campaign," MCHC, Martin Codel Papers, box 6, file: Misc. Loose Papers.

21. "January Eventful in Radio Realm," *New York Times*, Feb. 3, 1929, sec. 9, p. 24; "Radio Chain Plans for Inauguration," *New York*

Times, Feb. 19, 1929, 32; "Millions to Hear Hoover Take Presidential Oath," *New York Times,* Feb. 24, 1929, 13; "Radio Nets Prepare for Inaugural Ball," *New York Times,* Feb. 25, 1929; "Schools and Trains to Hear Broadcasts," *New York Times,* Mar. 4, 1929, 4; "Radio to Cover Every Feature of the Inauguration," *New York Times,* Mar. 3, 1929, 16; and "Will Television Be Ready for the Next Inaugural?" *New York Times,* Mar. 10, 1929, sec. 11, p. 17.

22. "Radio," *New York Times,* Mar. 17, 1929, sec. 10, p. 23; "Asks Cleared Air for Inauguration," *New York Times,* Mar. 2, 1929.

23. "Radio Advisory Council Plans for the Future," *New York Times,* Mar. 17, 1929, 18.

24. Jack Woodford, "Radio—A Blessing or a Curse?" *Forum,* Mar. 1929, 169–71.

25. General J. G. Harbord, "Radio and Democracy," *Forum,* Apr. 1929, 214–16.

26. Hawley, *The Great War,* 173–91.

27. Ibid., 173–84.

28. Ibid., 184–91.

29. Ibid., 180–85.

30. Sterling and Kittross, *Stay Tuned,* 141–96.

31. Frank Arnold, "Planning a Campaign of Broadcast Advertising," *NBC's Little Books on Broadcasting,* MCHC, James Papers, box 4, file 2: NBC Advertising Devices.

32. Leuchtenburg, *The Perils of Prosperity,* 261.

33. Jack Perilla to WEAF, Sept. 12, 1930; Elwood to McClelland, Sept. 19, 1930; Perilla to NBC, Oct. 1, 1930; Interdepartment Correspondence—John Elwood to M. H. Aylesworth, Nov. 6, 1930, and Aylesworth to Elwood, Nov. 10, 1930, MCHC, NBC Papers, Central Files, Correspondence, box 4, file: Political Broadcasts, 1930.

34. M. Zeroff to NBC, Oct. 22, 1930, MCHC, NBC Papers, Central Files, Correspondence, box 4, file: Political Broadcasts, 1930.

35. "California Slander Law Passed, Covers Radio," *New York Times,* June 16, 1929.

36. "Libel Bill in Texas," *New York Times,* Mar. 16, 1930.

37. "Guilty of 'Radio Slander,'" *New York Times,* Apr. 20, 1950.

38. "States Urged to Keep Pace with Radio Law," *New York Times,* Dec. 7, 1930, sec. 10, p. 12.

39. *Sorenson v. Wood,* 243 N.W. 82 (1932); "Special Dispatch to the Enquirer," *Editor and Publisher,* Apr. 18, 1931; and "Radio Libel Liability to be Tested," *Cincinnati Enquirer,* Apr. 12, 1931, ACLU Papers.

40. *Sorenson v. Wood,* 82.

41. Ibid.; "Radio Libel Liability to be Tested," ACLU Papers.

42. *Sorenson v. Wood,* 82, 84.

43. Ibid.

44. 360 U.S. 525 (1959). In *WDAY,* the Supreme Court unanimously held that Section 315 prohibited broadcaster censorship of candidates. The Court also held in a more narrow five-to-four vote that Section 315 preempted state defamation law and created an absolute privilege that protected licensees, but not the candidates themselves, from liability for statements so made.

45. "To Appeal Radio Libel Decision," ANPA Bulletin 6093, Mar. 10, 1933.

46. "Radio Speech Law Cited," *New York Times,* Sept. 13, 1932, 17; "Political Broadcasting," *Broadcasters' News Bulletin,* Sept. 3, 1932, NAB Library, NAB Headquarters, Washington, D.C.

47. "The KFKB Decision," *Broadcasters' News Bulletin,* July 16, 1932, NAB Library.

48. "WCCO Cuts Speech Alleging Libel," and "Libel on the Air!" *Editor and Publisher,* Nov. 12, 1932; Arthur Scharfeld to Gordon Moss, Nov. 12, 1932, ACLU Papers.

49. "WCCO Cuts Speech Alleging Libel."

50. Arthur Scharfeld to Gordon Moss, Nov. 16, 1932, ACLU Papers.

51. "Attack on Shuler Barred by KNX as Copy Is Switched," *Variety,* Nov. 1, 1932; "Hearst Is Attacked as Political Boss," *Editor and Publisher,* Dec. 31, 1932, ACLU Papers.

52. Scharfeld to Moss, Nov. 16, 1932, and Moss to Louis Caldwell, Nov. 22, 1932, ACLU Papers.

53. Gordon Moss to Bethuel Webster, Dec. 15, 1932, ACLU Papers.

54. Moss to Scharfeld, Nov. 1, 1932; Victor Gettner to Gordon Moss, Dec. 26, 1932; and "Tentative Draft of Model Federal Bill Pertaining to Scandal by Radio," National Council on Freedom from Censorship, Dec. 29, 1932, ACLU Papers.

55. Hearings, in Re Application of William B. Schaeffer, Docket No. 837 (hereafter cited as "Hearing, Docket 837"), and Statement of Facts and Grounds for Decision No. 5228 (hereafter cited as "Statement of Facts, Decision 5228"), NA, RG 173, FCC Docket Section 837, vols. 2 and 3, box 116; "Fate of KGEF up to Commission," newspaper clipping, Oct. 7, 1930, and "First Conviction Won for Law Forbidding Obscenity on Radio," newspaper clipping, no date, ACLU Papers, vol. 385.

56. Hearings, Docket 837, vol. 3, 10–17.

57. Ibid., 155.

58. Ibid., 156.

59. Ibid., 157–58.

60. Ibid., 156, 158–59.

61. Ibid., 24, 132–52; "Faces 5-Year Term for Profanity on Radio in Oregon," no date; "Jailed for Radio Language," Nov. 17, [1931]; "First Conviction Won for Law Forbidding Obscenity on Radio," ACLU Papers.

62. Hearings, Docket 837, vol. 3, 29–32, 152–60.

63. Ibid., 210.

64. Ibid., 254.

65. Statement of Facts, Decision 5228, vol. 2, box 116, 12–13.

66. Ibid., 14.

67. Ibid.

68. Ibid., 15.

69. Hearings, Docket 837, vol. 3, 156–60.

70. Ibid., 14–21; Statement of Facts, Decision 5228, vol. 2, box 116, 11.

71. Statement of Facts, Decision 5228, 11–12.

72. Ibid., 12.

73. Ibid., 15–16; Hearings, Docket 837, vol. 3, 9–10.

74. "First Conviction Won for Law Forbidding Obscenity on Radio," ACLU Papers.

75. Robert Duncan to Forrest Bailey, Nov. 10, 1930, ACLU Papers, vol. 424.

76. *Duncan v. U.S.*, 48 F2d 128 (1931); and "Profanity Sentence Valid," *New York Times,* Mar. 10, 1932, 19.

77. *Duncan v. U.S.*, 128, 134; "What Is Profane Language?" *Broadcasters' News Bulletin,* May 2, 1931, NAB Library.

78. "Profanity Sentence Valid," 19.

79. Hawley, *The Great War,* 213–29.

80. "Radio Prepares for Barrage of Political Oratory," *New York Times,* June 5, 1932, sec. 10, p. 8.

81. Orrin E. Dunlap Jr., "Two Hundred Broadcasters Join Convention Hook-Up," *New York Times,* June 12, 1932, sec. 9, p. 5; "Mail Reveals American's Reaction to Politics on the Air," *New York Times,* July 17, 1932, sec. 8, p. 5.

82. Hawley, *The Great War,* 213–29.

83. Orrin E. Dunlap Jr., "Lessons of the Campaign," *New York Times,* Nov. 13, 1932, sec. 8, p. 6; "Radio Broadcasting in the 1932 Campaign," MCHC, Mass Communication Ephemera Collection, box 5: National Association of Broadcasters, General.

84. "Radio 'Debunking' the Campaigns," *Literary Digest,* Dec. 1, 1928, 13.

85. "Preparing for the Crusade," *New York Times,* Sept. 4, 1932; "Personal Touch Survives," *New York Times,* Oct. 29, 1932, 14.

86. Ibid.

87. Ibid.

88. Ibid.

89. "Wisconsin Provides for Politics," *New York Times,* Sept. 4, 1932.

90. "Broadcasters Plan Busy Days," *New York Times,* Oct. 30, 1932, sec. 8, p. 6; Orrin E. Dunlap Jr., "Elaborate Plans for Tuesday," *New York Times,* Nov. 6, 1932, sec. 8, p. 6.

91. Dunlap, "Lessons of the Campaign," 6.

92. "Politics Irks Broadcasters," *New York Times,* Oct. 23, 1932, sec. 8, p. 6; "Politics on Air Ousts Regular Programs," *New York Times,* Nov. 2, 1934, 16.

93. "Campaign Wind-Up Upsets Radio Plans," *New York Times,* Nov. 4, 1932, 11.

94. "$5,000,000 Spent on Radio," *New York Times,* Nov. 8, 1932, 7; Clarence Dill, "Radio Broadcasting in the 1932 Campaign," an address over NBC, Nov. 7, 1932, printed by the National Association of Broadcasters, MCHC, Mass Communication Ephemeria Collection, box 5, folder 12: National Association of Broadcasters, General.

95. "Radio and the New Oratory," editorial, *Christian Century,* Nov. 30, 1932, 146.

96. "Today's Town Crier," editorial, *New York Times,* Nov. 6, 1930, 24.

97. "Radio Will Carry Event to the World," *New York Times,* Mar. 4, 1933, 4.

98. "Party Control for Official Radio Talks," *New York Times,* Sept. 24, 1933, ANPA Bulletin 6179, Oct. 6, 1933; "President Employs Air, Press to Educate Nation," *Literary Digest,* Jan. 27, 1934, 9; "Roosevelt Bars Radio in Talk to Bankers; To Keep Broadcasts for 'Fireside Chats,'" *New York Times,* Oct. 9, 1934, 2; and "Roosevelt and Cabinet," *New York Times,* Dec. 24, 1934, 9.

8. Speak No Evil: The Early 1930s

1. "Board Recommends First Code of Ethics," *NAB News,* Feb. 27, 1928; "Who Owns the Air?" editorial, *World Tomorrow,* Mar. 22, 1933, 271.

2. "January Eventful in Radio Realm," 24; "Paganism Scored by Presbyterians," *New York Times,* May 31, 1932; "Our Bad Taste Deplored," letter to the editor, *New York Times,* Nov. 8, 1934, 22; "Speaking of Blasphemy," letter to the editor, *New York Times,* Nov. 12, 1934, 18; "One Talent Action," letter to the editor, *New York Times,* Nov. 18, 1934, sec. 4, p. 5; and letters in NA, RG 173, FCC, box 308, Office of Executive Director, General Correspondence, 1927–46, file: Censorship 76-1, and Radio Division, box 279, BG-1-8, Broadcasting.

3. "8,000 Druggists Insulted by Old Vaudeville Gag as Used on Radio," *Variety,* May 6, 1931; Jack Foster, "Radio Wit Has Worries," *New York Telegram,* Dec. 12, 1931; and Dawson, "Censorship on the Air," 257–68.

4. "Amos 'n' Andy, Guests at Negro Picnic, Answer Hostile Race Press," *Variety,* Aug. 18, 1931, ACLU Papers.

5. "Too Realistic," *Variety,* Dec. 15, 1931, ACLU Papers.

6. Ibid.

7. Jay Robert Nash, *Encyclopedia of World Crimes* (Wilmett, Ill.: Crime Books, Inc., 1990), 2806–10.

8. Vita Lauter and Joseph Friend, "Radio and the Censors," *Forum,* Dec. 1931, 359–65.

9. Paul Hutchinson, "Is the Air Already Monopolized?" *Christian Century,* Apr. 1, 1931, 441–44.

10. "Stalin and the Air Censors," loose clipping, Dec. 1932, ACLU Papers.

11. Correspondence between Mannheimer, Milner, and Allen, Nov. and Dec. 1933, ACLU Papers.

12. Edward Ervin to Theodore Nathan, Apr. 20, 1934, reprinted in *New York Post,* May 1, 1934, ACLU Papers.

13. "Anti-Nazi Radio Ban Stirs Talk of U.S. Censorship," *New York Post,* May 1, 1934, ACLU Papers.

14. "Protests Barring of Speech by WRNY," *New York Times,* May 5, 1929.

15. Lauter and Friend, "Radio and the Censors," 359–65.

16. Ibid.

17. "Catholic Priest Shut Off Air for Talk on Race Issue," *Christian Century,* Dec. 14, 1932, ACLU Papers.

18. "Liberty on the Air," *Philadelphia Record,* Apr. 26, 1930, ACLU Papers, vol. 385; Lauter and Friend, "Radio and the Censors," 359–65.

19. "Year Changes Things," *New York Telegram,* Nov. 18, 1931, ACLU Papers.

20. Press release, "Senator Robert F. Wagner's Unemployment Radio Speech," scheduled for Friday evening, Oct. 2, 1931, ACLU Papers.

21. "Wagner Speech on Jobs Rejected by Radio Chain," Oct. 3, 1931; Gordon Moss to Merlin Aylesworth, Oct. 5, 1931; and "For Immediate Release (10/3/31)," ACLU Papers.

22. Lawrence W. Lowman to Gordon Moss, Oct. 6, 1931; W. E. Mulholland to Moss, Oct. 7, 1931; Moss to Lowman, October 7, 1931; Moss to Merlin Aylesworth, Oct. 7, 1931; Aylesworth to Moss, Oct. 9, 1931; and "Censoring Unemployment Discussion on the Air," editorial, *Editor and Publisher,* Oct. 10, 1931, ACLU Papers.

23. "Truth Is Off the Air," draft of an editorial; letter to the editor, *The Nation,* Mar. 9, 1933; and correspondence between Roger Baldwin, Sophie Trefon, Hatcher Hughes, Gordon Moss, Lewis Tonks, and Kolin Hager, Mar. 30, 1933, ACLU Papers.

24. RNB to Sophie Trefon, Mar. 11, 1933, ACLU Papers.

25. H. K. Randall to Roger Baldwin, Mar. 20, 1933, ACLU Papers.

26. "Indirect Radio Censorship Used to Hush Protests by Veterans," *New York Herald Tribune,* June 20, 1934; "Radio 'Gag' Is Attacked," *New York Times,* Jan. 10, 1934; and "Barred Talk Put Back on the Radio," *New York Times,* no date, ACLU Papers.

27. "Radio's Slender Base," *Editor and Publisher,* Jan. 20, 1934.

28. 1930 Advisory Council Report, MCHC, NBC Papers, box 107, Advisory Council, Reports and Minutes, 1927–36; Hutchinson, "Is the Air Already Monopolized?" 441–44.

29. Albert Day to Forrest Bailey, Jan. 14, 1931; Bailey to Day, Jan. 17, 1931; Bailey to Harry Ward, Jan. 20, 1931; Day to Bailey, Jan. 22, 1931; and Bailey to Day, Jan. 23, 1931, ACLU Papers, vol. 498.

30. Forrest Bailey to Harry Ward, Jan. 20, 1931; Albert Day to Bailey, Jan. 22, 1931; and Bailey to Day, Jan. 23, 1931, ACLU Papers, vol. 498.

31. "Mothers Fighting the Radio Bogies," *Literary Digest,* Mar. 18, 1933.

32. "Protest on Radio Songs," *New York Times,* Mar. 6, 1933, 11.

33. "Censorship Issue Looms on Horizon," *New York World,* Apr. 8, 1933, ACLU Papers.

34. "Safeguard," *New Yorker,* Oct. 10, 1931; "Coy Reason, Eh What?" *New York Telegram,* Mar. 9, 1932; "The Jazz Jingles," Dec. 1932; and "CBS Dirt Drive Strikes Coast," *Variety,* Apr. 25, 1933, ACLU Papers.

35. James Cannon, "Indecency in Humming," *New York World-Telegram,* June 13, 1933, ACLU Papers.

36. "Song Censorship for Radio Begun," *New York Times,* Aug. 15, 1934, ACLU Papers.

37. "Radio Heads Laud Song Censorship," *New York Times,* Aug. 16, 1934.

38. "Networks 'Clean,' Song 'Censors' Say," *New York Times,* Aug. 23, 1934.

39. "Coast Radio Going Blue," *Variety,* Dec. 13, 1932, ACLU Papers.

40. "Change in Conan Doyle Text," *New York Telegram,* Dec. 4, 1931, ACLU Papers.

41. "Program Censored in Mid-Broadcast by Phone," *Variety,* Nov. 17, 1931, ACLU Papers.

42. "Roosevelt Air Dictator, Too?" *World Telegram,* May 16, 1933, ACLU Papers.

43. "Hell Over the Radio," *Literary Digest,* May 23, 1931, 22; and "What Is Profane Language?" May 2, 1931, NAB Library.

44. "Uphold Radio Station in Butler Speech Cut," *New York Times,* Apr. 27, 1931, 24.

45. Dawson, "Censorship on the Air," 257.

46. "Butler Radio Cut-Off Condemned by V.F.W.," *New York Times,* Oct. 6, 1934, 6.

47. Joseph Mitchell, "Radio Officials Mild Censors, Is Own Defense," *New York Telegram,* Nov. 25, 1931, ACLU Papers.

48. Release to Joseph Mitchell, Nov. 28, 1931, ACLU Papers.

49. "Speech of Senator Antonio R. Barcelono [*sic*] of Porto Rico [*sic*] Refused by WMCA and Columbia Broadcasting System, October

19th, 1931," and notarized statement of Henry S. Ortega, Oct. 30, 1931, ACLU Papers.

50. James Baldwin to Hatcher Hughes, Nov. 11, 1931, and press release, Nov. 22, 1931, ACLU Papers.

51. Press release, Nov. 22, 1931; "Responsibility for Radio Censorship Becomes Open Issue," *ACLU Bulletin,* Nov. 25, 1931; "Indirect Censorship," editorials in *Toledo (OH) News Bee,* Nov. 28, 1931, and *Knoxville (TN) Sentinel,* Nov. 27, 1931; and "Responsibility for Radio Censorship," *Information Service,* Jan. 9, 1932, ACLU Papers.

52. Roger Baldwin to Antonio Barcelo, Nov. 30, 1931, ACLU Papers.

53. RNB to Oswald Garrison Villard, Jan. 20, 1930; M. H. Aylesworth to Villard, Apr. 2, 1930; Villard to Baldwin, Apr. 10, 1930; Villard to Aylesworth, July 31, 1930; Alice Smith to Villard, Aug. 1, 1930; Maude Kimberley to Baldwin, Oct. 27, 1930; and Baldwin to Kimberley, Oct. 28, 1930, ACLU Papers, vol. 385.

54. "Censorship Investigated," *Broadcasters' News Bulletin,* Apr. 4, 1931.

55. See letters in file labeled "Liberal Radio Stations," various dates in Mar. 1931, ACLU Papers.

56. Stanley Hubbard to ACLU, Mar. 25, 1931, and Gordon Moss to Hubbard, Mar. 27, 1931, ACLU Papers.

57. "Fan Demands Patriots Get Off the Air," *Illinois Miner,* Feb. 22, 1930, ACLU Papers, vol. 385.

9. Gimme That Ol' Time Religion: Religious Issues on Radio to 1934

1. John Calahan Jr., "The Hour of Power," *Commonweal,* Jan. 28, 1931, 343–45.

2. Purcell to ACLU, Jan. 5, 1931; FB (Forrest Bailey) to CBS, Jan. 8, 1931; FB to Reverend Charles E. Coughlin, Jan. 8, 1931; FB to Purcell, Jan. 9, 1931; FB to FRC, Jan. 9, 1931; Forrest Bailey to Caroline Parker, telegram, Jan. 9, 1931; Parker to Bailey, telegram, Jan. 10, 1931; James Baldwin to Bailey, Mar. 4, 1931; and newspaper articles on file, ACLU Papers.

3. Lauter and Friend, "Radio and the Censors," 359–65. Also cited in Hutchinson, "Is the Air Already Monopolized?"

4. Purcell to ACLU, Jan. 5, 1931; FB to CBS, Jan. 8, 1931; FB to Reverend Charles E. Coughlin, Jan. 8, 1931; FB to Purcell, Jan. 9, 1931; FB to FRC, Jan. 9, 1931; Forrest Bailey to Caroline Parker, telegram, Jan. 9, 1931; Parker to Bailey, telegram, Jan. 10, 1931; James Baldwin to Bailey, Mar. 4, 1931; and newspaper articles on file, ACLU Papers.

5. Jane Butler, CBS, letter to the editor, "The Case of Father Coughlin," *Christian Century,* Mar. 23, 1932.

6. "The Coughlin Puzzle," *Michigan Christian Advocate,* Dec. 24,

1931, 5, NA, RG 173, FCC General Correspondence, 1927–71, box 199, file 44-3, Rev. Charles E. Coughlin.

7. Minutes of Board of Directors Meeting, Jan. 5, 1931, ACLU Papers.

8. Memorandum to Colonel Brown, Feb. 8, 1933, NA, RG 173, FCC General Correspondence, 1927–71, box 199, file 44-3, Rev. Charles E. Coughlin.

9. "Deplores 'Too Much Talk,'" *New York Times*, Apr. 18, 1932, 17; "Priest Defends His Radio Talks," *New York Times*, May 10, 1932, 23.

10. See NA, RG 173, FCC General Correspondence, 1927–71, boxes 199–200, file 44-3, Rev. Charles E. Coughlin.

11. H. J. Hahn, "Jesus' Way Out," speech, Jan. 3, 1932, ACLU Papers.

12. Robert Hoffman to Roger Baldwin, Jan. 3, 1932; flier, "Free Speech Suppressed!"; and Hahn, "Jesus' Way Out," ACLU Papers. "Freedom for the Radio Pulpit," *Christian Century*, Jan. 27, 1932, 112–13.

13. Robert Hoffman to Roger Baldwin, Jan. 3, 1932; ACLU telegrams, Jan. 4, 1932; John Vollenweider to Dr. John Haynes Holmes, Jan. 6, 1932; and James Myers to WGR, Jan. 6, 1932, ACLU Papers.

14. See various news clippings on Hahn's situation, ACLU Papers.

15. John Haynes Holmes to Buffalo Broadcasting Company, telegram, Jan. 4, 1932, ACLU Papers.

16. Robert Hoffman to Roger (Baldwin), Jan. 9, 1932, ACLU Papers.

17. Edward Letchworth to Roger Baldwin, Jan. 9, 1932, and Baldwin to Letchworth, Jan. 11, 1932, ACLU Papers.

18. Robert Hoffman to Roger Baldwin, Jan. 17, 1932, ACLU Papers.

19. H.R. 110, 72nd Cong., 1st Sess., Jan. 18, 1932. "Action Urged to Insure Free Speech over Radio," *U.S. Daily*, Jan. 19, 1932; "Hahn Carries Radio Dispute to Capital," Jan. 20, 1932; and other newspaper clippings, Jan. 18–21, 1932, ACLU Papers.

20. Robert Hoffman to Gordon West, Jan. 23, 1932, ACLU Papers.

21. Gordon Moss to Robert Hoffman, Jan. 28, 1932. Also see Morris Ernst to Moss, Jan. 27, 1932; Louis Manchester to Roger Baldwin, Jan. 27, 1932; Roger Baldwin to Louis Manchester, Jan. 28, 1932, ACLU Papers.

22. Gordon Moss to Louis Manchester, Mar. 9, 1932, ACLU Papers.

23. Gordon Moss to Robert Hoffman, Feb. 26, 1932, ACLU Papers.

24. Lauter and Friend, "Radio and the Censors," 359–65.

25. FB to Mrs. F. Robertson Jones, Oct. 24, 1930; Gustav Peck to Harry Elmer Barnes, Oct. 17, 1930; Gustav Peck, "Economic Philosophies: An Essay on the Principle of Population," speech, Oct. 8, 1930, ACLU Papers, vol. 431; Lauter and Friend, "Radio and the Censors," 359–65; Dawson, "Censorship on the Air," 263; and "Dr. Parran Quits Council," *New York Times*, Nov. 21, 1934, 20.

26. James Rorty, "The Impending Radio War," *Harper's Monthly Magazine*, Nov. 1931, 725.

27. "Protest Censorship Birth Control Talk by Broadcasting Co.," "Birth Control 'Hour' Starts Radio Litigation," "Broadcast Censorship of Birth Control Hit," and "Ministers' Talks on Birth Control Barred on Radio," newspaper clippings, ACLU Papers, vol. 366.

28. Louise Benjamin, "NBC, the Advisory Council, and the American Birth Control League: A Study in Access to the Media and Freedom of Speech," *Free Speech Yearbook*, vol. 28, 1990.

29. "Birth Control Body Protests Radio Ban," newspaper clipping, no date; "Birth Control Group Criticizes Radio Ban," *Buffalo Evening News*, Jan. 17, 1930; "Air Censorship on Birth Control Talks Assailed," *New York Herald Tribune*, Jan. 17, 1930, ACLU Papers, vol. 385.

30. ACLU to John Elwood, Nov. 22, 1929, ACLU Papers, vol. 375.

31. HFW (Harry F. Ward), Chairman, to Walter Damrosch, Nov. 23, 1929, and Ward to Ira E. Robinson, Nov. 23, 1929, ACLU Papers, vol. 375.

32. Frank H. Lovette to Harry F. Ward, Nov. 26, 1929, ACLU Papers, vol. 375.

33. Ira Robinson to Harry F. Ward, Nov. 29, 1929, ACLU Papers, vol. 375.

34. Carl Butman to Harry Ward, Dec. 17, 1929, ACLU Papers, vol. 375.

35. See, for example, F. D. Farrell to Harry F. Ward, Nov. 26, 1929, and Charles MacFarland to Ward, Nov. 27, 1929, ACLU Papers, vol. 375.

36. Owen Young to Harry Ward, Dec. 3, 1929, ACLU Papers, vol. 375.

37. Ibid.

38. Ibid.

39. Harry Ward to Owen Young, Dec. 10, 1929, ACLU Papers, vol. 375.

40. Ibid.

41. Ibid.

42. "Advisory Council of the National Broadcasting Company: The President's Report and Resume of Programs, Committee Reports," Fourth Meeting, 1930, ODY, 11-14-82, box 156, Advisory Council.

43. "Detailed Report," Feb. 14, 1930, ODY, 11-14-82, box 156, Advisory Council.

44. Ibid.

45. Ibid.

46. Ibid.

47. Ibid.

48. Ibid.

49. Everett Case to Harry Ward, Feb. 13, 1930; FB to Case, Feb. 14, 1930; and Case to Bailey, Feb. 20, 1930, ACLU Papers, vol. 431.

50. "Protests Radio Chain Ban," *New York Times,* Nov. 26, 1929; "Leaders Point the Way to New Opportunities," *New York Times,* Feb. 12, 1930, 12.

51. "Birth Control Talk Goes on Air Tonight," *New York Times,* Mar. 25, 1930; press release, "For Release Tuesday," Mar. 25 (1930), ACLU Papers, vol. 431.

52. Maude Toffefson to Forrest Bailey, Jan. 13, 1930, and Bailey to Toffefson, Jan. 14, 1930, ACLU Papers, vol. 385.

53. FB to F. Robertson Jones, Oct. 24, 1930, ACLU Papers, vol. 431.

54. "Birth Control Publicity," *Commonweal,* May 6, 1931, 2–3.

55. "Censor Deletes Radio Mention of Birth Control," *New York Tribune,* Nov. 12, 1932, in ACLU Papers.

56. Rorty, "Order on the Air!" 20–21.

57. Ibid., 7–11.

10. Freedom of the (Radio) Press?

1. Edwin Emery, *History of the American Newspaper Publishers Association* (Minneapolis: University of Minnesota Press, 1950), 197–98.

2. "WMAQ News Programs, 1922–1931," BPL, 134, Judith Waller.

3. "Assails the Radio as News Carrier," *New York Times,* Oct. 8, 1929.

4. ANPA Bulletin 5400, July 15, 1927.

5. Orrin E. Dunlap Jr., "Listening-In," *New York Times,* Feb. 21, 1932, sec. 8, p. 14.

6. "Pleas That Are 'Blindfolded,'" *New York Times,* Mar. 13, 1932, sec. 8, p. 14.

7. Dunlap, "Listening-In."

8. "Complaints on Radio News Inaccuracy," ANPA Bulletin 6095, Mar. 17, 1933.

9. "Report of the Forty-Seventh Annual Meeting," ANPA Bulletin 6114.

10. "Tomorrow's News Today," ANPA Bulletin 6063, Jan. 19, 1933; Neal Gabler, *Winchell* (New York: Alfred A. Knopf, 1994), 213–15.

11. "Forecasts More News Broadcasts," ANPA Bulletin 6068, Jan. 27, 1933.

12. Ibid.

13. Sterling and Kittross, *Stay Tuned,* 175–79.

14. "100 Publishers Here; Hoover Is Awaited," *New York Times,* Apr. 21, 1929, 19; "Hoover Speaks Here to Publishers Today," *New York Times,* Apr. 22, 1929, 29; and "Associated Press Pays Stone Tribute," *New York Times,* Apr. 23, 1929.

15. "Newspapers Warn Radio," *New York Times,* Jan. 25, 1931, 27.

16. "Green Warns Press on Foes of Labor," *New York Times,* Apr. 18, 1931, 26.

17. "Publishers Study Radio Use of News," *New York Times*, Dec. 7, 1932, 25.

18. Bickel to Palmer, Mar. 9, 1933, cited in "Bickel Outlines U.P. Stand on News Broadcasting," ANPA Bulletin 6095, Mar. 17, 1933.

19. "Report of the Forty-Seventh Annual Meeting," ANPA Bulletin No. 6114; "Ask Consideration of Ban on Programs," ANPA Bulletin 6191, Nov. 3, 1933.

20. "Robinson Pledges Caution on Money," *New York Times*, Apr. 25, 1933, 1.

21. "A.P. Resolution on News Broadcasting," ANPA Bulletin 6112, May 3, 1933. Also see "A.P. Majority Against Giving News to Radio," ANPA Bulletin 6109, Apr. 18, 1933; and "Associated Press Curbs Broadcasts," *New York Times*, Apr. 23, 1933, sec. 2, p. 1.

22. "New Rules Put A.P. Resolution into Effect," ANPA Bulletin 6112, May 3, 1933; "Publishers Favor Radio Program Ban," *New York Times*, Apr. 27, 1933, 15; and "Report of the Forty-Seventh Annual Meeting," ANPA Bulletin 6114.

23. "Radio 'Piracy' Charged in Associated Press Suit," ANPA Bulletin 6090, Mar. 3, 1933.

24. "Bars Broadcasts of the A.P.'s News," *New York Times*, Feb. 26, 1933, 7; "Move to Dismiss A.P. News Piracy Suit," ANPA Bulletin 6098, Mar. 31, 1933; "Affirms Injunction in News Piracy Case," ANPA Bulletin 6102, Apr. 7, 1933; and "Station Appeals Against 'News Piracy' Injunction," ANPA Bulletin 6109, Apr. 18, 1933.

25. "Stops News Broadcast," *New York Times*, Mar. 14, 1933; "News Injunction Signed," *New York Times*, Mar. 15, 1933; and "Appeal Dropped in 'News Piracy' Case," ANPA Bulletin 6179, Oct. 6, 1933.

26. "Broadcaster Admits 'Lifting' News," ANPA Bulletin 6132, June 23, 1933; "New Orleans Papers Win Radio Injunction," *New York Times*, June 30, 1933; "Newspapers Win New Orleans Radio Case," ANPA Bulletin 6136, July 7, 1933; and "Newspaper Answers Radio Attack," ANPA Bulletin 6142, July 20, 1933.

27. "Service Gathers News for Radio," ANPA Bulletin 6167, Sept. 8, 1933.

28. "A.P. and A.N.P.A. Declare War on Radio," *Broadcasting*, May 1, 1933; "Commentators 'Gathering Own Material,'" ANPA Bulletin 6119, May 26, 1933.

29. Martin Codel's article cited in "Suggests 'Radio News Association,'" ANPA Bulletin 6112, May 3, 1933.

30. "A.P. Sets Charge for Broadcasting," ANPA Bulletin 6183, Oct. 19, 1933.

31. "Press Rates for Radio News," ANPA Bulletin 6183, Oct. 19, 1933.

32. "News Service for Radio Organized," ANPA Bulletin 6169, Sept.

21, 1933; "C.B.S. Adds News Broadcasts," ANPA Bulletin 6179, Oct. 6, 1933.

33. "C.B.S. Adds News Broadcasts," ANPA Bulletin No. 6179.

34. "Press Galleries Exclude Radio Men," ANPA Bulletin 6195, Nov. 10, 1933.

35. "News and Comment from the National Capital," *Literary Digest,* Nov. 11, 1933, 12; "The Press and the Microphone," *Christian Century,* Nov. 22, 1933, 1462.

36. Sterling and Kittross, *Stay Tuned,* chap. 4.

37. "Galleries Barred to Radio Reporters," *New York Times,* Nov. 8, 1933.

38. "Pirating of News by Radio Barred by Court," ANPA Bulletin 6521, Dec. 20, 1935.

39. "Conference on News Broadcasting," ANPA Bulletin 6211, Dec. 13, 1933. For further information on the Press-Radio War, see Gwenyth L. Jackaway, *Media at War: Radio's Challenge to the Newspapers, 1924–1939* (Westport, Conn.: Praeger, 1995).

40. "Radio News Plan Ends Long Fight," *New York Times,* Dec. 16, 1933; "News Broadcasting Agreement Reached," *New York Times,* Feb. 1, 1934; and "Report of the Forty-Eighth Annual Meeting of the American Newspaper Publishers Association," ANPA Bulletin 6266, May 3, 1934.

41. "Radio to Drop Spot News," *New York Times,* Feb. 8, 1934; "Two Radio Systems Get Press Service," *New York Times,* Feb. 20, 1934.

42. "Radio News Plan in Effect Today," *New York Times,* Mar. 1, 1934.

43. "'Human' News Rules in Press Broadcast," *New York Times,* Mar. 2, 1934.

44. "Publishers Urged to Aid Broadcasts," *New York Times,* Apr. 26, 1934.

45. "Radio Press Fails, Senator Dill Says," *New York Times,* Sept. 18, 1934.

46. Ibid.

47. "Schall Fights Air News," *New York Times,* Sept. 26, 1934.

48. "Report of the Forty-Ninth Annual Meeting of the American Newspaper Publishers Association," ANPA Bulletin 6413, May 7, 1935.

49. "Transradio Press Service vs. A.N.P.A. et al.," ANPA Bulletin 6440, June 26, 1935; Sammy Danna, "The Rise of Radio News," in *American Broadcasting: A Source Book on the History of Radio and Television,* ed. Lawrence Lichty and Malachi Topping (New York: Hastings House, 1975), 338; and Sterling and Kittross, *Stay Tuned,* 123, 175.

50. "UP and INS May Sell Radio News," *Broadcasting,* Apr. 15, 1935, 11; "UP and INS Offer News to Radio," *Broadcasting,* May 15, 1935, 11; Sterling and Kittross, *Stay Tuned,* chap. 5; and Jackaway, *Media at War.*

11. "Rogue" Stations and Controversial Issues of Public Importance: Protecting Nonconformist Speech

1. Lauter and Friend, "Radio and the Censors," 359–65. Also, see Nathan Godfried, *WCFL: Chicago's Voice of Labor* (Urbana: University of Illinois Press, 1997).

2. In Re: Paramount Broadcasting Corporation, WFOX, Hearings Before the Federal Radio Commission, Monday, Apr. 27, 1931, NA, RG 173, FCC Docket Section 1151, box 188 (hereafter cited as "WFOX Hearings, Apr. 27, 1931"); Statement of Facts and Grounds for Decision, In Re Application of Debs Memorial Radio Fund, Inc. (WEVD), No. 969, NA, RG 173, FCC Docket Section 969, box 153 (hereafter cited as "Statement and Grounds, WEVD"); and Hutchinson, "Is the Air Already Monopolized?" 441–44.

3. Report of Elmer W. Pratt, Examiner, Dec. 11, 1930, NA, RG 173, FCC Docket Section 969, box 153 (hereafter cited as "Pratt Report, Dec. 11, 1930"); Statement and Grounds, WEVD. G. August Gerber to Frederick Libby, Jan. 10, 1931; Forrest Bailey, ACLU, to National Broadcasting Company, no date; "Gerber to Oppose Closing of WEVD," "Debs Radio in Fight for Life," "Radio Station WEVD Fights for Its Life," "U.S. Tries to Take WEVD Off the Air," newspaper clippings, no date; "Charges Preferred Against Sta. WEVD," Oct. 14 (1930); "Debs Radio Permit Gets Turned Down," *Oklahoma Leader,* Oct. 17, 1930, ACLU Papers, vol. 385.

4. Pratt Report, Dec. 11, 1930. Examiner's Report No. 176 and Applicant's Exceptions to Examiner's Report No. 176, Docket No. 969, NA, RG 173, FCC Docket Section 969, box 153; ACLU to FRC, Oct. 9, 1930; and G. August Gerber to Frederick Libby, Jan. 10, 1931, ACLU Papers, vol. 385.

5. News release, Wednesday, Dec. 24, 1930; Forrest Bailey to Harry Elmer Barnes, Dec. 27, 1930; Elisabeth Gilman to Bailey, Dec. 29, 1930; Bailey to Mary E. Dreier, Dec. 27, 1930; Dorothy Detzer to Bailey, Dec. 29, 1930; John Haynes Holmes to Bailey, Dec. 29, 1930; Bailey to Robert Morse Lovett, Dec. 27, 1930; Florence Kelly to Bailey, telegram, Dec. 31, 1930; Bailey to Jesse Jolmes, Dec. 27, 1930; "Radio Commission Extends WEVD License," newspaper clipping, no date, ACLU Papers, vol. 385.

6. Applicant's Exceptions to Examiner's Report No. 176, 32–44, Docket No. 969, NA, RG 173, FCC Docket Section 969, box 153.

7. Hearings, in Re Application of Debs Memorial Radio Fund, Inc. (WEVD), No. 969, Sept. 26, 1931, 6–7, NA, RG 173, FCC Docket Section 969, box 153.

8. Ibid., 7–11.

9. Ibid., 12–17.

10. Ibid., 17–20, 24, and 25–29.

11. Ibid., 29.

12. Ibid., 30–33.

13. Ibid., 34–35.

14. Statement and Grounds, WEVD; G. August Gerber to Frederick Libby, Jan. 10, 1931, ACLU Papers, vol. 385.

15. Statement and Grounds, WEVD.

16. "WEVD License Revoked Without Warning; Radio Board Reverses Itself," *New Leader,* Jan. 24, 1931; various other newspaper clippings, Jan. 24, 1931; and stories in ACLU Bulletin, Jan. 16–22, 1931, ACLU Papers.

17. WFOX Hearings, Apr. 27, 1931.

18. "WEVD License Revoked Without Warning; Radio Board Reverses Itself"; various other newspaper clippings, Jan. 24, 1931; and stories in ACLU Bulletin, Jan. 16–22, 1931, ACLU Papers.

19. Statement of Facts, Grounds for Decision and Order of the Commission, in Re: Paramount Broadcasting Corporation, WFOX, Nov. 6, 1931, NA, RG 173, FCC Docket Section 1151, box 188 (hereafter cited as "Statement and Grounds, WFOX, Nov. 6, 1931").

20. Report of Examiner Elmer W. Pratt, in Re: Paramount Broadcasting Corporation, WFOX, Aug. 29, 1931, NA, RG 173, FCC Docket Section 1151, box 188.

21. Respondent's Exceptions to Examiner's Report No. 243, in Re: Paramount Broadcasting Corporation, WFOX, Sept. 18, 1931, and Request for Oral Argument, in Re: Paramount Broadcasting Corporation, WFOX, Sept. 18, 1931, NA, RG 173, FCC Docket Section 1151, box 188.

22. "A Test Case Concerning the Freedom of the Air," *Christian Century,* Sept. 30, 1931, in ACLU Papers.

23. Forrest Bailey to August Gerber, Jan. 3, 1931; Aylesworth to Baily [*sic*], Jan. 3, 1931; and Bailey to Aylesworth, Jan. 6, 1931, ACLU Papers.

24. Letter signed by ten trustees of WEVD to "Dear Friend," May 2, 1931, ACLU Papers.

25. "Report of the Committee on the Reorganization of WEVD," no date, but with papers of May–June 1931, and Norman Thomas to Roger Baldwin, June 13 and July 7, 1931, ACLU Papers.

26. Statement and Grounds, WFOX, Nov. 6, 1931.

27. "Television Limited to After Midnight," *New York Times,* Jan. 8, 1929; "Back Indiana Radio Plea," *New York Times,* Apr. 19, 1929, 31.

28. In Re Application of Chicago Federation of Labor (WCFL), Docket No. 881, Exceptions of the Tribune Company (WGN), Respondent, to the Report of Ellis A. Yost, Chief Examiner; Construction Permit to Change Location of Transmitter, October 6, 1930; Objections to Examiner's Report; *The Tribune Company v. Federal Radio Commission,* No. 5461; NA, RG 173, FCC Docket Section 881, box 137.

29. Laurence Todd, "Labor's Broadcasting Station in Vigorous Plea," *Federated Press,* Jan. 22, 1930, ACLU Papers, vol. 385.

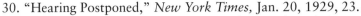

30. "Hearing Postponed," *New York Times,* Jan. 20, 1929, 23.

31. Morrison to Borah, Mar. 24, 1931, and Edward Nockels, "Labor's Rights on the Air," speech, Mar. 1931, LC, Manuscript Division, Borah Papers, General Office Files, box 324, Radio, 1930–31.

32. "Report of the Standing Committee on Communications," *American Bar Association Reports* 55 (1930): 99–104, 350–437.

33. E. N. Nockels, "Appeals to Honor of American Bar," *Federation News,* Oct. 7, 1931.

34. "Prejudice Charged in Allocation of Cleared Broadcast Channels," *U.S. Daily,* Mar. 16, 1932, ACLU Papers.

35. Hutchinson, "Is the Air Already Monopolized?" 441–44.

36. "Cleared Channel for Special Use of Labor Opposed," *U.S. Daily,* Mar. 17, 1932.

37. Herbert Pettey to E. N. Nockels, Oct. 20, 1934; Commission Order No. 3, Sept. 28, 1934; and press release, Sept. 15, 1934, NA, RG 173, FCC General Correspondence, 1927–71, box 497, file 201-4, Allocation in Broadcast Frequencies.

38. "Radio Board Assailed as Unfair in Hearings," *New York Times,* Sept. 2, 1932.

39. J. D. Secrest, "Peace for Broadcasters until December Comes," *New York Times,* July 20, 1930, sec. 4, p. 12.

40. Baldwin to Dill, Oct. 28, 1931; Dill to Baldwin, Nov. 5, 1931; and Minutes of Board of Directors Meeting, Dec. 28, 1931, ACLU Papers.

41. Gordon Moss to Bethuel Webster, Feb. 29, 1932; Tentative draft of congressional resolution to define the term "public interest, convenience, and/or necessity" as it affects radio broadcasting, ACLU Papers.

42. Baldwin to Dill, Nov. 21, 1931; Dill to Baldwin, Nov. 23, 1931; Webster to Moss, Mar. 1, 1932; Webster to Moss, Mar. 2, 1932; Baldwin to Dill, Mar. 2, 1932; Marguerite Owen to Baldwin, Mar. 5, 1932; Webster to Moss, Mar. 9, 1932; Ernst to Moss, Mar. 10, 1932; Moss to Dill, Mar. 31, 1932; Hatcher Hughes to Smith Brookhart, Mar. 31, 1932; Moss to Members of the National Council, Mar. 31, 1932; and ACLU Press Service, Bulletin 484, Nov. 25, 1931, ACLU Papers.

43. Moss to Members of the National Council, Mar. 31, 1932; A Bill to Amend Section 18 of the Radio Act of 1927, draft of proposed legislation, ACLU Papers.

44. Baldwin to Dill, Nov. 31, 1931; Dill to Baldwin, Nov. 23, 1931; Webster to Moss, Mar. 1, 1932; Webster to Moss, Mar. 2, 1932; Baldwin to Dill, Mar. 2, 1932; Marguerite Owen to Baldwin, Mar. 5, 1932; Webster to Moss, Mar. 9, 1932; Ernst to Moss, Mar. 10, 1932; Moss to Dill, Mar. 31, 1932; Hatcher Hughes to Smith Brookhart, Mar. 31, 1932; Moss to Members of the National Council, Mar. 31, 1932; Dill to Moss, Apr. 2, 1932; and A Bill to Amend Section 18 of the Radio Act of 1927, ACLU Papers.

45. "Memorandum on Senate Amendment to H.R. 7716 Affecting Radio Censorship," Dec. 1932, ACLU Papers.

46. Ibid.

47. Ibid.

48. Ibid.

49. Norman Thomas to Roger Baldwin, Dec. 8, 1932, ACLU Papers.

50. "Protection for Radio as American Project Is Urged at Hearing" and "Grant of Appeals to Court in Radio Cases Is Opposed," *U.S. Daily,* Dec. 23 and 24, 1932; Gordon Moss to Dorothy Detzer, Dec. 27, 1932, ACLU Papers.

51. Gordon Moss to Bethuel Webster, Dec. 15, 1932, and Moss to Morris Ernst, Dec. 15, 1932, ACLU Papers.

52. Webster to Dill, Dec. 17, 1932, ACLU Papers.

53. See letters in ACLU Papers between Moss, Dill, Ernst, and Webster, Dec. 1932.

54. Moss to Ernst, Dec. 20, 1932, and Hatcher Hughes to James Couzens, telegram, Dec. 22, 1932, ACLU Papers.

55. "Senate Radio Bill Favorably Reported," *U.S. Daily,* Jan. 11, 1933, and Ewin Davis to Hatcher Hughes, Jan. 16, 1933, ACLU Papers. Also see Hughes to James Couzens, telegram, Dec. 22, 1932; Gordon Moss to Dorothy Detzer, Dec. 27, 1932; and Moss to Norman Thomas, Dec. 27, 1932, ACLU Papers.

56. Hatcher Hughes to C. C. Dill and Edwin [Ewin] Davis, Jan. 11, 1933, and "House Votes Measure on Lotteries by Radio," *U.S. Daily,* Feb. 27, 1933, ACLU Papers.

57. *Amending the Radio Act of 1927,* 72nd Cong. 2nd sess., H. Rept. 2106, Feb. 23, 1933.

58. Herbert Hoover, *Memoirs of Herbert Hoover: The Great Depression, 1929–1941* (New York: The Macmillan Company, 1952), 176–95; *To Amend the Radio Act of 1927,* 73rd Cong., 1st sess., H.R. 1735, Mar. 9, 1933; George Manning, "Lotteries Evade Ban," *Editor and Publisher,* Mar. 18, 1933. "Dill Amendments Pop Up in New Bland Radio Bill," *Variety,* Mar. 21, 1933; Dill to Roger Baldwin, Feb. 26, 1933; Hatcher Hughes to Schuyler Otis Bland, Mar. 29, 1933; Dill to Gordon Moss, Apr. 6, 1933, ACLU Papers.

59. "Bill for a Communications and Power Board, as Roosevelt Proposed, Is Offered in House," *New York Times,* Jan. 31, 1933, 2.

60. "Ernst Predicts Radio Control by Roosevelt," *New York Herald,* Feb. 28, 1933; "Warns of Curbs on Radio Stations," *New York Times,* Feb. 26, 1933, ACLU Papers.

61. "Radical Truth Goes Off the Air," *World Tomorrow,* Mar. 22, 1933, 272.

62. Ibid.

63. Walter Nelson to Harold LaFount, Apr. 5, 1933, ACLU Papers.

64. Walter Nelson to Roger Baldwin, Mar. 30, 1933; Baldwin to Nelson, Apr. 1, 1933; and Nelson to Harold LaFount, Apr. 5, 1933, ACLU Papers.

65. "Memorandum, On Radio in Relation to Free Speech," May 19, 1933, ACLU Papers.

66. RNB to Henry Eskstein, Nov. 8, 1933, ACLU Papers.

67. RNB to Dr. Tracy Tyler, Oct. 24, 1933, ACLU Papers.

68. RNB to Morris Ernst, Dec. 4, 1933, ACLU Papers.

69. Senate, statement of Senator Henry Bellows, Chairman of the Legislative Committee of the National Association of Broadcasters, hearings on S. 2910 before the Committee of Interstate Commerce, 73rd Cong., 2nd sess., Mar. 15, 1934, 63 (hereafter cited as "Bellows's Statement").

70. Senate Committee on Interstate Commerce, *A Bill to Provide for the Regulation of Interstate and Foreign Communications by Wire or Radio, and for Other Purposes: Hearings on S. 2910,* 73rd Cong., 2nd sess., Mar. 9, 1934, 19 (hereafter cited as "Hearings on S. 2910").

71. Bellows's Statement, 66–68.

72. "One Board Asked on Wire and Radio," *New York Times,* Jan. 28, 1934, 28; and "Broadcasters Hit New Control Bill," *New York Times,* Mar. 10, 1934, 27.

73. "Broadcasters Hit New Control Bill," 27, and "Gifford Attacks Wire Control Bill," *New York Times,* Mar. 14, 1934, 27.

74. "Unifying Communications," *New York Times,* Feb. 3, 1934.

75. "One Board Asked on Wire and Radio," 28.

76. House, H.R. 7986, *To Amend the Radio Act of 1927, Approved February 23, 1927, as Amended,* 73rd Cong., 2nd sess., 1934; "Radio," ANPA Bulletin 6255, Apr. 12, 1934.

77. *Congressional Record,* 73rd Cong., 2nd sess., 1934, 78, pt. 10: 10307–9.

78. H.R. Conf. Rep. No. 1918, 73rd Cong., 2nd sess., 1934, 78, pt. 10: 10968; *Congressional Record,* 78, pt. 10: 10307–9, 10968–95.

12. Congress Acts—Again

1. *Congressional Record,* 78, pt. 8: 8828. Also, see Hearings on S. 2910.

2. In the Matter of the Application of the Great Lakes Broadcasting Co., FRC Docket No. 4900, 3 FRC Ann. Rept. 32 (1929).

3. House Committee on Interstate and Foreign Commerce, *Hearings on H.R. 8301,* 73rd Cong., 2nd sess., 1934, 117.

4. Senate, S. Doc. 144, Message from the President of the United States recommending that Congress Create a New Agency to be known as the Federal Communications Commission, 73rd Cong., 2nd sess., 1934, 78, pt. 3: 3181.

5. McChesney, *Telecommunications, Mass Media, and Democracy*, 223.

6. "In the Days of Recovery," *New York Times*, Apr. 29, 1934.

7. Rorty, "Order on the Air!" 17; Sterling and Kittross, *Stay Tuned*, 632.

8. "Educational Groups Marshall at Washington for Radio Onslaught," *Variety*, Oct. 2, 1934, ACLU Papers.

9. Rorty, "Order on the Air!" 17; Sterling and Kittross, *Stay Tuned*, 632.

10. Federal Radio Commission, *Annual Report*, 1928, 49–50; McChesney, *Telecommunications, Mass Media, and Democracy*, 25.

11. "Calls Parley on Using Radio in Education," *New York Times*, May 22, 1929.

12. "Hoover's Aid Asked on Radio Education," *New York Times*, May 25, 1929.

13. McChesney, *Telecommunications, Mass Media, and Democracy*, 42.

14. John Jensen to L. A. Kalbach, Aug. 13, 1929, NA, RG 12, Office of Education Manuscripts, box 31; Armstrong Perry to Ella Crandall, Sept. 2, 1929, Payne Fund, container 56, folder 1068; Crandall to Perry, Nov. 18, 1929, Payne Fund, container 56, folder 1069; and McChesney, *Telecommunications, Mass Media, and Democracy*, 42.

15. Advisory Committee on Education by Radio, *Report of Advisory Committee on Education by Radio Appointed by the Secretary of the Interior* (Columbus, OH: F. J. Heer Printing Company, 1930), 35–37, 66–67, 76.

16. McChesney, *Telecommunications, Mass Media, and Democracy*, 43.

17. "Education Group Assails Tobacco," *New York Times*, July 4, 1930, 13.

18. Ira Robinson, "Who Owns Radio?" *NEA Journal* 19 (1930): 286.

19. "Education Group Assails Tobacco," 13; "The Public's Rights in Radio," *NEA Journal* 19 (1930): 285; and Willis Sutton to William Cooper, Oct. 8, 1930, Payne Fund, container 38, WRHS, Subseries F: Radio Projects, National Committee on Education by Radio.

20. "Minutes of the Conference on Educational Radio Problems," Oct. 13, 1930, NA, RG 12, Office of Education, Manuscripts, box 31.

21. "Reservation of Broadcasting Channels for Educational Institutions," *School and Society* 32 (1930): 722–23, and reported in *Education by Radio*, Mar. 19, 1931, ACLU Papers. These organizations were the National Education Association, the Association of College and University Broadcast Stations, the National University Extension Association, the National Association of State Universities, the Jesuit Education Association, the Association of Land Grant Colleges and Universities, the National Catholic Education Association, the National Council of State Superintendents, and the American Council on Education.

22. John Henry MacCracken, "The Fess Bill for Education by Radio," *Education by Radio*, Mar. 19, 1931, ACLU Papers.

23. Hutchinson, "Is the Air Already Monopolized?" 441–44.

24. James Rorty, "Free Air: A Strictly Imaginary Educational Broadcast," *The Nation*, Mar. 9, 1932, 280–82.

25. Barnouw, *A Tower in Babel*, 261; Ellen Condliffe Lagemann, *The Politics of Knowledge: The Carnegie Corporation, Philanthropy, and Public Policy* (Middletown, Conn.: Wesleyan University Press, 1989), 106–8.

26. McChesney, *Telecommunications, Mass Media, and Democracy*, 55.

27. James Rorty, "The Impending Radio War," *Harper's Monthly Magazine*, Nov. 1931, 717–18.

28. Armstrong Perry, "Freedom of Speech Almost Lost," *Education by Radio*, Mar. 19, 1931, ACLU Papers.

29. "Educational Programs Analyzed," *Broadcasters' News Bulletin*, Mar. 14, 1931.

30. "Superpower," *Education by Radio*, May 7, 1931, ACLU Papers.

31. Rorty, "Free Air," 280–82.

32. "Radio Men Warned on Advertising Evil," *New York Times*, May 22, 1931.

33. Ibid.; "Educational Radio Developments," *Broadcasters' News Bulletin*, Feb. 14, 1931.

34. "The Public's Rights in Radio," *Education by Radio*, Mar. 19, 1931, ACLU Papers.

35. Paul Hutchinson, "Education and Radio," *Christian Century*, Apr. 8, 1931, 478–79.

36. Harold A. LaFount, FRC Commissioner, "Contributions of the Federal Radio Commission to Education by Radio," address delivered before the Second Annual Institute for Education by Radio at Columbus, Ohio, June 8, 1931, NA, RG 173, box 310, FCC, file: DE-4-e.

37. Perry, "Freedom of Speech Almost Lost."

38. Rorty, "The Impending Radio War," 718, 725.

39. "Senate Seeks Data on Radio Advertising," *New York Times*, Jan. 13, 1932, 31.

40. Memorandum for Mr. Baldwin, Nov. 18, 1933, Re: National Committee on Education by Radio, ACLU Papers.

41. Editorial, *New Republic*, Sept. 26, 1934, ACLU Papers.

42. "Use of Broadcasts by Schools Gains," *New York Times*, Apr. 19, 1934; "In the Days of Recovery," *New York Times*, Apr. 29, 1934.

43. "Ickes Sees Radio Force in Education," *New York Times*, Oct. 9, 1934, 9.

44. William Orton, "A Future American Radio Policy," *Education by Radio*, Dec. 20, 1934, ACLU Papers.

45. "Time for Religion," *Commonweal*, Mar. 30, 1934, 592–93; Sen-

ate, statement of Rev. Father John B. Harney, New York City, hearings on S. 2910.

46. House, statement of Rev. John B. Harney, hearings on H.R. 8301 before the Committee on Interstate and Foreign Commerce, 73rd Cong., 2nd sess., May 9, 1934, 156–57.

47. House, supplementary statement by the National Association of Broadcasters regarding the amendment to H.R. 8301 proposed by Father John B. Harney, hearings on H.R. 8301 before the Committee on Interstate and Foreign Commerce, House of Representatives, on H.R. 8301, 73rd Cong., 2nd sess., May 8, 1934, 117.

48. Ibid., 118.

49. Ibid., 119.

50. Statement of Rev. John B. Harney, hearings on H.R. 8301, 162.

51. Hearings on S. 2910; *Congressional Record*, 78, pt. 8: 8830, 8843–45.

52. *Congressional Record*, 78, pt. 8: 8830–37.

53. Ibid., 8845–46; "Wire-Radio Board Voted by Senate," *New York Times*, May 16, 1934.

54. *Congressional Record*, 78, pt. 10: 10315–17.

55. *Communications Act of 1934*, 73rd Cong., 2nd sess., Apr. 17, 1934, S. Rept. 781, 2; House, *Communications Act of 1934*, 73rd Cong., 2nd sess., Conference Rept., Section 307, 22; and "New Deal in Radio Law to Regulate All Broadcasting," *New York Times*, June 24, 1934.

56. "Agree on Wires Measure," *New York Times*, June 8, 1934; "Text of the House Conferees' Statement on the Communications Bill," *New York Times*, June 10, 1934.

57. "Keep Radio Free Roosevelt Urges," *New York Times*, June 14, 1934; "40 Bills Signed by the President," *New York Times*, June 21, 1934, 2.

58. Rowland, "The Meaning of 'The Public Interest' in Communications Policy, Part II," 388–89; Sterling and Kittross, *Stay Tuned*, chap. 5.

59. "Educational Groups Marshall at Washington for Radio Onslaught."

60. "Radio Groups Open Wave Length Fight," *New York Times*, Sept. 10, 1934, ACLU Papers.

61. Clifton Read to Members of the Radio Committee, memorandum, Sept. 12, 1934, ACLU Papers.

62. Levering Tyson to Clifton Read, Sept. 14, 1934; Morris Ernst to Read, Sept. 14, 1934; Read to Roger Baldwin, telegram, Sept. 18, 1934; Read to Norman Thomas, Sept. 19, 1934; Read to Ernst, Sept. 19, 1934; Baldwin to ACLU, telegram, Sept. 19, 1934; Read to Alexander Lindey, Sept. 22, 1934; Baldwin to Read, Sept. 24, 1934, ACLU Papers.

63. Roger (Baldwin) to Clif (Read), Sept. 24, 1934, ACLU Papers.

64. "A Proposal to Promote Public Discussion over the Radio," remarks by Bethuel Webster, Oct. 1934, and press release, Oct. 5, 1934,

ACLU Papers. Also see "Civil Liberties Union Protests Radio Censoring," *Salt Lake City Tribune*, Oct. 6, 1934; "Radio Stations Accused of Undue Censorship," *Buffalo News*, Oct. 6, 1934; "Radio Asked to Give Educational Time," *Washington Herald*, Oct. 6, 1934; "Censorship of Radio Attacked by Webster," *Chattanooga Times*, Oct. 6, 1934; "Censorship of Programs Laid to Radio Stations," *New York Herald Tribune*, Oct. 6, 1934; "New Chains Taking Form," *Syracuse Herald*, Oct. 6, 1934; "Attacks Radio for Censorship," *Toledo Blade*, Oct. 8, 1934; and "Scores Censorship of Radio Programs," *New Orleans Item*, Oct. 13, 1934, ACLU Papers.

65. "For Better Broadcasting," *New Republic*, Oct. 3, 1934, 201–2.

66. "More Education over Radio Asked," *New York Times*, Oct. 2, 1934; "Educational Groups Marshall at Washington for Radio Onslaught," ACLU Papers.

67. "W. S. Paley Against 'Forced' Programs," *New York Times*, Oct. 18, 1934, 26; "Statement of William S. Paley to the Federal Communications Commission," ACLU Papers.

68. "Statement of William S. Paley to the Federal Communications Commission," ACLU Papers.

69. "Federal System Proposed in Radio," *New York Times*, Oct. 20, 1934, 17.

70. "A Proposal to Promote Public Discussion over the Radio," remarks by Bethuel Webster, Oct. 1934, and press release, Oct. 5, 1934; "Civil Liberties Union Protests Radio Censoring," *Salt Lake City Tribune*, Oct. 6, 1934; "Radio Stations Accused of Undue Censorship," *Buffalo News*, Oct. 6, 1934; "Radio Asked to Give Educational Time," *Washington Herald*, Oct. 6, 1934; "Censorship of Radio Attacked by Webster," *Chattanooga Times*, Oct. 6, 1934; "Censorship of Programs Laid to Radio Stations," *New York Herald Tribune*, Oct. 6, 1934; "New Chains Taking Form," *Syracuse Herald*, Oct. 6, 1934; "Attacks Radio for Censorship," *Toledo Blade*, Oct. 8, 1934; "Scores Censorship of Radio Programs," *New Orleans Item*, Oct. 13, 1934; and "Radio No Open Forum," *Lexington Herald*, Oct. 25, 1934, ACLU Papers.

71. "A Proposal to Promote Public Discussion over the Radio," remarks by Bethuel Webster, Oct. 1934, and press release, Oct. 5, 1934, ACLU Papers.

72. Baldwin to Bethuel Webster, Oct. 23, 1934, ACLU Papers.

73. "U.S.-Operated Network Urged to Solve Radio Problem," *Christian Science Monitor*, Nov. 2, 1934, ACLU Papers.

74. "More Education Over Radio Asked," *New York Times*, Oct. 2, 1934, 16; "Federal Dictation Opposed for Radio," *New York Times*, Oct. 10, 1934; and "Freedom of Speech Upheld," *New York Times*, Oct. 14, 1934, ACLU Papers.

75. "Radio Industry Presents United Front Against Educational Leaders' Claims," *New York Times*, Oct. 16, 1934, ACLU Papers.

76. "Radio 'Education Use' by Government Cited," *New York Times,* Oct. 21, 1934, ACLU Papers.

77. "Federal System Proposed in Radio," *New York Times,* Oct. 20, 1934, 17.

78. "Education 'Time' on Radio Opposed," *New York Times,* Oct. 19, 1934, 6; Orrin E. Dunlap Jr., "Tracking the Likes of the Radio Fan," *New York Times,* Nov. 25, 1934, sec. 6, p. 7.

79. "Radio as School," editorial, *New York Times,* Oct. 20, 1934, 14.

80. "Radio Report to Await Submission to Congress," *New York Times,* Nov. 18, 1934, sec. 9, p. 1B.

81. Report of the Federal Communications Commission to Congress Pursuant to Section 307(c) of the Communications Act; E. O. Sykes to the President, Jan. 22, 1935; and Sykes to Augustine Lonergan, Jan. 31, 1935, NA, RG 173, FCC General Correspondence, 1927–71, box 497, file 201-4, Allocation in Broadcast Frequencies.

82. Report of the Federal Communications Commission to Congress Pursuant to Section 307(c) of the Communications Act, NA.

83. Ibid.

84. "Opposes Fixed Law for Radio Time," *New York Times,* Jan. 23, 1935, 12.

➤ INDEX

Louise M. Benjamin is an associate professor in the Department of Telecommunications at the Henry W. Grady College of Journalism and Mass Communication at the University of Georgia, where she teaches broadcast history and mass media and telecommunications policy. Her research has also appeared in the *Journal of Broadcasting and Electronic Media, Journalism Quarterly, American Journalism, Journalism History,* the *Historical Journal of Film, Radio and Television, Communications and the Law, Free Speech Yearbook,* and *Journal of Advertising.*